D1268034

THEORIES OF GROUP BEHAVIOR, ed. by Brian Mullen and George R. Goethals. Springer-Verlag, 1987. 243p bibl indexes 86-6626. 40.00 ISBN 0-387-96351-0. HM 131. CIP

Over the past two decades, the area of social psychology has largely ignored one of the most important aspects of social behavior: behavior in groups. This book contains essays by well-known contemporary social psychologists that discuss major social-psychological theories and their applications to the study of behavior in groups. Theoretical approaches include social comparison theory, cognitive dissonance theory, self-presentation theory, drive theory, social impact theory, self-attention theory, social cognition theory, and transactive memory theory. However, the book does not try to encompass theoretical approaches to group behavior that are sociological, anthropological, political, or historical. Each chapter includes an independent introduction to the respective theory, reviews relevant literature, and discusses areas of application. Chapters contain careful reviews of previous research, and current research questions are discussed; each chapter is well written and includes an extensive reference list. Well suited for advanced undergraduate courses or honors courses in social psychology, as well as a valuable resource for students interested in conducting research in this area.— *T. Hill, University of Tulsa*

SSSP

Springer
Series in
Social
Psychology

SSSP

Theories of Group Behavior

Edited by
Brian Mullen and
George R. Goethals

Springer-Verlag New York Berlin Heidelberg
London Paris Tokyo

Brian Mullen
Department of Psychology
Syracuse University
Syracuse, New York 13210
U.S.A.

George R. Goethals
Department of Psychology
Williams College
Williamstown, Massachusetts 01267
U.S.A.

With 13 Figures

Library of Congress Cataloging in Publication Data
Theories of group behavior (SSSP)
    (Springer series in social psychology)
    Bibliography: p.
    Includes index.
    1. Social groups. 2. Social interaction.
I. Mullen, Brian, 1955–   . II. Goethals, George R.
III. Title. IV. Series.
HM131.T446   1986   302.3   86-6626

Typeset by Ampersand Publisher Services, Rutland, Vermont.
Printed and bound by R.R. Donnelley, Harrisonburg, Virginia.
Printed in the United States of America.

9 8 7 6 5 4 3 2 1

ISBN 0-387-96351-0 Springer-Verlag New York Berlin Heidelberg
ISBN 3-540-96351-0 Springer-Verlag Berlin Heidelberg New York

For Lou and Marion

Preface

In the fall of 1983, we began to organize a symposium entitled "General Social Psychological Theories of Group Behavior." Our goal was to encourage the extension and application of basic current social psychology to group behavior. The symposium was presented in the spring of 1984 at the Eastern Psychological Association convention in Baltimore and the interest that it generated led to discussions with colleagues and friends about similar efforts by social psychologists, eventually resulting in the present book.

Some clarification about the contents is in order. First, the theories presented here are clearly social psychological in scope and level of analysis, as discussed in the Introduction (Chapter 1). However, we are not trying to encompass sociological, anthropological, political, or historical theoretical approaches to group behavior.

Second, while the theories comprise a wide-ranging and representative, if not quite exhaustive, selection of social psychological theories of group behavior, there are some interesting and general perspectives that are not represented. For example, one perspective that is conspicuous by its absence is some variant of learning theory. Aside from the rare, notable exception (e.g., Buss, 1979), little work currently is being done on group behavior from a learning theoretic perspective. Our inclusion or exclusion of a theory reflects our judgment regarding its currency and accessibility to social psychological researchers.

Third, and most striking, is the generality of the theories included in this book. We use generality here to refer to a theory's capacity to help us understand a wide range of group behaviors. This type of generality is a double-edged sword: On the one hand, discussion of general theories often circumvents large research literatures that have crystallized around highly specific, phenomena-bound theories (such as group polarization, coalition formation, and the relationship between attitude similarity and attraction). On the other hand, such discussion often provides a broader understanding of group phenomena, in all of their diversity and complexity. We hope that consideration of general theoretical perspectives will allow us to put the more common, highly specific, phenomena-bound theories into a meaningful context.

Following the Introduction and concluding with the Overview, the eight theories are arranged in an approximate historical sequence. Undoubtedly, most or all of these perspectives can be traced back to LeBon, Pareto, Simmel, Mead, Cooley, Allport, McDougall, and/or Freud. However, returning to the first formal presentations of most of the perspectives, we progress through Festinger (1954) (Chapter 2: social comparison theory), Festinger (1957) (Chapter 3: cognitive dissonance theory), Goffman (1959) (Chapter 4: self-presentation theory), Zajonc (1965) (Chapter 5: drive-arousal theory), Latane and Nida (1980) (Chapter 6: social impact theory), Carver and Scheier (1981) (Chapter 7: self-attention theory), the general social cognition zeitgeist of the early 1980s (Chapter 8: social cognition theory), and Wegner and Giuliano (1982) (Chapter 9: transactive memory theory).

We anticipate that this book can be used in at least three important ways: (1) It is an introduction to these general theories for the upper-level student in social psychology, providing an in-depth presentation of the general theories of group behavior that are currently being developed by social psychologists. (2) It is a valuable resource for practitioners in a wide range of areas, as the theories are systematically applied to such diverse phenomena as participation in the classroom and in religious groups, worker productivity, antisocial behavior, and jury deliberations. Professionals involved in these domains will appreciate the applications section of each chapter. (3) By presenting these theories in a consistent format, and considering how they apply to a common pool of behavioral domains, the similarities among theories will become apparent, and the discrepancies cast into sharp relief. While the overview in Chapter 10 has begun the task of delineating these similarities and differences, the careful reader will undoubtedly unearth some that we did not anticipate. These gems are the stuff of which dissertations are made. We hope the book will provide an increased concern for broad theoretical issues and an appreciation for the similarities and differences among the general social psychological theories of group behavior.

We would like to acknowledge the support provided to us by Syracuse University and the Naval Training Systems Center (B.M.) and by Williams College and the University of California, Santa Barbara (G.R.G.). Thanks go to the many friends and colleagues who have read, commented, suggested, and encouraged us throughout this project. Special thanks go to the people at Springer-Verlag for their support and good advice. Finally, we would like to express our appreciation and gratitude to our wives, to whom this book is dedicated.

September 29, 1986

References

Buss, A.H. (1983). Social wards and personality. *Journal of Personality and Social Psychology, 44,* 553–563.

Carver, C.S., & Scheier, M.F. (1981). *Attention and self-regulation: A control theory approach to human behavior.* New York: Springer-Verlag.

Festinger, L. (1954). A theory of social comparison processes. *Human Relations, 7,* 117–140.

Festinger, L. (1957). *A theory of cognitive dissonance.* Stanford, CA: Stanford University Press.

Goffman, E. (1959). *Presentation of self in everyday life.* Garden City, NY: Doubleday.

Latané, B., and Nida, S. (1980). Social impact theory and group influence: A social engineering perspective. In P. Paulus (Ed.), *The psychology of group influence* (pp. 3–34). Hillsdale, NJ: Erlbaum.

Wegner, D.M., & Guiliano, T. (1982). The forms of social awareness. *Personality, roles, social behavior.* New York: Springer-Verlag.

Zajonc, R.B. (1965). Social facilitation. *Science, 149,* 269–274.

Contents

Contributors

Roy F. Baumeister, Department of Psychology, Case Western Reserve University, Cleveland, Ohio 44106 U.S.A.

Brad J. Bushman, Department of Psychology, University of Missouri, Columbia, Missouri 65201, U.S.A.

John M. Darley, Department of Psychology, Princeton University, Princeton, New Jersey 08540 U.S.A.

Russell G. Geen, Department of Psychology, University of Missouri, Columbia, Missouri 65201, U.S.A.

George R. Goethals, Department of Psychology, Williams College, Williamstown, Massachusetts 01267 U.S.A.

Debra G. Hutton, Department of Psychology, Case Western Reserve University, Cleveland, Ohio 44106, U.S.A.

Jeffrey M. Jackson, Department of Psychology, Fordham University, New York, New York 10023, U.S.A.

Brian Mullen, Department of Psychology, Syracuse University, Syracuse, New York, 13210, U.S.A.

Thomas M. Ostrom, Department of Psychology, Ohio State University, Columbus, Ohio 43210, U.S.A.

John B. Pryor, Department of Psychology, Illinois State University, Normal, Illinois 61761, U.S.A.

Gerald N. Sande, Department of Psychology, University of Manitoba Winnipeg, Manitoba R3T 2N2, Canada

Daniel M. Wegner, Department of Psychology, Trinity University, San Antonio, Texas 78284, U.S.A.

Mark P. Zanna, Department of Psychology, University of Waterloo, Waterloo, Ontario N2L 3G1, Canada

Chapter 1

Introduction: The Study of Group Behavior

Brian Mullen

> Hell is alone, the other figures in it merely projections.
> T.S. Eliot (1950) *The Cocktail Party.*

> Hell is—other people!
> Jean Paul Sartre (1944) *Huis-Clos.*

We all belong to countless groups: family groups, work groups, play groups, political groups. The major events of our lives almost invariably occur to us as members of groups: births, deaths, celebrations, bereavements, achievments, and entertainments all occur in group contexts. The possibility that groups are inherently good (Anderson, 1978) or inherently bad (Buys, 1978) has been discussed ad infinitum. As the foregoing epigrams suggest, it is probably accurate to adapt Aristophanes' dictum to groups: we can't live with them, and we can't live without them.

The major headlines of the day can be used to highlight the pervasive, if subtle, importance of groups. For example, the tragic violence exhibited by British soccer fans at an international soccer match in Belgium held the attention of the world media for several weeks in the spring of 1985 (Lacayo, 1985). When the Spy Run Creek in Fort Wayne, Indiana, began to flood its banks in late winter of 1985, a group of the community's youths voluntarily participated in efforts to hold back the rising waters (*New York Times,* 2/27/85). Fred Postlewaite's 20-year, cross-country, one-man crime wave against the Sigma Alpha Epsilon fraternity from which he had been rejected as a youth might be viewed in terms of a group which one person wanted to, but could not, join (*Murray Ledger-Times,* 1/10/85). These headlines may already be receding into the past. However, comparable news stories will continue, temporarily but vividly, to illustrate the importance of groups.

For almost a century, social scientists have been intrigued by many elements of group behavior. This book represents a collection of the best recent efforts on the part of several social psychologists to further our understanding of group behavior. The present chapter is intended to set the stage for the presentation of eight current, general theories of group behavior. This introduction does not attempt to predict or explain the behavior of people in groups. Such prediction and explanation are the tasks set for the eight theories to be presented later in this book. The stage will be set for these theories by elucidating the nature of a group. This introduction to the study of group behavior involves four sections. The first section is devoted to the prerequisite treatment of the definition of the group. Next, the topographical, or physical, characteristics of groups are detailed. Third, the temporal dimension of group phenomena is examined. Finally, the remaining chapters are outlined.

Definition of the Group

There are really three issues that are intertwined in any study of group phenomena. These are: definition of the group: the reality of the group: and the appropriate unit of analysis (i.e., the group or the individual). One's definition of the group will be determined by, and will further reify, one's beliefs regarding the reality of groups. Further, one's definition of the group will reflect and help guide a level of analysis focused upon the individual or upon the group. Before we turn to any particular theory of group behavior, it is important to come to terms with these three interrelated issues.

Because it seems almost mandatory to begin any work on group behavior with some definition of the group, there is an (over-) abundance of definitions from which to choose. For example, a group has been defined as:

> two or more people who share a common social identification of themselves, or, which is really the same thing, perceive themselves to be members of the same social category. (Reicher, 1982)
> a collection of individuals whose existence as a collection is rewarding to the individuals. (Bass, 1960)
> a set of individuals who share a common fate, that is, who are inter-dependent in the sense that an event which effects one member is likely to affect all. (Fiedler, 1967)
> two or more persons who are interacting with one another in such a manner that each person influences and is influenced by each other person. (Shaw, 1981)

These definitions seem to capture many critical elements of what a group is: social categorization, a rewarding social stimulus, interdependence, inter-action, and influence.

It should be recognized that many authors have found it useful to draw distinctions between group, collective, mass, public, crowd, mob, and assemblage, as well as between various strains within each of these species of social entities. However, the term "group" is used in the most general sense in this book. The research discussed in the following chapters is based upon such diverse aggregates of people as the intimate dyad (Wegner,

Chapter 7) and the savage lynch mob (Mullen, Chapter 6). This does not belie some inviious assumption of "structural homology" (Golembiewski, 1962). Simply because we use the term "group" to refer to both types of phenomena, it is not necessary to assume that lynch mobs and intimate dyads are equivalent in all structural and functional aspects.

Most general definitions of the group can usually be interpreted as being consistent with either the group level of analysis or the individual level of analysis. At one extreme is the position that the group is more real than the individual and that the appropriate unit of analysis is the group. The preeminent proponent of this perspective was Emile Durkheim:

> If, then, we begin with the individual, we shall be able to understand nothing of what takes place in the group.... Consequently, everytime a social phenomenon is directly explained by a psychological phenomenon, we may be sure that the explanation is false. (Durkheim, 1938, p. 104)

At the other extreme is the position that the individual is more real than the group, and that the appropriate unit of analysis is the individual. The preeminent proponent of this perspective was Floyd Allport:

> All theories which partake of the group fallacy have the unfortunate consequence of diverting attention from the true locus of cause and effect, namely, the behavior mechanisms of the individual. (F.H. Allport, 1920, p. 9)

Although Durkheim and Allport might have agreed with the definitions of the group presented above, they would undoubtedly have disagreed as to what the definitions mean.

One attempt to integrate the individual level of analysis with the group level of analysis involves positing a parallelism between the individual and the group. Historically, it has been fairly common to assert that the group is just like the individual in some ways. For example, Saint Peter is accredited with developing such an analogy regarding Jesus and the early Christian Church. John of Salisbury (d. 1180) elaborated on the parallel between the king and the state in his *Polycraticus*. Early in the development of contemporary social psychology, conceptualizations of the group mind (e.g., Boodin, 1913; LeBon, 1895/1960; McDougall, 1920) and the collective unconscious (Jung, 1922) illustrate this tendency to analogize the individual and the group. The terms *syntality* (Cattell, 1948) and *groupality* (Borgardus, 1954) each attempt to parallel at the level of the group the concept of personality employed at the level of the individual.

The parallelism between processes and mechanisms observed in the individual and those observed within a group has fallen out of vogue. However, in spite of the decline in the popularity of this approach, positing such a parallelism continues to be a fruitful heuristic strategy. Some of the chapters in this book report on the extension of individual psychological principles to social contexts. For example, Ostrom and Pryor's contribution (Chapter 9) considers the correspondence between social structures and cognitive structures. In a similar vein, Wegner's contribution (Chapter 7) extends fundamental memory processes to transactive memory processes, or memory processes that occur at an interpersonal level.

Another, more powerful, reconciliation between the individual level of analysis and the group level of analysis was developed by Donald Campbell (1958). Campbell proposed that social aggregates vary in their degree of *entitativity,* or in the extent to which they have the nature of an entity or real existence. Thus, in some instances, the group may be quite real, and in such instances the group may be the more appropriate unit of analysis. In other instances, the group may be a fictitious abstraction, and in such instances the individual may be the more appropriate unit of analysis. Entitativity was proposed to be a reflection of the Gestalt principles of perceptual organization (e.g., proximity, similarity, common fate, pregnance). To the extent that the elements of a social aggregate can be characterized in terms of high proximity, high similarity, a common fate, and "good form," that social aggregate will have higher entitativity and will thereby be seen more as a real group. In other words, to the extent that an aggregate of people are close to one another, are similar to one another in appearance, seem to be doing the same things over time, and are spatially arranged in a cohesive pattern, those people will be more likely to be seen as a real group. Robinson (1981) has proposed a similar gage of the reality of groups. According to Robinson, a social aggregate will be perceived, and will function, as a group to the extent that it stays the same size (similarity, common fate) and continues to engage in the same kind of activity over time (similarity, common fate, pregnance).

Although Campbell's proposal is often cited in introductions such as this, it does not seem to have had the integrative and heuristic effects that it might have had. It is true that some current efforts are directly aimed at using Gestalt principles to understand the effects of group composition (e.g., Brewer, 1979; Mullen, 1983; Wegner & Schaefer, 1978). Nonetheless, the major trends in social psychological research seem to have ignored this intriguing approach. Consider, by way of illustration, the amount of research devoted to group phenomena such as coalition formation (e.g., Komorita & Moore, 1976). The social aggregates studied in this research domain can be characterized in terms of the barest minimum of entitativity. On the other hand, consider Mann's (1969: Mann & Taylor, 1969) unique work on long-term queues, or waiting lines. These social aggregates would be calculated by Campbell to have relatively high entitativity, and yet queues have been almost completely ignored. It would seem that if Campbell's reconciliation (between the individual level of analysis and the group level of analysis) had been taken to heart by social psychology, there would have been at least as many studies devoted to people in queues as there have been devoted to people in coalitions.

The emphasis on the individual that has developed in social psychology in the United States has received a considerable amount of critical examination (e.g., G.W. Allport, 1968; Knowles, 1982; Latta & Gorman,

1984; Pepitone, 1981; Reicher, 1982; Shaffer, 1978; Smith & White, 1983; Steiner, 1974). This emphasis has been variously labeled *individualistic* (Steiner, 1974), *individuocentric* (Pepitone, 1981), *methodological individualism* (Vapnarsky, 1967), and *egocentric contractual* (Shweder & Bourne, 1982). Numerous reasons have been suggested for this preference for the individual as the appropriate unit of analysis: experimental control can become more refined when focused upon the individual rather than upon the social system (Steiner, 1974); research programs emphasizing the individual produce results more easily, more quickly, and with less risk (Steiner, 1974); the focus upon the individual is consistnet with the mores of American capitalistic society (Taylor & Brown, 1979); because of specialization in graduate education, a growing ignorance of sociology and anthropology among psychological social psychologists (Shaffer, 1978), and the general failure of the group mind hypothesis (the one truly molar and group-oriented hypothesis that was inherently psychological) to survive the transition to behaviorism in the 1920s and 1930s (G.W. Allport, 1968; Knowles, 1982; Wegner, Guiliano, & Hertel, 1984). This individualistic emphasis is probably both a reflection of and a contribution to the methodological concentration on social aggregates of exceedingly low entitativity (described above).

It is certainly desirable to attempt to balance the American individualistic emphasis with a more vigorous concern with the group level of analysis. Indeed, a number of the chapters in this book represent a movement in this direction. However, Taylor and Brown (1979) eloquently cautioned against viewing this emphasis on the individual as wholly inappropriate for a social psychology of group behavior:

> To theorize using the individual as the unit of analysis is not in any way to ignore social processes, but merely to be a psychologist interested in psychological issues.... While it is true that the dynamics have with a few exceptions been neglected, redressing the balance does not require a new level of theorizing; to do so would be to abdicate the central focus of psychology. (pp. 176–177)

It seems that the many critical examinations of the individualistic emphasis in current American social psychology (cited above) have made us more sensitive to social contexts and the group level of analysis. However, it does not seem likely that the individual will be, or should be, supplanted by the group as the primary unit of analysis. Rather, the individual is being progressively better understood in the context of the group. In turn, a deeper understanding of the behavior that occurs within the group is fostered through this appreciation of the effects of the group on the individual.

Topographical Aspects of Groups

With the term "topographical aspects of groups" we are referring to such attributes as group size, density, and interrelatedness of group members.

Table 1.1. Categorization Schemes for Describing Groups of Various Sizes

Group size	Brown (1954)	Caplow (1957)[a]	Simmel (1902)[a]
1			
2		Small primary	Dyad (2)
3		(2–20)	Triad (3)
4	Room size	Small nonprimary	The few (4–20)
5		(3–100)	
10			
20			The society (20–30)
30			
40			
50	Public hall		The large group
100	size		
1,000		Large (1,000–10,000)	
10,000	Too large	Largest (10,000+)	The largest group
100,000	to congregate		

[a]Numbers in parentheses represent the number of people proposed to comprise that particular type of group.

These attributes might be thought of as the kind of information one might try to obtain about a group from a photograph. An overview of these topographical aspects of groups should complement the definitional approach to understanding groups presented in the previous section.

A number of different categorization schemes have been developed for describing groups of various sizes. Table 1.1 presents three such categorization schemes. Clearly, one goal of this type of framework is to try to capture a critical attribute of various types of groups.

While such categorizations may be interesting in their own right, it is always problematic whether such a priori schemes fit the reality of groups. Consider, for example, James' (1951, 1953) series of observations of naturally occurring, free-forming groups. In a wide variety of settings, under a wide range of circumstances, free-forming groups tended to be rather small in number (ranging from two to seven persons, with a mean size of about three). This finding has been replicated many times (e.g., Bakeman & Beck, 1974; Hollingshead, 1949; Jorgenson & Dukes, 1976; Lyndsay, 1972, 1976).

One topographical aspect of groups that is related to the mere number of people in the group is the set of interrelated concepts of density, proximity, and crowding. John Q. Stewart's (1941, 1952) early efforts to develop a social physics laid the foundation for the current and active interest in crowding (cf. Baum & Valins, 1977; Freedman, 1975; Knowles, 1979, 1980; Stokols, 1978). Density refers to some ratio between the number of people present and the area that they occupy. Given a constant area, as the number of people increases, density also increases. By the same token, as the density increases, the interpersonal proximity (or the inverse of interpersonal distance) also increases (Knowles, 1979; Stokols, 1978). The term "crowding" has come to refer to a reaction to, rather than an alternative label for, increased density. Current research suggests that increased density results in perceived crowding only under certain conditions. For example, increased density in conjunction with a perceived loss of control (Rodin & Baum, 1978) may result in an experience of crowding. Similarly, increased density in conjunction with an attributional labeling of arousal in terms of the presence of other people may result in an experience of crowding (Worchel, 1978).

From the point of view of the individual group member, the larger group carries with it the possibility of a larger number of relationships. For example, Bossard (1945) noted that the possible number of symmetrical relationships (PR) between individuals in a group of size N is:

$$PR = \frac{N^2 - N}{2}$$

Thus, for a group of two people, the number of possible relationships between individuals is simply $PR = 1$; for a group of seven people the number of possible relationships between individuals is $PR = 21$.

Alternatively, consider the possibility that a relationship exists as an interaction between two individuals, or between an individual and a subgroup, or between two subgroups. Kephart (1950) observed that when relationships are defined in this way the number of possible relationships for a group of size N is:

$$PR = \frac{3^N - 2^{N+1} + 1}{2}$$

Thus, for a group of two people, the number of possible relationships is simply $PR = 1$; for a group of seven people, the number of possible relationships is $PR = 966$. This inherent complexity of groups is a subtle consequent of the mere number of people in the group. This adds elements of efficiency and convenience to the often observed tendency for people in groups to perceptually distinguish group members into subgroups of "us" and "them," rather than perceiving each person as a distinct entity (Brewer, 1979; Koffka, 1935; Lyndsay, 1976; Mullen, 1983; Rytina & Morgan, 1982; Sumner, 1906; Tajfel, 1978, 1983). This perceptual distinction of a group into subgroups of "us" and "them" can often be stimulated or exaggerated by differences between group members in such things as gender or handedness (McGuire & McGuire, 1982), attitudes (Gerard & Hoyt, 1974), or roles (Mullen, 1983; Wegner & Schaefer, 1978).

The work of Jacob Moreno (1934) stimulated efforts in the 1930s that continue today to try to capture the topography of the group. One of

Moreno's major contributions was the now familiar *sociogram,* wherein circles are drawn to represent group members, and lines are drawn between the circles to represent relationships, communication, or friendship choices between group members. Early applications of matrix algebra to socio-metric data (e.g., Festinger, 1949; Forsyth & Katz, 1946; Katz, 1947; Luce, 1949) provided a means of operationalizing group structure. An $N \times N$ matrix could be developed from a sociogram, where a 1 in the jth row and the kth column indicated that person k was a friendship choice of person j, whereas a 0 in that cell indicated the absence of such a choice. Analyses of these matrices to identify clusters of mutual choices along the main diagonal constitutes an operationalization of "cliques" or subgroups. In the 1960s, the extension of graph theoretical principles to the analysis of sociometric matrices (e.g., Harary, Norman, & Cartwright, 1965) represented a further refinement in the description of the topography of the group. This work has largely been conducted, and read, by sociologically oriented researchers and has not had much direct impact on the types of psycho-logically oriented theories presented in this volume (cf. Leinhardt, 1977; Scott & Scott, 1981).

An analogous approach to the topography of the group has been the communication network perspective. This work attempts to characterize the group in terms of who communicates or exchanges information with whom. One way of operationalizing this facet of the group is referred to as *adjacency density.* This index of the overall interrelatedness of the group is defined as:

$$\text{adjacency density} = \frac{a}{[N(N-1)]/2}$$

where a is the number of links between group members and N is the number of group members. This group measure actually represents the percentage of all possible links that do in fact occur in a group. Thus, a high adjacency density indicates that most of the people in the group communicate with everyone else: a low adjacency density indicates that most of the people in the group communicate with very few other group members.

Another possible means of operationalizing the communication network of a group is called the *centrality index.* This index of the interrelatedness for a given group member is defined as:

$$\text{centrality index} = \frac{\Sigma d_{jk}}{\Sigma d_{xk}}$$

where d_{jk} is the shortest distance between any two group members, and d_{xk} is the shortest distance between group member x and any other group member. Distance here refers to the number of communication steps, or the number of people, involved in conveying a message from one person to another. This individual measure represents the degree of communication a

Network	Adjacency Density	Centrality Index for Position				
		A	B	C	D	E
Wheel 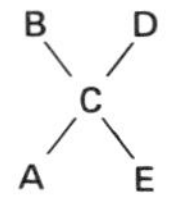	.40	4.6	4.6	8.0	4.6	4.6
Y 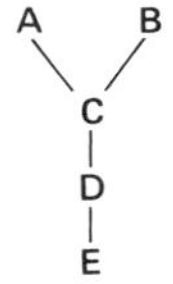	.40	4.5	4.5	7.2	6.0	4.0
Chain 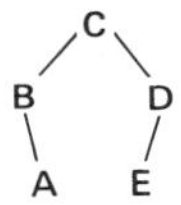	.40	4.0	5.7	6.7	5.7	4.0
Circle 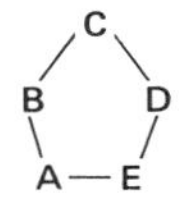	.50	5.0	5.0	5.0	5.0	5.0
Comcon 	1.00	5.0	5.0	5.0	5.0	5.0

Figure 1.1. Illustrations of adjacency density and centrality index for some five-person communication networks. (Letters represent group members, lines between letters represent communication between group members.)

given individual shares with all other group members. Thus, an individual with a high centrality index communicates with most of the other people in the group; an individual with a low centrality index communicates with very few other group members. Examples of adjacency density and centrality index are presented in Figure 1.1.

The distinction between the group level of analysis (adjacency density) and the individual level of analysis (centrality index) is represented by these two indices of communication network interrelatedness. Note that, as illustrated in Figure 1.1, high levels of centrality (individual) will only be possible for at least some of the group members under conditions of low adjacency density (group). At the group level, it has been demonstrated that the mean group member satisfaction is highest in groups with a higher adjacency density. At the individual level, it has been demonstrated that the individual group member's satisfaction is highest in a position of high centrality.

Thus, one might be led to expect group members to favor the wheel, or to favor the circle, depending upon whether the unit of analysis used was the individual or the group. For example, refer to the circle and the wheel depicted in Figure 1.1. Leavitt (1951) found higher mean group member satisfaction in the five-person circle (adjacency density = 0.50) than in the wheel (adjacency density = 0.40). However, the satisfaction of group member in position C was higher in the wheel (centrality = 8.0) than in the circle (centrality = 5.0); the satisfaction of group members in positions A, B, D, and E was lower in the wheel (centrality = 4.6) than in the circle (centrality = 5.0). These results have received subsequent replication (e.g., Cohen, 1961; Hirota, 1953).

More recent attempts to characterize the topography of the group can be found in Latané's social impact theory (Latané, 1981; Jackson, Chapter 5, this volume) Knowles' (1979, 1980) development of a social physics perspective, Mullen's (1983, Chapter 6, this volume) extension of self-attention theory, and Tanford and Penrod's (1984) social influence model. These more recent approaches to the effects of group composition are illustrated in later chapters in this volume.

Temporal Aspects of Groups

Just as groups may vary in a number of physical, topographical ways, groups may also change over time. Such changes may be thought of as the kind of information one can obtain about a group from a tape recording of the group members' interactions. As indicated in the earlier discussion of the definition of the group, members of an aggregate must change together in order for the aggregate to be seen as a real group in some sense. For example, Campbell (1958) noted that a band of gypsies would be more likely to be perceived as an entity than would a ladies aid society. This was based on the notion of a higher covariation over time between the members of the gypsy band than between the members of the ladies aid society. Thus, some dynamic element of change may actually be necessary in order for an aggregate to be perceived as a group.

Less attention has been devoted to the temporal dimension of groups than to the topographical dimension described in the previous section. Nonetheless, groups do change over time, and a certain consistency in the pattern of such changes has emerged. Many different frameworks have been proposed for describing the changes that occur in groups over time. Tuckman (1965; Tuckman & Jensen, 1977) provided a simple and accessible set of terms to describe the phases of development through which groups progress. As can be seen in Table 1.2, a number of other writers have observed similar general patterns of temporal changes.

During the phases of *forming*, the group is concerned with orientation. Group members come together and begin to arrive at definitions of tasks and requirements of group members. They exchange information and begin to develop the interpersonal relations that are to define membership in the group. *Storming*, obviously, refers to a phase of polarization and conflict. Disagreements arise and may become exaggerated. Group members may become dissatisfied with other group members or with the group process as a whole. During the phase of *norming*, conflicts are resolved and the group members agree upon definitions of tasks and group member requirements. *Performing* describes a phase in which the group members actively strive toward group goals. The major emphasis is on working toward task achievement. Finally, *adjourning* may occur if the group is expected or required to disband upon task completion. The nature of the task, the heterogeneity of the group, and the cyclical or repetitive nature of certain types of groups may modify the manner in which groups progress through these various stages (Cissna, 1984; Shaw, 1981; Tuckman & Jensen, 1977). Still, the general pattern of sequential stages does appear to be a relatively consistent and replicable phenomenon.

This phenomenon of phases of group development has generated a research literature of its own. However, an implicit connection exists between particular phases of group development and general bodies of social psychological research. In a sense, it seems that certain domains of social psychological research have been based upon the following methodological paradigm: bring a group of people together, force them (through task structuring, instructions, and manipulations) through to some particular phase of group development, and then study the behavior that occurs during this artificially attained phase. For example, the research literatures on such phenomena as group polarization effects (Stoner, 1961), the reactions of the group to deviants (Schachter, 1951), and intergroup conflict (Brewer, 1979) might illustrate a methodological focus upon groups that have been arrested at the storming phase of development. The research literatures on such phenomena as conformity behavior (Asch, 1956), the establishment of group norms (Sherif, 1936), and the symbolic interactionist perspective on role definition (Shibutani, 1961) may illustrate a methodological focus upon groups that have been accelerated into, and then arrested at, the norming phase of group development. The research literatures on such phenomena as group performance (Steiner, 1972) and the effects of cooperation and competition (Blake & Mouton, 1979) may illustrate a methodological focus upon groups that have been accelerated into, and then arrested at, the performing phase of group development.

This correspondence between phases of group development and general bodies of social psychological research casts into sharp relief the things that

Table 1.2. Phases of Group Development

Source	Forming	Storming	Norming	Performing	Adjourning
Bales & Strodbeck (1951)	Orientation	Evaluation	Control		—
Fisher (1970)	Orientation	Conflict	Emergence	Reinforcement	—
Mabry (1975)	Boundary seeking	Ambivalence	Actualization		—
Hare (1976)	Pattern maintenence	Adaptation	Integration	Goal attainment	—
Winter (1976)	Encounter	Differentiation	Norm building	Production	Separation
Caple (1978)	Orientation	Conflict	Integration	Achievement	Order
LaCoursiere (1979)	Orientation	Dissatisfaction	Production		Termination
Leventhal (1979)	Preconflict	Onset	Stabilized conflict	Termination	Postconflict

Phases (according to Tuckman's terminology)

we do know about the temporal aspects of groups and the things that we do not know about the temporal aspects of groups. We know a great deal about the events that occur during storming, norming, and performing, by virtue of the research literatures that have developed around the study of groups that have been artificially accelerated into these phases. However, the process of forming has generally been accomplished through the mechanisms of subject pool sign-up procedures and random assignment based on pretest scores. Thus, we know very little about the events that occur during the initial phases of forming. Notable exceptions to this are studies of voluntary association memberships (McPherson & Lockwood, 1981; Zander, 1972), the small but intriguing literature on conversion and recruitment into cults (e.g., Halperin, 1982; Stark & Bainbridge, 1980), and Moreland and Levine's (1982, 1984; Pavelchek, Moreland, & Levine, 1985) seminal efforts on reconnaissance activities and joining groups. The temporal aspect of groups about which we know the least is the phase of adjourning. This phase of group development is generally accomplished through the "subjects were debriefed and dismissed" mechanism of the research paradigm.

Before moving away from the general topic of temporal aspects of groups, it is interesting to speculate on the connections between levels of analysis, definitions of groups, and the different research emphasis on events occuring during different phases of group development. Recall the numerous reasons delineated above for the use of the individual rather than the group as the appropriate unit of analysis in social psychological research. The methodological and procedural concentration on some (artificially created) phases of group development may be an epiphenomenon of this preference for the individual as the unit of analysis. The paradigm that emerged in the context of a focus on the individual allowed researchers to examine in detail the events occurring during storming, norming, and performing. However, this paradigm made it very easy to "create" the groups being studied and dismiss them when the study was done (thereby skipping over the processes of forming and adjourning).

Overview of the Rest of the Book

If the reader were to survey the tables of contents of current books on group behavior, certain consistencies would emerge. Invariably, one would find a chapter devoted to leadership behavior, another chapter devoted to group performance, a third chapter devoted to group decisions, a fourth chapter devoted to coalition formation, and so on. This common format of group behavior books follows very closely the tendency for the field to develop theories that are devoted to particular behavioral domains. For example, theories of coalition formation were developed to account for the particular behavioral phenomena associated with coalitions. Coalitions may be inherently interesting in many respects, and some authors have been very creative in generalizing theories of coalition formation beyond the laboratory paradigm (cf. Caplow, 1968, for a compellingly broad perspective on coalition-type behaviors). Nonetheless, no one would expect theories of coalition formation to describe, predict, or explain phenomena that fall outside of the behavioral domain within which these theories were developed. Thus, the typical format for books on group behavior involves a topical consideration of heavily researched behavioral domains, along with the theories developed to describe, predict, or explain these behavioral domains.

The table of contents for the present book breaks from the pattern described above. Throughout the remainder of this book, theories will be presented that are not tied to some particular behavioral domain. Each of these theories is general in the sense that each theory is constructed to deal with group behavior at a broad level, with reference to many different behavioral domains. For each theory, the mechanisms, processes, and patterns that are important for understanding one example of group behavior are important for understanding many other examples of group behavior as well. Each of the theories presented in the remaining chapters of this book is extremely ambitious in scope. Thereby, the book as a whole becomes particularly ambitious, in bringing together for the first time such a wide range of general theories of group behavior.

Each theoretical perspective described in the next eight chapters is presented in a consistent format. In the first section of each chapter, the vocabulary, concepts, principles, and assumptions of each theoretical orientation are presented. Next, the operation of each theory's principles in group settings is discussed. In the third section of each chapter, each theory is applied to a variety of specific group phenomena. Finally, each chapter concludes with a general summary and conclusion section.

Chapter 2 by George Goethals and John Darley describes the processes by which people come to evaluate themselves, their abilities, and their opinions through comparisons with others. The operation of social comparison processes in group settings, and the effects of social comparison on group behavior, are examined. Chapter 3 by Gerald Sande and Mark Zanna considers the processes by which cognitive dissonance mechanisms are engaged in group contexts. The influence of cognitive dissonance on attitude change and diffusion of responsibility on the part of group members are discussed. Chapter 4 by Roy Baumeister and Debra Hutton examines the effects of the group on the individual's desire to match one's self-presentations to others' expectations, and to one's ideal self. The attributes of groups that influence these audience-pleasing and self-construction motives are delineated. Chapter 5 by Russell Geen and Brad Bushman examines group phenomena in terms of arousal mechanisms. The processes by which group settings influence arousal are addressed along with the processes by which arousal influences the behavior of group members. Chapter 6 by Jeffery Jackson presents social impact theory's characterization of the relation between stimulus magnitude (the strength, immediacy, and number of people in a group) and sensation intensity (social impact). Chapter 7 by Brian Mullen describes group effects in terms of the influence of group composition on individuals' attentional focus. The Other–Total Ratio, an algorithm that characterizes these group effects on self-attention processes, is employed to predict various types of group behavior. Chapter 8 by John Pryor and Thomas Ostrom considers group behavior from the perspective of social cognition theory. This chapter reviews and integrates current research on the processes by which information regarding groups is processed and recalled. Chapter 9 by Dan Wegner examines group phenomena in terms of transactive memory processes. This perspective describes how information is encoded, stored, and retrieved by social units, rather than by single individuals.

The final chapter by George Goethals provides an overview of these theoretical perspectives and characterizes the foregoing presentations in terms of broad, underlying dimensions. Similarities and differences between theoretical perspectives are highlighted, and directions for future research are suggested.

Acknowledgments. The author would like to thank George R. Goethals, Li-tze Hu, Eric Knowles, Sally Tanford, and Daniel Wegner for their helpful comments on earlier drafts of this manuscript.

References

Allport, F.H. (1920). *Social Psychology*. Boston: Houghton-Mifflin.

Allport, G.W. (1968). The historical background of modern social psychology. In G. Lindzey & E. Aronson (Eds.), *Handbook of social psychology* (2nd ed.). Reading, MA: Addison-Wesley.

Anderson, L.R. (1978). Groups would do better without humans. *Personality and Social Psychology Bulletin, 4*, 557–558.

Asch, S.E. (1956). Studies of independence and a minority of one against a unanimous majority. *Psychological Monographs, 70*, No. 9 (whole no. 416).

Bakeman, R., & Beck, S. (1974). The size of informal groups in public. *Environment and Behavior, 6*, 378–390.

Bales, R.F., & Strodtbeck, F.L. (1951). Phases in group problem solving. *Journal of Abnormal and Social Psychology, 46*, 485–495.

Bass, B.M. (1960). *Leadership, psychology and organizational behavior*. New York: Harper & Row.

Baum, A., & Valins, S. (1977). *Architecture and social behavior: Psychological studies of social density*. Hillsdale, NJ: Erlbaum.

Blake, R.R., & Mouton, J.S. (1979). Intergroup problem solving in organizations: From theory to practice. In W.G. Austin & S. Worchel (Eds.), *The social psychology of intergroup relations*. Monterey, CA: Brooks/Cole.

Bogardus, E.S. (1954). Group behavior and groupality. *Sociology and Social Research, 38*, 401–403.

Boodin, J.E. (1913). The existence of social minds. *American Journal of Sociology, 19*, 1–47.

Bossard, J.H.S. (1945). Law of family interaction. *American Journal of Sociology, 50*, 292–294.

Brewer, M.B. (1979). In-group bias in the minimal intergroup situation: A cognitive motivational analysis. *Psychological Bulletin, 86*, 307–324.

Brown, R.W. (1954). Mass phenomena. In G. Lindzey (Ed.), *Handbook of social psychology*. Cambridge, MA: Addison-Wesley.

Buys, C.J. (1978). Humans would do better without groups. *Personality and Social Psychology Bulletin, 4*, 123–125.

Campbell, D.T. (1958). Common fate, similarity and other indices of aggregates of persons as social entities. *Behavioral Science, 3*, 14–25.

Caple, R.B. (1978). The sequential stages of group development. *Small Group Behavior, 9*, 470–476.

Caplow, T. (1957). Organizational size. *Administrative Science Quarterly, 1*, 484–505.

Caplow, T. (1968). *Two against one: Coalitions in triads*. Englewood Cliffs, NJ: Prentice-Hall.

Cattell, R.B. (1948). Concepts and methods in the measurement of group syntality. *Psychological Review, 55*, 48–63.

Cissna, K.N. (1984). Phases in group development: The negative evidence. *Small Group Behavior, 15*, 3–32.

Cohen, A.M. (1961). Changing small group communication networks. *Journal of Communication, 11*, 116–124, 128.

Durkheim, E. (1938). *The rules of sociological method*. Glencoe, IL: Free Press.

Festinger, L. (1949). The analysis of sociograms using matrix algebra. *Human Relations, 2*, 153–158.

Fiedler, F.E. (1967). *A theory of leadership effectiveness*. New York: McGraw-Hill.

Fisher, B.A. (1970). Decision emergence: Phases in group decision making. *Speech Monographs, 37*, 53–66.

Forsyth, E., & Katz, L. (1946). A matrix approach to the analysis of sociometric data: A preliminary report. *Sociometry, 9*, 340–347.

Freedman, J.L. (1975). *Crowding and behavior*. San Francisco: Freeman.

Gerard, H.B., & Hoyt, M.F. (1974). Distinctiveness of social categorization and attitude toward ingroup members. *Journal of Personality and Social Psychology, 29*, 836–842.

Golembiewski, R.T. (1962). *The small group*. Chicago: University of Chicago Press.

Halperin, D.A. (1982). Group processes in cult affiliation and recruitment. *Group, 6*, 13–24.

Harary, F., Norman, R.Z., & Cartwright, D. (1965). *Structural models: An introduction to directed graphs*. New York: Wiley.

Hare, A.P. (1976). *Handbook of small group research* (2nd ed.). New York: Free Press.

Hirota, K. (1953). Group problem solving and communication. *Japanese Journal of Psychology, 24*, 176–177.

Hollingshead, A.B. (1949). *Elmstown's youth*. New York: Wiley.

James, J. (1951). A preliminary study of the size determinant in social group interactions. *American Sociological Review, 16*, 474–477.

James, J. (1953). The distribution of free-forming small group size. *American Sociological Review, 18*, 569–570.

Jorgenson, D.O., & Dukes, F.O. (1976). Deindividuation as a function of density and group membership. *Journal of Personality and Social Psychology, 34*, 24–29.

Jung, C.G. (1922). *Collected papers on analytic psychology* (2nd edition). London: Bailliere, Tindall & Cox.

Katz, L. (1947). On the matrix analysis of sociometric data. *Sociometry, 10*, 233–241.

Kephart, W.M. (1950). A quantitative analysis of intragroup relationships. *American Journal of Sociology, 55*, 548.

Knowles, E.S. (1979). The proximity of others: A critique of crowding research and integration with the social scences. *Journal of Population, 2*, 3–17.

Knowles, E.S. (1980). An affiliative-conflict theory of personal and group spatial behavior. In P.B. Paulus (Ed.), *Psychology of Group Influence*. Hillsdale, NJ: Erlbaum.

Knowles, E.S. (1982). From individuals to group members: A dialectic for the social sciences. In W.J. Ickes & E.S. Knowles (Eds.), *Personality, roles and social behavior*. New York: Springer-Verlag.

Koffka, K. (1935). *Principles of gestalt psychology*. New York: Harcourt, Brace.

Komorita, S.S., & Moore, D. (1976). Theories and processes of coalition formation. *Journal of Personality and Social Psychology, 33*, 371–381.

Lacayo, R. (1985). Blood in the stands. *Time, 125(23)*, 39–41.

LaCoursiere, R. (1974). A group method to facilitate learning during stages of psychiatric affiliation. *International Journal of Group Psychotherapy, 24*, 342–351.

Latané, B. (1981). The psychology of social impact. *American Psychologist, 36*, 343–356.

Latta, R.M., & Gorman, M.E. (1984). The small group: A bridge between sociology and social psychology. *Psychological Reports, 54*, 947–950.

Leavitt, H.J. (1951). Some effects of certain communication patterns on group performance. *Journal of Abnormal and Social Psychology, 46*, 38–50.

LeBon, G. (1895/1960). *The Crowd*. New York: Viking.

Leinhardt, S. (Ed.) (1977). *Social networks: A developing paradigm*. New York: Academic Press.

Leventhal, G.S. (1979). Effects of external conflict on resource allocation and fairness within groups and organizations. In W.G. Austin & S. Worchel (Eds.), *The Social Psychology of Intergroup relations*. Monterey, CA: Brooks/Cole.

Lyndsay, J.S.B. (1972). On the number in a group. *Human Relations, 25*, 47–64.

Lyndsay, J.S.B. (1976). On the number and size of subgroups. *Human Relations, 29*, 1103–1114.

Luce, R.D. (1949). A method of matrix analysis of group structure. *Psychometrika, 14*, 95–116.

Mabry, E.A. (1975). Sequential structure of interaction in encounter groups. *Human Communication Research, 1*, 302–307.

Mann, L. (1969). Queue culture: The waiting line as a social system. *American Journal of Sociology, 75*, 340–350.

Mann, L., & Taylor, K.F. (1969). Queue counting: The effect of motive upon estimates of numbers in waiting lines. *Journal of Personality and Social Psychology, 12*, 95–103.

McDougall, W. (1920). *The group mind*. Cambridge: Cambridge University Press.

McGuire, W.J., & McGuire, C.V. (1982). Significant others in self-space: Sex differences and developmental trends in the social self. In J. Suls (Eds.), *Psychological perspectives on the self* (vol. 1). Hillsdale, NJ: Erlbaum.

McPherson, J.M., & Lockwood, W.G. (1981). The longitudinal study of voluntary association memberships: A multivariable analysis. *Journal of Voluntary Action Research, 10*, 74–84.

Moreland, R., & Levine, J.M. (1982). Socialization in small groups: Temporal changes in individual-group relations. In L. Berkowitz (Ed.), *Advances in experimental social psychology* (Vol. 15). New York: Academic.

Moreland, R., & Levine, J.M. (1984). Role transitions in small groups. In V. Allen & E. van de Vliert (Eds.), *Role transitions: Explorations and explanations*. New York: Plenum.

Moreno, J.L. (1934). *Who shall survive?* Washington, DC: Nervous and Mental Disease Publishing.

Mullen, B. (1983). Operationalizing the effect of the group on the individual: A self-attention perspective. *Journal of Experimental Social Psychology, 19*, 295–322.

Murray Ledger-Times (1/10/1985). Newsbriefs. p. 2.

New York Times (2/27/1985) Section I, p. 12.

Pavelcheck, M.A., Moreland, R.L., & Levine, J.M. (1985). Effects of prior group memberships on subsequent reconnassiance activities. *Journal of Personality and Social Psychology, 50*, 56–66.

Pepitone, A. (1981). Lessons from the history of social psychology. *American Psychologist, 36*, 972–985.

Reicher, S. (1982). The determination of collective behavior. In H. Tajfel (Ed.), *Social identity and intergroup relations.* Cambridge: Cambridge University Press.

Robinson, M. (1981). The identity of human social groups. *Behavioral Science, 26*, 114–129.

Rodin, J., & Baum, A. (1978). Crowding and helplessness: Potential consequences of density and loss of control. In A. Baum & Y. Epstein (Eds.), *Human responses to crowding.* Hillsdale, NJ: Erlbaum.

Rytina, S., & Morgan, D.L. (1982). The arithmetic of social relations: The interplay of category and network. *American Journal of Sociology, 88*, 88–113.

Schachter, S. (1951). Deviation, rejection and communication. *Journal of Abnormal and Social Psychology, 46*, 190–207.

Scott, W.A., & Scott, R. (1981). Intercorrelations among structural properties of primary groups. *Journal of Personality and Social Psychology, 41*, 279–292.

Shaffer, L.S. (1978). On the current confusion of group-related behavior and collective behavior: A reaction to Buys. *Personality and Social Psychology Bulletin, 4*, 564–567.

Shaw, M.E. (1981). *Group dynamics: The psychology of small group behavior.* New York: McGraw-Hill.

Sherif, M. (1936). *The psychology of social norms.* New York: Harper.

Shibutani, T. (1961). *Society and personality.* Englewood Cliffs, NJ: Prentice-Hall.

Shweder, R.A., & Bourne, E.J. (1982). Does the concept of the person vary cross-culturally? In A.J. Marsella & G.M. White (Eds.), *Cultural conceptions of mental health and therapy.* London: Reidel.

Simmel, G. (1902). The number of members as determining the sociological form of the group. *American Journal of Sociology, 8*, 1–46, 158–196.

Smith, K.K., & White, G.L. (1983). Some alternatives to traditional social psychology of groups. *Personality and Social Psychology Bulletin, 9*, 65–73.

Stark, R., & Bainbridge, W.S. (1980). Networks of faith: Interpersonal bonds and recruitment to cults and sects. *American Journal of Sociology, 85*, 1376–1395.

Steiner, I.D. (1972). *Group process and productivity.* New York: Academic Press.

Steiner, I.D. (1974). Whatever happened to the group in social psychology? *Journal of Experimental Social Psycholgoy, 10*, 94–108.

Stewart, J.Q. (1941). An inverse distance variation for certain social influences. *Science, 93*, 89–90.

Stewart, J.Q. (1952). A basis for social physics. *Impact of Science on Society, 3*, 110–133.

Stokols, D. (1978) In defense of the crowding construct. In A. Baum, J.E. Singer, & S. Vallins (Eds.), *Advances in environmental psychology* (Vol. 1). Hillsdale, NJ: Erlbaum.

Stoner, J.A.F. (1961). A comparison of individual and group decisions involving risk. Unpublished master's thesis. Massachusetts Institute of Technology, 1961; cited by D.G. Marquis (1962). Individual responsibility and group decisions involving risk. *Industrial Management Review, 3*, 8–23.

Sumner, W.G. (1906). *Folkways*. New York: Ginn.

Tajfel, H. (Ed.) (1978). *Differentiation between social groups: Studies in the social psychology of intergroup relations*. London: Academic Press.

Tajfel, H. (1983). Experiments in intergroup discrimination. In H.H. Blumberg, A.P. Hare, V. Kent, & M.F. Davies (Eds.), *Small groups and social interaction*. Chinchester: Wiley.

Tanford, S., & Penrod, S. (1984). Social influence model: A formal integration of research on majority and minority influence processes. *Psychological Bulletin, 95*, 189–225.

Taylor, D.M., & Brown, R.J. (1979). Towards a more social social psychology? *British Journal of Social and Clinical Psychology, 18*, 173–180.

Tuckman, B.W. (1965). Developmental sequence in small groups. *Psychological Bulletin, 63*, 384–399.

Tuckman, B.W., & Jensen, M.A.C. (1977). Stages in small group development revisited. *Group and Organizational Studies, 3*, 419–427.

Vapnarsky, C.A. (1967). On methodological individualism in social sciences. *Cornell Journal of Social Relations, 2*, 1–18.

Wegner, D.M., Giuliano, T., & Hertel, P.T. (1984). Cognitive interdependence in close relationships. In W.J. Ickes (Ed.), *Compatible and incompatible relationships*. New York: Springer-Verlag.

Wegner, D.M., & Schaefer, D. (1978). The concentration of responsibility: An objective self-awareness analysis of group size effects in helping situations. *Journal of Personality and Social Psychology, 36*, 147–155.

Winter, S.K. (1976). Developmental stages in the roles and concerns of group coleaders. *Small Group Behavior, 7*, 349–362.

Worchel, S. (1978). The experience of crowding: An attributional analysis. In A. Baum & Y. Epstein (Eds.), *Human response to crowding*. Hillsdale, NJ: Erlbaum.

Zander, A. (1972). The purposes of national associations. *Journal of Voluntary Action Research, 1*, 20–29.

Chapter 2

Social Comparison Theory: Self-Evaluation and Group Life

George R. Goethals and John M. Darley

When psychologists think of social comparison theory, they initially recall Leon Festinger's classic paper on a theory of social comparison processes. However, in the three decades since the publication of this work, social comparison theory has evolved in several ways. First, there have been many restatements and amendments to the theory, some connecting it with other theories current in social psychology. Second, several discrete areas of empirical investigation have flourished that are closely connected to the theory. A modern theory of social comparison draws on both these developments for its formulation.

In this chapter we first make a few historical comments about the origins of the theory, next present what we take to be an adequate revised statement of the theory, and finally turn to developing its implications for various group processes and behaviors.

The Origins of Social Comparison Theory

Two related propositions comprise what most psychologists would regard as the core of the original theory of social comparison processes: (1) Individuals evaluate their opinions and abilities by comparing them with the opinions and abilities of other people. (2) In order to do this, they chose similar others with whom to compare. Obviously, then, social comparison is an *interpersonal* process, in that one person evaluates his or her own opinion or ability by comparing it with the opinions expressed or abilities displayed by other people. However, in this formulation, social comparison is not a *group* process; the focus of the theory is on the individual engaged in self-evaluation. This is not accidental. Festinger made several contributions to experimental social psychology, and one of the major ones was to take many of Lewin's theoretical formulations, which wavered between the individual and the group level, and ground them unambiguously at the individual level. This made them accessable to empirical verification using the experimental procedures so ingeniously developed by Festinger himself, by Schachter, and by their students.[1]

However, that many of the ideas in Fstinger's formulation of social comparison theory had their origins in considerations of group processes becomes clear when one examines the work Festinger had been engaged in just before the development of the theory. The 1954 theory of social comparison processes had its roots in two research areas that had concerned Festinger prior to 1954. The first involved the determinants of group members' aspirations for their level of performance on various ability-related tasks, and particularly the ways in which group standards affected individual levels of aspiration. The second, theoretically summarized in the 1950 paper on informal social communication, reviewed studies showing that people seek opinion uniformity in groups in order to establish a social definition of reality against which to validate their opinions. Interestingly, the processes discussed in both the 1950 and the 1954 papers are similar, but the papers differ as to their implied levels of analysis of the phenomena. The 1950 paper proposed that groups strive for opinion uniformity in order to establish a social reality. The 1954 paper argues that individuals are attracted to groups in which the members have opinions similar to their own so that they can evaluate their own opinions with precision. In both cases the end result is the same, preference for groups that are homogeneous with respect to opinion. In the 1950 theory this opinion uniformity serves the group's requirements, it is a prerequisite for "group locomotion" (a term taken from Lewin). In the 1954 theory, the same uniformity serves the individual's requirements.

Other examples of this move away from the group level and toward the individual level of analysis could be cited, but the implication for the present chapter is clear. The theory of social comparison processes exists at the level of the individual, but because of its historical origins, can be expected to have a number of implications for group process. These implications will need to be made explicit, and that is the purpose of the present chapter.

---

[1]One of the consequences of Festinger's grounding of social comparison theory at the individual level was that researchers were led away from studying group processes. To this day research done on social comparison processes at the group level has lagged behind research done at the individual level. Yet writing in 1959, in his *The Psychology of Affiliation*, Schachter reported that the only empirical support for the major propositions of social comparison theory came from Festinger, Riecken, and Schachter's (1956) book on *When Prophecy Fails*. This book reported a case study of group processes. Ironically, most social psychologists remember this book as the origins of a new construct at the individual level, cognitive dissonance. Thus in yet another way were researchers, Festinger included, led away from research at the group level and, in this instance, from research on social comparison processes.

A Modified Theory of Social Comparison Processes

Festinger began his theory of social comparison with the postulate that people have a "drive" to evaluate their abilities (Hypothesis I). The "drive" vocabulary seems to us to be a dated one, and one that may move the theoretical discussion in nonuseful ways. We think this postulate reflects two ideas: first, during the course of development, people learn it is useful to know how well they can do various things. By having a fairly accurate idea of their talents and skills, they are able to avoid various physical and social disasters that otherwise might befall them. Second, this accuracy motive can be situationally induced or enhanced in specific social contexts. If I know, for instance, that I have a choice of competing for prizes by ring tossing or dart throwing, I am suddenly very interested in how well I can do those two skills.

This example hints at the second important postulate of social comparison theory. In the absence of physical realities or standards of comparison, individuals seek to compare their abilities and opinions with the abilities and opinions of others (Hypothesis II). If anything, we would suggest that Festinger understated the strength of this point (see Tajfel, 1978). It sounds as if social comparison is a somewhat deficient substitute for physical comparison. In fact, it strikes us that social comparison is often, as a matter of logic, the only comparison possible. Rarely do physical facts give conclusive evidence on the truth of an opinion. ("I prefer the paintings of Monet to those of Manet.") Rarely is there a physical reality to which we can compare our performance in the case of abilities. ("I ran a mile in four minutes" seems to refer to an objective standard but is given meaning and translated into a level of running ability only because we know how few people could run as fast.) Social realities seem to us frequently to be the preferred information for establishing one's own abilities and opinions.

As noted above, a third major postulate of Festinger's social comparison theory was the proposition that people prefer comparison with other people whose opinions and abilities are similar (Hypothesis III). This preference for comparison with similar others was explained in terms of the first postulate, the need to precisely evaluate opinions and abilities. For example, evaluation of our chess playing ability is best served by comparison to others who play about the same level that we do, rather than to grand masters or preschool children. To anticipate a fundamental modification of social comparison theory discussed below, comparison with similar others may serve needs to validate as well as evaluate ourselves. In opinion comparison, for example, similar others are the most likely to validate our opinions. It is not as clear that they provide the most objective source of disinterested evaluation.

The foregoing material summarizes the fundamental concepts of social comparison theory as set forth in Festinger's original 1954 statement. In the decades since the publication of that paper, there have been a number of empirical discoveries and theoretical developments both in the social comparison literature and in psychology in general, which require modifications of various aspects of the theory. (Latané, 1966, and Suls and Miller, 1977, are both useful collections of many writers' thinking on social comparison.) Here we will suggest the modifications to the theory that are particularly useful in developing it in directions that facilitate its applications to group processes.

The drive for self-validation or self-esteem. While it is probably true that people have a generalized desire, need, wish, or want to know how good they are at various ability-linked tasks, it is certainly the case that they also want to discover that they are good at the tasks. More formally, it has been suggested by numerous theorists that people have a desire to think well of their abilities—that is, to think that their abilities are high.[2] The same is true for opinions. People want to believe that their opinions are correct. They may wish objectively to evaluate them in many cases, but often they simply wish to establish that they are correct.

It can be argued that Festinger's original theory contained a recognition of this motive, in the case of ability comparison, in the form of the well-known but enigmatic postulate of the "unidirectional drive upward" (Hypothesis IV). Festinger also noted that people of lower ability who are forced into comparison with those of higher ability will have "deep experiences of failure and feelings of inadequacy" with respect to the ability in question, and, it is fair to infer, with respect to their self-esteem in general (Festinger, 1954, p. 137).

As evidence for the role of self validation concerns in social comparison processes, we would cite the evidence that shows that the interpretation of information obtained through social comparison is biased by the need to maintain a positive self-evaluation. Several studies of "attributional egotism" indicate that people make self-serving attributions about their own performances but do not make parallel "other-serving" attributions about other people's performances (M.L. Snyder, Stephan, & Rosenfield, 1976, 1978). That is, people take credit for their own successes, and deny responsibility for their own failures (Greenwald, 1980), but do not make similar attributions for the successes and failures of others. People also overestimate the magnitude of their contributions to joint products if the

---

[2]William James (1890) has written charmingly and insightfully about this. He points out that people generally want to think that they have high abilities, but that there is an interesting maneuver, which he calls "adjusting one's pretentions," that people can do when they have discovered that they do not possess a high level of some ability. They can simply cease to regard the possession of that ability as important to people in general or themselves in particular. As James implies, therefore, what is really at issue here is the person's self-esteem, which is complexly connected to possession of abilities.

products are successful, but not if they are failures (M. Ross and Sicoly, 1979). There is considerable debate about why people make these self-serving attributions (Bradley, 1978; Miller and Ross, 1975; M. Ross & Fletcher, 1985; Tetlock and Levy, 1982; Zuckerman, 1979), but the argument centers around whether people make irrational esteem-enhancing or esteem-maintaining attributions or whether they make rational attributions consistent with a positive self-evaluation. There is general agreement that people either already have or are trying to achieve or enhance a positive self-evaluation. It we assume that the average person's flattering view that he or she is better than average reflects a need rather than a reality (this seems a safe assumption, because the average person cannot consistently be better than the average), we see evidence for the emergence of the self-validation drive in social comparisons.

Further evidence for a self-validation component in the social comparison of opinions comes from studies showing that people remember data about a set of other people's opinions to contain a higher rate of agreeing opinions than in fact the set did contain (Goethals, 1986). In general, there are several sources of evidence that people make self-validating interpretations about their own performances, about the performances of other people as compared to their own, and about the frequency of agreement between other people's opinions and their own.

We have been discussing the self-validation motive with regard to abilities and opinions specifically. Singer (1966) made the important point that social comparison theorists have become increasingly concerned with self-evaluation and self-esteem, and not just opinion and ability assessment. Elsewhere we have argued that this is one of the reasons that there is continuing interest in social comparison theory (Goethals, in press). For purposes of future discussion, we propose that social comparison theory be viewed as being concerned with overall self-evaluation and self-validation as well as the evaluation of specific personal characteristics and opinions.

Saving face in group settings. On occasion the exigencies of the situation require that a performance be given in public. The anxieties created by that point out the existence of another motive that figures into social comparison situations, which is that of preserving or even enhancing ones face in the eyes of others. That what we think of ourselves is connected to what others think of us is certainly true in the long run, but in the short run it seems worth distinguishing the two motives. Even though we academics do not ourselves care about how well we dance, we would feel acute concerns for saving face—or losing it—were we required to perform in front of people who judged one another on how well they danced.

The performance–ability distinction. It is particularly useful, for a social comparison theory that is aimed at illuminating group phenomena, to distinguish between underlying dispositions and their various manifestations in observed behavior. This is particularly important in the case of abilities; what we can observe are not the abilities of another (or, for that matter, of ourselves), but some product or performance that we assume to be a manifestation of that ability. From our observations, we make an *inference*, which may be more or less conscious and reflective, about the level of ability that a person holds. As the reader will recognize, making this distinction creates a role for attributional considerations within social comparison theory (Goethals & Darley, 1977). A second set of theoretical possibilities are also accessed. By recognizing that people are motivated in social comparison settings by concerns for both self-validation and what others think of them, and also drawing on the recently developed notion of "excusing conditions" (J. Austin, 1956; C. Snyder, Higgens, & Stukey, 1984) room is made within social comparison theory for self-presentational considerations (see Baumeister and Hutton, Chapter 4, this volume). Without going into great detail here, an example may convey the general notion. A college professor who loudly announces, just before a squash game, that he has forgotten his regular glasses and must play with his (performance-degrading) bifocals, is making a self-presentational move that is easily understood.[3]

The related attributes hypothesis. A further modification of social comparison theory also ties it to attribution theory (Jones and Davis, 1965; Kelley, 1967, 1971, 1972, 1973). Festinger's original statement concerning choice of comparison other was that one sought out "similar" others for comparison purposes. We (Goethals and Darley, 1977) pointed out that it would be useful to construe this statement as meaning similarity on background attributes related to the opinion or ability in question, a proposition that Wheeler and Zuckerman (1977) refered to as "the related attributes hypothesis." Intuitively, it seems likely that in order accurately to determine the correctness of one's opinion or the level of one's ability, one must compare with others who are similar on background attributes related to the opinion or ability being evaluated. For example, in evaluating one's opinion about disinvestment in South African businesses, an American would want to compare with others who are similar in general political orientation and dislike of apartheid, believing that these factors are related to and predictive of opinions on disinvestment. Similarly, in evaluating one's tennis-playing ability, one would wish to compare with a person of about the same age, degree of physical stamina, and amount of recent practice, because it is generally held that these factors are related to current level of performance, independent of underlying ability.

---

[3]If somewhat transparent. Particularly if repeated. The authors are grateful to Professor E.E. Jones for bringing this example to their attention.

The related attributes hypothesis has generated considerable research in recent years. While it is clear that people do compare with others who are similar on related attributes (Zanna, Goethals, & Hill 1975), recent research suggests that sometimes we compare with others who are similar in terms of performance levels as well (Wheeler, Koestner, & Driver, 1982). In addition, whether people compare with similar or dissimilar others is affected by a variety of factors (Mettee & Smith, 1977). The important point is that what it means to compare with similar others needs to be understood in terms of the related attributes hypothesis as well as by the traditional interpretation of the similarity hypothesis, which holds that we wish to compare with others whose opinions and performance levels are similar.

Avoiding social comparison. We have suggested that concerns for self-validation and face saving need to be added to concerns for self-evaluation as determinants of social comparison processes. In some situations, in which the context does not induce strong needs accurately to assess new abilities, and the possibilities of harming one's self-esteem or losing face are high, people may actively seek to avoid social comparison. In their influential chapter on "pleasure and pain in social comparison," Brickman and Bulman (1977) make the intuitively correct point that there are many cases in which people avoid situations because they do not wish to receive the social comparison information that is available there. (Class reunions are an example that will remind many of us of these fears.) An individual risks two kinds of pain in these situations. First is the self-esteem damage done by the discovery that another's abilities outstrip ones own. Second, one also risks losing face in the eyes of others. This is so because the norms in many group settings foster or even require disclosure of one's own achievements, abilities, and opinions, in a pattern of reciprocal disclosure with others. Here the reader can imagine the pain inflicted by the discovery that another's achievements surpass one's own, followed instantly by the necessity, in response to her question, to reveal one's own suddenly pathetic-seeming achievements.

These suggestions fit nicely with the research on false consensus and false uniqueness effects. People want self-validating information and avoid social comparison when that might undermine it. Sometimes they go further and fabricate comparison information that is self-serving. They do this by generating self-serving estimates of consensus. For instance, people over-estimate the numbers of other people who share their socially undesirable or neutral behaviors and underestimate the numbers that share their socially desirable behaviors (Goethals, 1986; Mullen, Atkins, Champion, 1985; L. Edwards, Hardy, Story, & Vanderblok, Ross, 1977; Suls & Wan, in press).

The automaticity of the social comparison process. Recently, in social and cognitive psychology, it has been recognized that many inferential processes are of an automatic sort. By this it is meant that the initiation and perhaps the unfolding of the process are not under the control of the individual. It begins and goes on automatically. While we recognize that the extension of that notion to social comparison processes is a very considerable extension indeed, nevertheless we would like to suggest that at least some aspects of the social comparison process have this automatic quality. (One could almost refer to this as "mindless" social comparison.) When persons are in small, face to face groups, the actions of the other members of the group are extremely salient. It strikes us as likely that people will decode the social comparison implications of these actions and statements whether or not they would choose to do so if left to their own devices (D. Miller, 1983). The pleasure or the pain that these comparisons generate will be felt.

The downward comparison phenomenon. By adding to classic social comparison theory the notions that self-esteem and face-saving considerations are important determinants of social comparison choices, we are better able to make theoretical sense of one of the classic research areas created by social comparison theory. In the original study in what has come to be called the "downward comparison" area, Hakmiller (1966) showed that people who received threatening information about their personality traits chose to compare with others who were worse off than they were, in the sense of having even lower scores on tests of the personality traits in question. This "downward" or "defensive" comparison tendency differs markedly from the tendency to compare upwards or with similar people that is found in many other studies (e.g., Wheeler, 1966). Reviewing what was by that time a large literature, Wills (1981) developed a general theory that suggests that people's sense of subjective wellbeing can be maintained by comparing with others who are worse off. A desire for downward comparison is aroused whenever one's sense of wellbeing is threatened. Downward comparison may take either an active or a passive form. Passive downward comparison is done by simply noting that available, or perhaps remembered, comparison persons are worse off than oneself. This seems to fit the case of the Hakmiller study. Active downward comparison can take the form of active derogation of other people, which increases their social distance from the self and makes the self look better in comparison. It may also take the form of harming others in ways designed to lower their performance on the relevant dimensions. These sorts of harms are frequently aggressive actions, and we note that social comparison theory suggests an interesting relationship between competition and aggression. Both are ways of improving one's standing in the social comparison process. Competitive moves are generally designed to raise one's own performance level; aggressive moves, in the social comparison context, are designed to lower the performance level of the other. The social comparison outcome is the same, a relative improvement in one's own standing.

Social Comparison Theory in Group Contexts

In the original paper, Festinger spelled out several implications of social comparison theory for group processes. He proposed that if there were opinion or ability discrepancies within a group, action would be taken to reduce those discrepancies (Derivation D). These actions include changing one's own ability or opinion, changing those of other people, or ceasing comparison with continuingly dissimilar others. Changing other people's opinions entails engaging in social influence attempts. Changing one's own ability level or the ability level of others entails competing with others. Thus, social influence attempts and competition are two major ground-level consequences of social comparison processes.

In the case of opinions, cessation of comparison with other people will be accompanied by hostility and derogation (Corollary VI A). Schachter's thesis (1951), which was frequently cited by Festinger in the social comparison paper, showed that these attitudes of hostility and derogation could lead to rejection of the continuing deviant from the group. Although Festinger did not propose that there is also derogation of those performing less well in ability comparison situations, it seems reasonable to suggest a tendency for them to be derogated, and eventually to be excluded from the group, if they do not exclude themselves for self-esteem and face-saving reasons.

In short, the original theory did have implications for the kinds of groups that individuals will prefer for comparison purposes. These are groups in which others are similar. In addition, Festinger suggests what steps people will take to bring about similarity and homogeneity within groups. These steps include social influence attempts, competition, rejection, and derogation.

The formation of groups. Festinger also suggested that the social comparison perspective had important implications for group formation and social structure. A major one of these implications was that society would segment itself at the level of small groups according to what might be called "the principle of similarity." The multiplicity of small groups that form themselves do so of people of similar opinions and abilities. From within the bolstering atmospheres of these groups, people will regard people in other groups as incomparable. Thus the opinions and abilities of poeple in these incomparable groups will not be important for people's evaluations of their own abilities or opinions. We would point out that one important consequence of this segmentation of individuals into groups of similar people is that persons with relatively modest abilities can maintain a positive self-evaluation based on their comparisons with the restricted range of abilities that is represented within their group.

Automatic social comparison in groups. The motive to evaluate one's abilities and opinions is one reason people form groups, but it seems important to point out that it is not the only reason people do so. In fact, common sense suggests that there are a number of reasons groups are formed. Some of those reasons also have to do with the two other motives that we suggested operate in social comparison settings: self-esteem and face saving. However, on many occasions people join and remain in groups for reasons that have nothing to do with social comparison. There are problem-solving groups, groups formed by physical proximity on the job, and so on. However, the fact that these groups are formed for reasons having little or nothing to do with social comparison does not mean that no social comparison takes place within them. In fact, one of the more interesting applications of a theory of social comparison processes that includes motives to avoid comparison is to just such groups. If the reader accepts our previous argument, that social comparison processes have automatic components, then these "accidentally" formed groups, which may contain individuals who differ greatly on some opinions or may possess quite high levels of various abilities, are dangerous places, because they cause people automatically to come to conclusions about themselves that they feel are self-diminishing.

A study done by Morse and Gergen (1970) illustrates this point. Two individuals found themselves together because they were both applying for the same sort of job. Actually the experimenters had arranged the "coincidence," and one of the individuals was a confederate of the experimenters. When he was paired with some of the subjects, he presented himself in ways that made him seem very competent and qualified for the job. With others he appeared to be relatively unqualified. Measuring the self-estem of the subject just after the self-presentation of the confederate, the experimenters found that when the confederate appeared to be highly qualified, the self-esteem of the subject was lowered. When the confederate appeared to be less qualified, self-esteem increased. A revised theory that recognizes the self-esteem issues involved in social comparison and asserts that there are automatic components to social comparison processes nicely encompasses these results.

Group norms for the avoidance of comparison. Since many groups are formed for other than social comparison purposes, these groups are likely to contain people of widely ranging opinions and abilities. If, as we have argued, social comparison is a process with automatic elements, and one that can lead to conclusions that are damaging to the self-esteem or face of the comparing individual, then people will often experience painful comparisons in these groups. Intuitively, this strikes us as true. A great basketball player shows up in the faculty league, and considerably lowers everybody else's estimations of their abilities. Deviant opinions are revealed by a member of an office staff and derogation and exclusion processes are initiated, and so on. However, these processes are often detrimental to the functioning of the group, and it is reasonable to suppose, either because of internal loyalties or external constraints, that the group needs to continue to deal with the tasks for which it was formed. Therefore, it seems reasonable that groups would develop some barrier to social comparison processes taking place, and some ways of limiting the most negative effects of social comparison, if social comparison has taken place. We suggest that such barriers and limits exist. First the limits. Once social comparison has taken place, as, for instance, happens in pickup tennis games at the office picnic, it seems socially obligatory that the one who stood out as the best player minimizes the more stark, ability-driven aspects of his or her achievement by attributing it to a great deal of recent practice, or the luck of having some good lessons as a child, or some other non-ability-indexing factor. At future office picnics that person may choose some other sport in which to participate. His or her tennis playing is then confined to another group in which talents are less widely distributed. Second, the barriers. If a person has just given a modestly competent performance on a musical instrument, another person who, without some external pressure, immediately gives a much better one is being cruel. A person who egregiously comments on the poor quality of another's ability-linked performance is being cruel in a similar way. They are causing the performing individual to confront the possibility that he has a low ability at the talent in question, and has just lost face by giving what he now realizes was as inadequate performance in public.[4] A person who inflicts such social comparison wounds runs two sorts of risks: first of driving the wounded person to leave the group, incurring whatever costs are associated with that; second of being wounded at some future time following a poor performance of his own, because he has certainly made such retaliations toward him normative, from either the previously damaged individual or another group member. In general, it is our impression that groups of mixed abilities or opinions, constrained or rewarded for staying together as a group, are quite careful to avoid presenting the information that would trigger social comparison immediately following a poor performance; and quite accepting, at least on the surface, of any excuses the performer provides for the poor performance, no matter how implausible.

Similar norms operate with respect to avoiding opinion comparison, and they are most likely to operate in the kinds of heterogeneous groups we have been discussing—groups that are formed according to external constraint rather than personal choice. For many of us, gatherings of relatives are such a group. Not suprisingly, family reunions provide a vivid example of a

---

[4]In fact, the situation is worse. The person now realizes that he looks doubly foolish: first for giving a low-talent performance, and second for being so out of touch with reality as to give this low-talent performance in public, thereby signalling that he thought it was one to be proud of.

setting in which opinion comparison can produce unpleasant consequences, namely, hostility and derogation. Thus in many such settings the
discussion of national or world affairs is assiduously avoided. In his
important essay "On Face Work," Goffman (1955) discussed with great
sensitivity the subtleties of the norms suppressing social comparison of
opinions and abilities, and the ways people try to mend situations spoiled by
the unwanted eruption of social comparison.

Social comparison across groups. The principles of social comparison that we
have discussed to this point have concerned only self-evaluation within a
single group. However, research on outcome comparison has for many years
considered comparison with members of other groups, or with those other
groups as a whole (Levine & Moreland, in press; Runciman, 1961, 1966;
Stouffer Suchman, De Vinney, Star, & Williams, 1949). An approach to self-
evaluation that emphasizes across-group comparisons is Tajfel and Turner's
(1986) *social identity theory*. Here we will describe social identity theory in
some detail so that we can conclude our discussion of the operation of social
comparison principles in groups with an integration of social identity
considerations into a revised theory of social comparison processes. Putting
this another way, we propose that modern social comparison theory be
informed by the insights of Tajfel and Turner.

Social identity theory is concerned with the ways in which individuals
maintain a high level of self-esteem through comparison, or the avoidance
of comparison, with various other groups, including some usually known as
"outgroups." Many of its concepts are similar to the concepts of social
comparison theory, and many of them are compatable with the ways in
which we have found it useful to modify social comparison theory. Social
identity theory makes its unique contribution, however, in considering
social comparison on a between-groups or intergroup basis, rather than on a
within-groups or interpersonal basis.

Social identity theory defines social identity as "those aspects of an
individual's self-image that derive from the social categories to which he
perceives himself as belonging" (Tajfel and Turner, 1986, p. 16). It proposes
that people strive to maintain a positive self-concept and self-esteem (a
proposal that we have argued needs to be at the core of a theory of social
comparison processes). One way of maintaining or enhancing self-esteem,
according to this theory, is to achieve a "positive social identity." Positive
social identity is achieved by drawing favorable comparisons between
groups to which one belongs and other groups. More generally, the value,
positive or negative, of one's social identity is strongly influenced by
comparisons between one's own groups and others. Other groups are
regarded as suitable for comparison not only on the basis of similarity but
also on the basis of proximity and situational salience, dimensions that we
have argued are important in a revised theory of social comparison.

More specifically, social evaluation is determined by social comparison between various groups' standing on dimensions of valued attributes. If one's group compares favorably on a valued dimension with another salient group, then one's own group is valued positively and one possesses a positive social identity. If comparison with outgroups is unfavorable, then the person experiences a negative social identity. Individuals experiencing negative social identity are predicted to leave their groups or attempt to make them better. Making them better frequently involves causing them to engage in competition with other groups. Turner (1975) has long argued that competition among groups is motivated as much by the self-evaluation needs of the members as by real conflicts of interest. In fact, the simple possibility of social comparison between groups will produce "spontaneous" intergroup competition and at times groups will compete as a result of self-evaluation needs even when it is against their self-interest (Turner, 1978).

Groups are more likely to compete and discriminate against out-groups that are in some way comparable or salient (Turner and Brown, 1978). Finally, when comparisons continue to be unfavorable and social identity is threatened, assuming that there are barriers against individual members abandoning the group, groups may sometimes engage in a set of activities that facilitates cessation of comparison with high-status other groups. Although Tajfel and Turner (1986) do not explicitly say so, the implication is that they begin comparing with lower status out-groups.

It is worth noting how many of the ideas of social identity theory parallel the ideas of our modified theory of social processes. At the same time we should be clear about the differences between the two theories. A first point of comparison concerns the motivation for social comparison. Social identity theory regards self-validation, and not self-knowledge, as the usual motive for engaging in comparison. Social comparison theory now also recognizes the importance of self-validation in guiding the gathering and interpretation of social comparison information. However, social comparison theory maintains that people compare as well in order to evaluate opinions, performances, outcomes, emotions, and so on. Second, the two theories share the proposition that comparison is not always sought out, but will take place whenever another group is salient, available, or similar. Social identity theory makes this point in emphasizing the nearly automatic tendency for people to categorize individuals into ingroups and outgroups and the tendency to discriminate against people who can, on the flimsiest of bases, be regarded as belonging to outgroups. Social comparison theory implies this point in Brickman and Bulman's discussion of pleasure and pain in social comparison and makes it explicit in our own discussion above of the automaticity of social comparison processes.

There are three other instances in which social identity and social comparison theory make nearly identical points. First, the downward comparison principle discussed by Wills in individual cases is mirrored by the tendency of groups to shift from comparison with high- to low-status other groups. Second, groups seek to improve their standing by competition, just as individuals show Festinger's unidirectional drive upward. Finally the idea that competition is increased when out-groups are comparable is consistent with the related attributes hypothesis. When people or groups are similar on attributes related to an ability or characteristic being evaluated, they will compare more, and in the case of valued social attributes, they will compete more.

The reader will not have failed to notice that we think these similarities are not coincidental. To make the connections explicit, we think that all of the parallel processes above have their major origins in the individual's desire to think well of him or herself. Shifts in external circumstances can cause the major component of thinking well of oneself to involve comparisons between oneself and other individuals that are chosen as comparison others, or between oneself and other individuals among whom one happens to find oneself, or between the group to which one belongs and other groups. In order to think well of himself, the individual may shift among these comparisons in a motivated way, choosing to emphasize the importance of the comparison that currently makes him look best. The underlying realization that unites social comparison and social identity theories is that one's self-evaluation is to some extent anchored in comparisons between oneself and others, and to some extent anchored in comparisons between one's group and other groups.

Outcome comparison in groups. People who work in groups such as organizations get paid. They have an exchange relationship (Clark & Mills, 1979) with the organization and for certain inputs they receive certain outcomes. Social comparison processes are one of the central mechanisms for evaluating those outcomes (Levine and Moreland, in press). Recent research on both equity theory (Adams, 1965; Austin, 1977; Walster, Berscheid, & Walster. 1978), and relative deprivation (Cook, Crosby & Hennigan, 1977; Crosby, 1976; Walker & Pettigrew, 1984) considers the role of social comparison in the evaluation of outcomes. In the initial statements of equity theory (Adams 1965; Homans, 1961), it was suggested that an individual will feel that a relationship with another person is equitable if the ratio of the individual's outcomes to his or her inputs equals the outcome/ input ratio for the other person (also see Walster, *et al.*, 1978). Equity theory becomes more complex when the inputs made by various contributors are different in kind, and this complexity seems to us to be illuminated by a consideration of the related attributes hypothesis of a revised social comparison theory (Wheeler & Koestner, 1984; Wheeler & Zuckerman, 1977). In the usual social comparison case an opinion or ability is the "criterion," the attribute to be evaluated, and it is evaluated in terms of the individual's own and comparison persons' standing on related attributes, which in this case are the work inputs. Consider the situation that arises when a worker and a boss jointly produce some product. The worker can feel that his outcomes, in wage and benefit terms, are low relative to the contributions he made to the product (perhaps hard work and long hours). The boss recognizes that his wages and benefits are considerably higher than the worker's but feels that this is more than justified by the knowledge and brainpower he contributed to the product. Each defines the relevant background factors in a somewhat different way. Not coincidentally, they do so in ways that magnify their entitlements (Ross and Sicoly, 1979).

Relative deprivation is closely allied to inequity. There is debate about whether the two are truely different (Cook, *et al.*, 1977; Wheeler & Zuckerman, 1977). Feelings of inequity typically arise from comparison between two individuals in a group. Relative deprivation theorists have typically been more concerned with the affect and cognition of those at the lower end of the outcome hierarchy and they have been more concerned with comparisons that take place across groups. Like social identity theory, relative deprivation theory has reminded social comparison theorists of the importance of intergroup comparisons. It has also stressed a "feasibility of achievement" notion (Cook *et al.*, 1977; Folger, 1983; Olson & Ross, 1984); suggesting that people are more likely to feel deprived if they perceive that there is the possibility that they might receive a desired outcome, given their standing on related attributes, and then do not receive that outcome. A nurse in a hospital might experience relative deprivation if she observes another group receiving better outcomes, if she judges that group's entitlements to those outcomes as no better than the entitlements of her group. As relative deprivation theorists point out, the moves that can be made to deal with those feelings are many, ranging from generalized dissatisfaction through leaving the deprived group, to active ways of redressing the imbalance such as unauthorized appropriation of common resources, to revolution. (The explosive character of the feelings of entitlement provided by relative deprivation considerations has been recognized in political science, where it is known as the "revolution of rising expectations" hypothesis, and frequently used to explain revolutionary movements.)

The conclusion that we wish the reader to draw here is clear: Social comparison of outcomes, done according to the related attributes model, both between and within groups, is one of the major sources of feelings of inequity and relative deprivation.

Social Comparison Processes in Specific Group Settings

Using the principles that we have sketched above, we will now turn to applying them to the various settings suggested for consideration in this book. Because there seems to be more to say about certain group settings from a social comparison perspective, we will spend more time on those settings and discuss several others that seem to us to be particularly illuminated by social comparison considerations.

Elementary School Classrooms. People who work within the social comparison perspective find the elementary school classroom a frightening place. The potential for damage to children's self-esteem is high, as is the potential for children to adopt artificially low conceptions of their own abilities. [We have discussed some of the reasons for this evaluation of the elementary school setting in Darley and Goethals (1980). In his chapter on social comparison in educational settings, Levine (1983) reaches a similar conclusion based on his review of the evidence.[5]] The school system is the first authority system, aside from the parental one, that the child confronts in any sustained way. The school authority system has certain values which, although rarely articulated in any detailed way, are communicated implicitly in hundreds of day to day ways (Dweck & Goetz, 1978). One such message is that good moral character is shown by following the classroom rules of good behavior. Another message, and the central one for the purposes of our discussion, is that good performance on the various intellectual tasks set by the teacher is a good thing, specifically a better thing than less good performance. We would suggest that it is through the repitition of these kinds of messages that children acquire in academic achievement settings the "unidirectional drive upward" postulated by Festinger in his Hypothesis IV. Over time the child learns that good performance is taken by the teacher to mean high abilities, and prestige and privilege accrue to those who show good performance. Frequently this value system is echoed by the other children, so that prestige and privilege are granted by all children to those children who perform well in class—or at least this is the way it seems to the children. A sort of pluralistic ignorance may be at work here, in which children have very little opportunity to register their dissent with the value system, or their doubt about its specific conclusions. (However, we present some evidence later that suggests that fourth and fifth grade children begin to perceive some descrepancies between what other children vs. parents and teachers regard as important skills to possess.)

Since we think that social processes determine which performance dimensions are defined within a culture as "abilities" and thereby tightly linked to self-esteem, it seems worthwhile to comment that the school system is a central agent in our culture for this kind of socialization. [This is hardly a new conclusion. Bourdie and Passeron (1977) have a particularly interesting discussion of how many of the advantages conveyed by social

---

[5]Levine's (1983) paper, entitled "Social Comparison and Education," is a thoughtful and integrative review. Those who find their interest drawn by our discussion to the application of social comparison concepts to school settings would do well to begin with that reading.

class become translated by the school system into performances taken as evidences of high ability, thereby perpetuating the social class structure and apparently validating certain aspects of it.]

Ruble and her associates (Ruble, Boggiano, Feldman, & Loebel, 1980; Ruble, Parsons, & Ross, 1976) have done careful and detailed observational studies of the development of social comparison capabilities and interests in the primary school years. These have led Ruble (1983) to suggest that, while the cognitive capabilities are present earlier, the complex information-interpreting capabilities necessary for making social comparison inferences seem to begin to be present at about the second grade. Suls and Mullen (1982) have developed a lifespan perspective for the self-attributions of ability that includes the suggestion that an individual develops a tendency to compare with others rather than past instances of own performances during the middle childhood years. Working with children of that age group and higher, Harter (1985) and her associates have carried out a linked series of studies that trace the connections between a "Jamesian" conceptualization of abilities, self-esteem, and certain clinical phenomena. Briefly, she had children rate the degree to which they possessed certain common childhood skills and abilities and the degree of importance they placed on possessing those abilities. She then combined the two measures, assigning negative scores to cases in which the child felt that he or she possessed little or none of the skill, and increasing the negativity of the score depending on the importance the child placed on possessing the skill. Totalling this score across all cases of skills and abilities, she then correlated the resulting score with a measure of global self-esteem. The two scores correlated quite highly (around .60 in several studies), providing convincing evidence for James's notion that self-esteem is related to one's achievements weighted by one's pretentions, rather than to one's achievements alone (the achievement–self-esteem correlations were lower, although not greatly lower).

At first glance this seems to create an almost solipsistic possibility, in which an individual could perform poorly on many dimensions and yet remain high in self-esteem by abandoning the desire to do well on those dimensions, much as a baloonist maintains a high altitude by casting ballast over the side. However, this is not the way things work, at least at the level of the elementary school child. In a preliminary study one of us (JMD) assessed school children's abilities and aspirations, much as did Harter, and found similar results. However, the children were asked to rate not only which tasks they thought it was important to possess, but also what tasks peers, parents, and teachers though it was important for the child to possess. The correlations of all of these pairs of ratings were quite revealing. First, they were all strongly positive. Still, a pattern emerged. The correlation of the child's importance scores with the child's perceptions of the importance ratings of peers was .80, the same correlation with the perceived importance scores of parents and teachers was .62, and the correlation between the perceived importance scores of parents and teachers, and peers was .47.

These correlations hint at a fourth or fifth grade child's perception that there are somewhat different conceptualizations held by two important constituencies in his or her life as to what is important. However, when we looked at the correlation between the child's ratings of the degree to which he or she possessed the various skills, weighted by how important the parents and teachers considered it to be to possess those skills, and the child's self-esteem, we found it to be .68, a result we would interpret as showing that the children did not have the freedom to arrive an idiosyncratic interpretations of the importance of skills and abilities if those would differ from the interpretations held by the significant authority figures in their social networks.

Earlier we said that, from the perspective of the social comparison theorist, the elementary school is a claustrophobic setting for the child. Now we can say more about why that is so. The elementary school setting presents to the child an overwhelming case for the importance of being good at the skills and abilities that it teaches; likewise it brings the children into contact with their peers in a mercilessly public setting in which all quickly are able to assess the performance levels of others, does so at an age when the social comparison process is centrally interesting to the students, and at an age when, one suspects, they have few resources to resist its apparent conclusions. The playground, and sports in general, offer some possibility for the display of other kinds of abilities, and for some this may create the possibility for some self-esteem-bolstering displays of talent, but few other possibilities seem available, and those that are seem much less sustained than the hour after hour, day after day, comparison processes inflicted within the domains the school system designates as abilities. Given this, the reader will not be surprised by Harter's finding that fifth and sixth grade children identified by their teachers as manifesting the affective and motivational symptoms of depression showed very low self-ratings of global self-esteem. Second, they regarded themselves as being low on competence in performance domains that nonetheless were important to them. While the findings are correlational in nature, our interpretations of them are obvious. Discovering that one is doing poorly on the tasks the school system causes to be salient leads to feelings of low self-esteem (Stang, Smith, & Rogers, 1978), and eventually to depression.

Group decision making. People in organizations make decisions. Research on "groupthink" (Janis, 1982) suggests that they often do it very badly. We think that social comparison processes underly some aspects of the groupthink phenomenon.

"Groupthink" can be defined as the tendency to use inadequate decision-making procedures in groups because of the group's tendency to seek concurrence and disregard risk. Both tendencies can be understood from a social comparison perspective. From that perspective, the concurrence-seeking tendency is a reflection of the pressures toward uniformity that exist in groups. Notice that the concurrence-seeking tendency produces compliance rather than deeper opinion change and a fear- or loyalty-produced stifling of the expression of dissenting opinions. This compliance and stifling of dissent produces what Janis referred to as "an illusion of unanimity." Because group members do not hear each other's misgivings they overestimate the degree to which others agree with the authorative opinion—finally to the extent of thinking that others are unanimous in holding the opinion around which the consensus seems to be forming. This is the pattern one might expect if self-validation concerns dominated over the evaluative motive to discover the factually correct opinion. Consistent with the view that it is self-validation rather than self-evaluation that produces pressures toward concurrence seeking in groups is the finding that groups often experience high levels of self-esteem just when they are unanimously reaching decisions that turn out to be disastrous.

Social comparison is also important in explaining the collective disregard of risk that contributes to groupthink. This disregard has been referred to as the "risky shift," the tendency for groups to make decisions that are riskier than the average of the decision perferences of the individuals making up the group (Pruitt, 1971; Wallach, Kogan, & Bem, 1962). [The risky shift is now seen as only one exemplar of the more general phenomenon of "group polarization," (Myers, 1983).] There are two ways in which social comparison phenomena contribute to a shift toward more risky decisions. First, risk is a value in our culture (Brown, 1965). People compete to compare favorably with others on this valued dimension, just as they compete in performance domains that are related to ability. Second, the risky shift can be tied directly to the social comparison of abilities. Risk is valued in our culture because it is associated with ability. Jellison and Riskind (1970) have shown that risk-choosing individuals are perceived to be creative, innovative, and talented and that persons with high levels of ability are thought to take more or greater risks. In short, ability is an attribute related to how much risk individuals choose to take. Goethals and Zanna (1979) then argued that the risky shift may occur in groups because individuals are implicitly striving to present themselves as possessing high ability by indicating that they are willing to take at least as much risk as others in the group. Their data indicated that when group members exchange ability self-ratings and come to perceive their group to be composed of persons who are similar in ability, they show shifts to risk through these information exchange procedures that are equal in magnitude to shifts found following group discussion. These data suggest that when ability similarity is established, social comparison on risk is fully engaged, and competition to be at least as risky as other group members produces the shift.[6]

---

[6]In pointing out that social comparison sometimes offers a full explanation of shifts to risk, we do not mean to overlook the fact that there are other approaches to the phenomenon. For instance, Burnstein and Vinokur's (1977) persuasive arguments theory is frequently a viable explanation of specific risky-shift phenomenon (Myers, 1983).

Worker productivity. Social comparison theory is helpful in trying to understand conflicting pressures that individuals in a group work setting experience. Understanding these pressures as they are experienced on an auto assembly line, in a secretarial pool, or among migrant farm workers may help us understand why worker productivity is a "problem" in some organizations. Earlier we discussed Festinger's notion of the "unidirectional drive upward in the case of abilities." Festinger argued that people strive to perform better than those around them, and, as each individual does this, an undamped competition is set up. Thus one might expect individuals in a work situation to strive to work more productively, up to the physical limits given for performances. One notices that this does not seem to happen always, or even often, in real life. To the extent that these competitive strivings to do better in comparison to one's co-workers are not observed, we must ask what other motivations or imposed limits constrain that process. Festinger suggested that "the unidirectional push to do better" conflicts with the pressures toward uniformity with respect to ability levels that exist in groups. These pressures can be seen in various forms of "norm sending" (Rommetveit, 1955) that workers bring to bear on each other so as to enforce norms regarding appropriate levels of productivity. Both those who perform at a lower rate than that specified by the norm, "chiselers," and those who exceed the norm, "rate busters," are subjected to pressure to reduce discrepancies in levels of performance (Roethlisberger & Dickson, 1939).

As with many other social comparison phenomena, the pressures toward performance uniformity seen in work situations are probably better understood in terms of needs for self-validation rather than self-evaluation. The unidirectional drive upwards for abilities and the segementation into similar ability-level groups that takes place in society are best seen as related to self-esteem. It is most plausible to view pressures to reduce discrepancies that might indicate different levels of ability in the same light. Basically, groups norms are developed that prevent individuals from displays of prowess that embarrass others.[7]

Festinger also notes that as a result of the conflicting tendencies to do better and to achieve performance uniformity in groups, each individual will prefer to be at the point of compromise between these two drives, the point where his or her performance level is just slightly better than other people's. Of course, it is impossible for everyone to be at this level. Thus there will be continued turmoil in groups as a result of these conflicting

---

[7]We do not wish to be thought naive. We recognize that these norms develop because bosses may fire those who perform comparatively poorly; and that bosses also may lower the rates of pay for each piece of worth, as the group average rate of productivity increases, and norms holding down work rates develop in response to these social facts. Social comparison has an interesting but partial application in the case that we are discussing.

pressures to excel and to conform to norms. How strong each of these pressures is can be expected to vary from group to group and to have a profound influence on the character of productivity in that group.

Group psychotherapy. One debate in the psychotherapeutic field concerns whether group psychotherapy is only a less costly but less desirable version of individual therapy, or one with some additional benefits caused by the group setting. From a social comparison-theoretic perspective, the answer is obvious: group settings have unique benefits, because they create the opportunity for comparing one's own anxieties, disabilities, and symptoms with those of other people, an opportunity that is important in breaking what Harry Stack Sullivan (1953) regarded as an important obstacle to mental wellbeing, the phenomenon he called the "fallacy of uniqueness." According to Sullivan many psychiatrically disturbed persons believed, erroneously, that their self-defeating behaviors or problems were unique. This added to their problems in a way that has been illuminated by recent studies by Jemmott, Ditto, & Croyle (in press). They showed that people who are told that they have a physical disease that is described as rare find the disease more serious than do individuals given an identical description, but told that the disease is more common. While we must be cautious in extrapolating from beliefs about physical illness to beliefs about psychiatric illness, these studies suggest that people may view their psychological problems as less severe if they receive information that they are more prevalent than they believed. Social comparison theory suggests that the face to face setting of a group therapy situation is a particularly forceful context in which to receive this information.

Social comparison theory would go on to suggest that, although this is the sort of information that is likely to come up in group-theraputic settings driven by almost any theory of psychotherapy, it would be a useful theraputic strategy to create occasions when this theme did arise and was systematically explored. Particularly it would be useful if those group members who seemed competent on a particular ability dimension could be led to reveal doubts or instances of past failure experiences on performances related to that ability.

Sullivan's "fallacy of uniqueness" is related in an interesting way to research on false consensus and false uniqueness effects. Recent studies show that normal people show false consensus effects, that is, overestimations, of the number of people who share their socially undesirable or neutral behaviors, but false uniqueness effects, that is, underestimates of the number of people who perform similar desirable behaviors (Campbell, 1986; Goethals, 1986; L. Ross, Greene, & House, 1977). Furthermore, data from Campbell (1987) and Tabachnik, Crocker, and Alloy (1983) showed that depressed individuals do not show typical false consensus effects. [Note that there is some controversy about the Tabachnik *et al.*, study. See

McCauley (1985) and Crocker, Kayne, and Alloy (1985).] This leads us to hypothesize that depressed individuals and other individuals whose difficulties are connected with self-esteem decrements might not show typical false uniqueness effects for desirable behaviors either. Instead they may show false uniqueness effects for their *un*desirable or *dis*ordered behaviors; precisely what Sullivan is suggesting by his notion of "the fallacy of uniqueness" displayed by those with certain kinds of psychological difficulties.

Conclusions

Social comparison theory is a theory concerned with self-evaluation and self-validation through comparative appraisal of the self. Because of the capacity of individuals for symbolic representations, social comparison can take place "within the head" of the individual, using information imaginatively cognitively represented by the individual.[8] However, because social comparison is a process with automatic aspects, and because the social realities that are its inputs present themselves in group settings, social comparison is a pervasive aspect of group life. Because of this, individuals in group settings often receive comparative information that is negative in its implications, which can lead to feelings of ability inferiority, to self-esteem loss, and eventually to depression.

Individuals strive to maintain positive self-regard within a group by achieving opinion uniformity and by demonstrating that they are slightly better than fellow group members on abilities and other valued personal characteristics. These strivings give rise to social influence processes and competition within groups, but because of concerns for face saving and control of the damage that can be done by social comparison processes, norms develop that somewhat mute the workings of social comparison processes within groups.

Individuals also strive to achieve positive self-regard through comparisons with members of other groups. As members of in-groups, they contribute to that group's competitions with out-groups to gain favorable comparisons.

These fundamental comparison motivations and behaviors lead to a variety of personal, interpersonal, and intergroup consequences. They affect the way we interpret information about self and others, how we interact with

---

[8]We would suggest that Walter Mitty is a little-noticed exemplar of one function of social comparison. Mitty was a mild-mannered man (created by James Thurber), henpecked by a domineering wife, who constantly slid into fantasies in which he performed high-risk, high-ability feats of heroism. It strikes us that the fantasies were preserving Mitty's self-esteem, allowing him to return to the real world with sufficient self-regard to withstand its buffetings.

others, and how groups relate to each other. Because self-evaluation is a basic psychological process and because it inevitably is set in motion by the presence of others, social comparison is always a major facet of the complex structure of group life, and social comparison theory will continue to play a major role in our understanding of group behavior.

Acknowledgments. This chapter was written while John Darley was a Fellow at the Center for Advanced Studies in the Behavioral Sciences. He is grateful for the financial support provided by the John D. and Catherine T. MacArthur Foundation and by the National Science Foundation, grant BNS-8011494.
The authors would like to thank Diane Mackie, Brian Mullen, and Jerry M. Suls for their helpful comments on the manuscript.

References

Adams, J.S. (1965). Injustice in social exchange. In L. Berkowitz (Eds.), *Advances in experimental psychology* (Vol. 2, pp. 269–299). New York: Academic Press.

Austin, J. (1956). A plea for excuses. *Proceedings of the Aristotelian Society*, 1–30.

Austin, W. (1977). Equity theory and social comparison processes. In J. M. Suls and R. L. Miller (Eds.), *Social comparison processes: Theoretical and empirical perspectives* (pp. 279–305). Washington, DC: Hemisphere Press.

Bourdieu, P., & Passeron, J. (1977). *Reproduction: In education, society, and culture.* Beverly Hills, Ca: Sage.

Bradley, G.W. (1978). Self-serving biases in the attribution process: A reexamination of the fact or fiction question. *Journal of Personality and Social Psychology, 36,* 56–71.

Brickman, P., & Bulman, R. (1977). Pleasure and pain in social comparison. In J. M. Suls and R. L. Miller (Eds.), *Social comparison processes: Theoretical and empirical perspectives* (pp. 149–186). Washington, DC: Hemisphere Press.

Brown, R. (1965). *Socal psychology.* New York: Free Press.

Burnstein, E., & Vinokur, A. (1977). Persuasive arguments and social comparison as determinants of attitude polarization. *Journal of Experimental Social Psychology, 13,* 315–322.

Campbell, J.D. (1986). Similarity and uniqueness: the effects of attribute type, relevance, and individual differences in self-esteem and depression. *Journal of Personality and Social Psychology, 50,* 281–294.

Clark, M.S. & Mills, J. (1979). Interpersonal attraction in exchange and communal relationships. *Journal of Personality and Social Psychology, 37,* 12–24.

Cook, T. D., Crosby, F., & Hennigan, K. M. (1977). In J. M. Suls and R. L. Miller (Eds.), *Social comparison processes: Theoretical and empirical perspectives* (pp. 307–334). Washington, DC: Hemisphere Press.

Crocker, J., Kayne, N., & Alloy, L. B. (1985). Comparing the self with others in depressed and nondepressed college students: Reply to McCauley. *Journal of Personality and Social Psychology, 48,* 1579–1583.

Crosby, F. (1976). A model of egoistical relative deprivation. *Psychological Review, 83,* 85–113.

Darley, J. M., & Goethals, G. R. (1980). People's analyses of the causes of ability-linked performances. In L. Berkowitz (Ed.), *Advances in experimental social psychology* (Vol. 13 pp. 1–37). New York: Academic Press.

Davis, J. A. (1966). The campus as frog pond: An application of the theory of relative deprivation to career decisions of college men. *American Journal of Sociology, 72,* 17–31.

Dweck, C., & Goetz, T. (1978). Attributions and learned helplessness. In J. Harvey, W. Ickes, and R. Kidd (Eds.), *New directions in attribution research* (Vol. 2 pp. 157–179). Hillsdale, NJ: Erlbaum.

Festinger, L. (1950). Informal social communication. *Psychological Review, 57,* 271–282.

Festinger, L. (1954). A theory of social comparison processes. *Human Relations, 7,* 117–140.

Festinger, L., Riecken, H., & Schachter, S. (1956). *When prophecy fails.* Minneapolis: University of Minnesota Press.

Folger, R., Rosenfield, D., Rheaume, K, and Martin, C. (1983). relative deprivation and referent cognitions. *Journal of Experimental Social Psychology, 19,* 172–184.

Goethals, G. R. (1986). Fabricating and ignoring social reality: Self-serving estimates of consensus. In J. M. Olson, C. P. Herman, and M. P. Zanna (Eds.), *Relative deprivation and social comparison: The Ontario Symposium* (Vol. 4, pp. 135–157). Hillsdale, NJ: Erlbaum.

Goethals, G. R. (in press). Social comparison theory: Psychology from the lost and found. *Personality and Social Psychology Bulliten.*

Goethals, G. R., & Darley, J. M. (1977). Social comparison, an attributional approach. In J. M. Suls & R. L. Miller (Eds.), *Social comparison processes: Theoretical and empirical perspectives* (pp. 259–278). Washington, DC: Hemisphere Press.

Goethals, G. R., & Zanna, M. P. (1979). The role of social comparison in choice shifts. *Journal of Personality and Soial Psychology, 37,* 1469–1476.

Goffman, E. (1955). On facework: An analysis of ritual elements in social interaction. *Journal of Psychiatry, 18,* 213–231.

Greenwald, A. G. (1980). The tolitarian ego: Fabrication and revision of personal history. *american Psychologist, 35,* 603–613.

Hakmiller, K. L. (1966). Threat as a determinant of downward comparison. *Journal of Experimental Social Psychology, 1966, Supplement 1,* 32–39.

Harter, S. (1985). Processes underlying the construction, maintenance, and enhancement of the self-conception in children. In J. M. Suls and A. Greenwald (Eds.), *Psychological perspectives on the self* (Vol. 3). Hillsdale, NJ: Erlbaum.

Homans, G. C (1961). *Social behavior: Its elementary forms.* New York: Basic Books.

James, W. (1890). *Principles of Psychology.* New York: Holt.

Janis, I. L. (1982). *Groupthink: Psychological studies in policy decisions and fiascoes* (2nd ed.). Boston: Houghton Mifflin.

Jellison, J. M., & Riskind, J. A. (1970). A social comparison of abilities interpretation of risk taking behavior. *Journal of Personality and Social Psychology, 15,* 375–390.

Jemmott, J., Ditto, D. H. & Croyle, R. T. (in press). Judging health status: The effects of perceived prevelance and personal relevance. *Journal of Personality and Social Psychology.*

Jones, E. E., & Davis, K. E. (1965). From acts to dispositions: The attribution process in person perception. In L. Berkowitz (Ed.), *Advances in experimental social psychology* (Vol. 2 pp. 219–266). New York: Academic Press.

Kelley, H. H. (1967). Attribution theory in social psychology. In D. Levine (Eds.), *Nebraska Symposium on Motivation* (Vol. 15, pp. 192–238).

Kelley, H. H. (1971). *Attribution in social interaction.* Morristown, NJ: General Learning Press.

Kelley, H. H. (1972). *Causal schemata and the attribution process.* Morristown, NJ: General Learning Press.

Kelley, H. H. (1973). The process of causal attribtuion. *American Psychologist, 28,* 107–128.

Latané, B. (Ed.). (1966). Studies in social comparison. *Journal of Experimental Social Psychology, Supplement 1.*

Levine, J. M. (1983). Social comparison and education. In J. M. Levine and M. C. Wang (Eds.), *Teacher and student perception: Implications for learning* (pp. 29–56). Hillsdale, NJ: Erlbaum.

Levine, J. M., & Moreland, R. L. (in press). Social comparison and outcome evaluation in group contexts. In J. C. Masters and W. P. Smith (Eds.), *Social comparison and social justice*. Hillsdale, NJ: Erlbaum.

McCauley, C. (1985). Depression and the false consensus effect: a note concerning the study by Tabachnik, Crocker, and Alloy. *Journal of Personality and Social Psychology, 48,* 1576–1578.

Mette, D. R., & Smith, G. (1977). Social comparison and interpersonal attraction: The case for dissimilarity. In J. M. Suls, & R. M. Miller (Eds.), *Social comparison processes: Theoretical and empirical perspectives*. Washington, DC: Hemisphere (pp. 69–102).

Miller, D. (1983). Paper presented at the Ontario Symposium on Relative Deprivation and Social Comparison. London, Ontario, October 13–15.

Miller, D. T., & Ross, M. (1975). Self-serving biases in the attribution of causality: Fact or fiction? *Psychological Bulletin, 82,* 213–225.

Morse, S., & Gergen, K. J. (1970). Social comparison, self-consistency, and the concept of self. *Journal of Personality and Social Psychology, 16,* 148–156.

Mullen, B., Atkins, J. L., Champion, D. S., Edwards, C., Hardy, D., Story, J. E., & Vanderklok, M. (1985). The false consensus effect: A meta-analysis of 115 hypothesis tests. *Journal of Experimental Social Psychology, 21,* 262–283.

Myers, D. (1983). *Social psychology*. New York: McGraw-Hill.

Olson, J. M., & Ross, M. (1984). Perceived qualifications, resource abundance, and resentment about deprivation. *Journal of Experimental Social Psychology, 20,* 425–444.

Pruitt, D. G. (1971). Choice shifts in group discussion: An introductory review. *Journal of Personality and Social Psychology, 20,* 339–360.

Roethlisberger, F., & Dickson, W. (1939). *Management and the worker*. Cambridge, MA: Harvard University Press.

Rommetveit, R. (1955). *Social norms and roles: Explorations in the psychology of enduring social pressures*. Minneapolis: University of Minnesota Press.

Ross, L. (1977). The intuitive psychologist and his shortcomings: Distortions in the attribution process. In L. Berkowtiz (Ed.), *Advances in experimental social psychology* (Vol. 10 pp. 173–220). New York: Academic Press.

Ross, L., Greene, D., & House, P. (1977). The "false consensus effect": An egocentric bias in social perception and attribution processes. *Journal of Experimental Social Psychology, 13,* 279–301.

Ross, M., & Fletcher, G. J. O. (1985). Attribution and social perception. In G. Lindzey and E. Aronson (Eds.), *The handbook of social psychology* (Vol. 2, pp. 73–122). New York: Random House.

Ross, M., & Sicoly, F. (1979). Egocentric biases in availability and attribution. *Journal of Personality and Social Psychology, 37,* 322–336.

Ruble, D. N. (1983). The development of social comparison processes and their role in achievement-related self-socialization. In E. T. Higgins, D. N. Ruble, & W. W. Hardup (Eds.), *Social cognition and social development: A socio-cultural perspective* (pp. 3–12). Cambridge: Cambridge University Press.

Ruble, D. N., Boggiano, A. K., Feldman, N. S., & Loebel, J. H. (1980). Developmental analysis of the role of social comparison in self-evaluation. *Developmental Psychology, 16,* 105–115.

Ruble, D. N., Parsons, J. E., & Ross, J. (1976). Self-evaluative responses of children in an achievement setting. *Child Development, 47,* 990–997.

Runciman, W. G. (1961). Problems of research on relative deprivation. *The European Journal of Sociology, 2,* 315–323.

Runciman, W. G. (1966). *Relative deprivation and social justice: A study of attitudes to social inequity in twentieth-century England.* London: Routledge and Kegan Paul.

Schachter, S. (1951). Deviation, rejection, and communication. *Journal of Abnormal and Social Psychology, 46,* 190–207.

Schachter, S. (1959). *The psychology of affiliation.* Stanford, CA: Stanford University Press.

Singer, J. E. (1966). Social comparison–progress and issues. *Journal of Experimental Social Psychology, Supplement 1,* 103–110.

Snyder, C., Higgins, R., & Stucky, R. (1983). *Excuses; masquerades in search of grace.* New York: Wiley.

Snyder, M. L., Stephan, W. G., & Rosenfield, D. (1976). Egotism and attribution. *Journal of Personality and Social Psychology, 33,* 435–441.

Snyder, M. L., Stephan, W. G., & Rosenfield, D. (1978). Attributional egotism. In J. H. Harvey, W. Ickes, and R. F. Kidd (Eds.), *New directions in attribution research* (Vol. 2 pp. 91–117). Hillsdale, NJ: Erlbaum.

Stang, L., Smith, M. D., & Rogers, C. M. (1978). Social comparison, multiple reference groups, and the self-concepts of academically handicapped children before and after mainstreaming. *Journal of Educational Psychology, 70,* 487–497.

Stouffer, S. A., Suchman, E. A., DeVinney, L. C., Star, S. A., & Williams, R. M. (1949). *The American soldier: Adjustment during Army life* (Vol. 1). Princeton, NJ: Princeton University Press.

Sullivan, H. S. (1953). *Interpersonal theory of psychiatry.* New York: W. W. Norton.

Suls, J. M., & Miller, R. L. (Eds.). (1977). *Social comparison processes: Theoretical and empirical perspectives.* Washington, DC: Hemisphere Press.

Suls, J. M., & Mullen, B. From the cradle to the grave: comparison and self-evaluation across the life span. In J. M. Suls (Ed.), *Social psychological perspectives on the self.* Hillsdale, NJ: Erlbaum.

Suls, J. M., & Wan, C. K. (in press). In search of the false uniqueness phenomenon: Fear and estimates of social consensus. *Journal of Personality and Social Psychology.*

Tabachnik, N., Crocker, J., & Alloy, L. B. (1983). Depression, social comparison, and the false consensus effect. *Journal of Personality and Social Psychology, 45,* 688–699.

Tajfel, H. (1978). Interindividual behavior and intergroup behavior. In H. Tajfel (Ed.), *Differentiation between social groups: Studies in the social psychology of intergroup relations* (pp. 27–60). London: Academic Press.

Tajfel, H., & Turner, J. C. (1986). The social identity theory of intergroup behavior. In S. Worchel and W. G. Austin (eds.), *Psychology of Intergroup Relations* (pp. 33–48). Chicago: Nelson-Hall Publishers.

Tetlock, P. E., & Levi, A. (1982). Attribution bias: On the inconclusiveness of the cognition-motivation debate. *Journal of Experimental Social Psychology, 18,* 68–88.

Turner, J. C. (1975). Social comparison and social identity: Some prospects for intergroup behaviour. *European Journal of Social Psychology, 5,* 5–34.

Turner, J. C. (1978). Social categorization and social discrimination in the minimal group paradigm. In H. Tajfel (ed.), *Differentiation between social groups: Studies in the social psychology of intergroup relations* (pp. 101–140). (European Monographs in Social Psychology). London: Academic Press.

Turner, J. C., & Brown, R. J. (1978). social status, cognitive alternatives and intergroup relations. In H. Tajfel (Eds.), *Differentiation between social groups: Studies in the social psychology of intergroup relations* (pp. 201–234). (European Monographs in Social Psychology). London: Academic Press.

Walker, I., & Pettigrew, T. F. (1984). Relative deprivation theory: An overview and conceptual critique. Special issue: Intergroup processes. *British Journal of Social Psychology, 23,* 301–310.

Wallach, M. A., Kogan, N., & Bem, D. J. (1962). Group influence on individual risk taking. *Journal of Abnormal and Social Psychology, 65* 75–86.

Walster, E., Berscheid, E., & Walster, G. W. (1978). *Equity: Theory and research.* Boston: Allyn & Bacon.

Wheeler, L. (1966). Motivation as a determinant of upward comparison. *Journal of Experimental Social Psychology, Supplement 1*, 27–31.

Wheeler, L., & Koestner, R. (1984). Performance evaluation: On choosing to know the related attributes of others when we know their performance. *Journal of Experimental Social Psychology, 20*, 263–271.

Wheeler, L., & Koestner, R., & Driver, R. E. (1982). Related attributes in the choice of comparison: It's all there but it isn't all there is. *Journal of Experimental Social Psychology, 18*, 489–500.

Wheeler, L., & Zuckerman, M. (1977). Commentary. In J. M. Suls and R. L. Miller (Eds.), *Social comparison processes: Theoretical and empirical perspectives* (pp. 335–357). Washington, DC: Hemisphere Press.

Wills, T. A. (1981). Downward comparison principles in social psychology. *Psychological Bulletin, 90*, 245–271.

Zanna, M. D., Goethals, G. R., & Hill, J. F. (1975). Evaluating a sex-related ability: Social comparison with similar others and standard setters. *Journal of Experimental Social Psychology, 11*, 86–93.

Zuckerman, M. (1979). Attribution of success and failure revisited, or: The motivational bias is alive and well in attribution theory. *Journal of Personality, 47*, 245–287.

Chapter 3

Cognitive Dissonance Theory: Collective Actions and Individual Reactions

Gerald N. Sande and Mark P. Zanna

Cognitive Dissonance Theory

The basic premise of Festinger's (1957) theory of cognitive dissonance is that an individual strives to maintain consistency or consonance among his or her cognitions. Inconsistent, or dissonant, cognitions lead to psychological discomfort, which motivates activity aimed at restoring consonance. For example, if I say something that hurts the feelings of a close friend the cognitions "I like that person" and "I hurt that person" are dissonant in light of the assumption that I ought not to hurt people I like. According to dissonance theory, a "drive-like" state of arousal will motivate me to reconcile the discrepancy. This may be accomplished in a number of ways. I may add consonant cognitions, for example, by performing some favor for the injured party, or perhaps by recalling previously performed favors. I may alter the importance of one of the cognitions, for example, by deciding that the remark was, in the overall course of the relationship, a minor incident. Finally, I may change one of the dissonant cognitions, for example, by deciding that I really did not like the target of the remark after all.

Most dissonance researchers have focused on the employment of postbehavioral attitude change as a means of reducing cognitive dissonance. Many of them have demonstrated this phenomenon using the "induced-compliance" paradigm, in which individuals are encouraged to perform an act that is inconsistent with their attitudes. For example, subjects in Festinger and Carlsmith's (1959) classic study were induced to tell a waiting subject that a boring task was actually exciting and enjoyable. In other studies subjects have been induced to write essays advocating a counterattitudinal position (Linder, Cooper, & Jones, 1967), eat grasshoppers (Zimbardo, Weisenberg, Firestone, & Levy, 1965), read aloud a list of obscene words (Aronson & Mills, 1959), and tolerate electric shocks (Gerard & Mathewson, 1966). Under certain conditions predicted by the theory subjects in these studies have reliably changed their attitudes, making them more consistent with their recent behaviors and, in the process, justifying those actions.

More than 25 years of research has investigated the mediating processes and boundary conditions of the cognitive dissonance phenomenon. In the words of Kiesler and Munson (1975), this research has demonstrated that

> A person will experience and reduce dissonance if he performs an act inconsistent with his beliefs and if the act has aversive consequences for the person or others, and if the person perceives that he bears some personal responsibility for the act. (p. 424)

Further experiments have demonstrated (a) that aversive consequences need not really occur, but that the subject must perceive that they are to occur, and (b) that these consequences must be irrevocable (Davis & Jones, 1960).

The individual's assumption of responsibility is a key mediator of the dissonance experience and plays a critical role in our discussion of dissonance in group settings that follows. Cooper and Fazio (1984) define the assumption of personal responsibility as "the attribution that the locus of causation for an event is internal" (p. 236). To date, researchers have focused on two components of responsibility assumption: choice and foreseeability. Only if a person perceives that he or she engaged in a behavior of his or her own volition does a counterattitudinal action produce dissonance (e.g., Linder *et al.*, 1967). An attribution that the behavior was the result of coercion will prevent the arousal of dissonance. In addition, dissonance will be aroused only if the aversive consequences of the behavior are judged by the subject to have been foreseeable (Goethals, Cooper, & Naficy, 1979).

Researchers have also studied the occurrence of cognitive dissonance in decision-making situations. Assuming that two options each have positive and negative features, postdecisional dissonance is aroused when one considers the negative attributes of the chosen alternative and the positive attributes of the rejected alternative (Festinger, 1964).

If I decide to visit my in-laws for Christmas instead of going to California, dissonance is aroused when I think of the relaxing time I would have lying on a California beach, and when I think of the cold climate in which my in-laws live. To resolve the dissonance I can (a) add cognitions consonant with the decision (e.g., remind myself of how much money I save by not flying to California), (b) alter the importance of a cognition (e.g., convince myself that Christmas is really a time to spend with family), or (c) change a cognition (e.g., decide that I really do not like lying on the beach all that much). The result of these efforts is that my evaluations of the two alternatives are spread apart, i.e., the chosen option is seen as more desirable, the rejected option as less desirable. Studies by Brehm (1956),

Knox and Inkster (1968), and others have demonstrated that postdecisional assessments are spread in the direction suggested.

As in the induced compliance paradigm, perceived personal responsibility is necessary for dissonance to occur. That is, (a) one must have a real choice between alternatives, (b) one must be committed to the decision (it cannot be revoked or denied), and (c) aversive consequences of the decision (the existence of positive attributes of the unchosen alternative and negative aspects of the chosen alternative) must be present and foreseeable.

In summary, cognitive dissonance theory proposes that people seek to maintain consonance among their cognitions. When dissonance is produced as a result of engaging in some action, such as a counterattitudinal behavior or a decision, attitude change may ensue in order to reestablish consonance. Postbehavioral attitude change will occur only if the action has irrevocable aversive consequences for which the actor takes personal responsibility.

Cognitive Dissonance in Groups

Although most of the existing research on dissonance has focused on individuals acting alone, some psychologists have considered the social context in which dissonance might arise. Zimbardo (1959, cited in Festinger & Aronson, 1962) investigated the effects of dissonance aroused by disagreeing with others. Aronson and Mills (1959) studied the effects of the severity of initiation into a group on how positively the group was rated by the individual being initiated. Other researchers have considered the effects of commitment to a group and group attractiveness on the dissonance produced by conformity with the group's wishes (Kiesler & Corbin, 1965; Kiesler & DeSalvo, 1967).

The present chapter also focuses on dissonance in a social context but differs from earlier work by considering how dissonance processes may be activated by *collective actions*. It is not difficult to imagine circumstances in which collective behaviors can produce dissonance in group members. For example, an individual may participate in counterattitudinal group behaviors because of such influences as peer pressure and organizational role constraints. Similarly, as members of formal (e.g., political and business) and informal (e.g., family and peer) groups, individuals are required to participate in making collective decisions capable of arousing dissonance. We have therefore begun to examine the occurrence of cognitive dissonance processes as they result from collective actions (Zanna & Sande, in press). The two basic questions we seek to address are: Will individuals acting as members of groups experience cognitive dissonance in the same manner and to the same degree as individuals acting alone? If so, when is dissonance likely to be reduced by means of postbehavioral attitude change and when may group members employ alternate avenues of dissonance reduction?

The Arousal of Dissonance in Groups

At this point we shall consider the characteristics of collective action that may increase or decrease the probability of arousing cognitive dissonance. Recall that the necessary conditions for the arousal of dissonance are (1) that an individual must engage in a counterattitudinal behavior, (2) that has aversive consequences, (3) for which he or she assumes personal responsibility. In the discussion that follows we consider group influences on those three primary components, namely, the probability of emitting counterattitudinal behavior, the actor's perceptions of the aversiveness of the consequences, and attributions of personal responsibility.

Behavior. We would suggest that individuals perform many, if not most, of their counterattitudinal behaviors in group settings. There is substantial evidence that people do things in a group that they would not normally do alone. Observations of crowd behavior (cf. LeBon, 1896; Mann, 1981) have suggested that otherwise law-abiding citizens engage in counternormative and counterattitudinal behaviors when afforded the anonymity of being in a large group. Festinger, Pepitone, and Newcomb (1952) called this relative anonymity deindividuation and showed that, even in small groups, it may lead to behaviors from which individuals would normally refrain. Small groups of students have been induced to engage in counternormative behaviors such, as expressing hostile statements about their parents (Festinger *et al.*, 1952), using obscene language (Singer, Brush, & Lublin, 1965), and shocking a fellow student (Zimbardo, 1970).

Given the pressures existing within a group that tend to produce uniformity of behavior (cf. Sherif, 1935; Asch, 1950), one may be particularly likely to engage in counterattitudinal behaviors in order to avoid sanctions from the other members of the group. For example, adolescents are subject to peer pressure to perform actions that might initially be contrary to their beliefs, such as dropping out of school, starting to smoke, taking drugs, etc. In more formal organizations, person–role conflict develops when an individual's personal values and beliefs are incompatible with the behavior prescribed by the position he or she occupies. In many organizations there exists a norm that encourages group members to compromise when there is disagreement over some course of action. The result is that nobody ends up acting in a totally attitude-consistent manner and everyone, to a greater or lesser extent, performs a counterattitudinal behavior. Other processes may operate in groups to suppress the expression of opposition to collective actions that run counter to individual values. Janis' (1972) analysis of the "groupthink" phenomenon suggests that pluralistic ignorance and the presence of self-appointed mindguards may cause the suppression of personal doubts about the group's intentions and eventually lead to collective counterattitudinal actions.

The above discussion suggests that one is more likely to engage in counterattitudinal behavior as a member of a group than when alone. When this does occur, the amount of dissonance a group member experiences depends, in part, on the extent of his or her personal involvement in the collective action. According to research on the "social loafing" effect (cf. Latané, Williams, & Harkins, 1979; Petty, Harkins, & Williams, 1980), the performance of group members is often characterized by decreased personal involvement and effort, compared to individuals performing alone. If group members do loaf, a corresponding decrease in the magnitude of dissonance aroused might ensue since, in effect, one engages in less counterattitudinal behavior in a group than when alone. Social loafing has, to date, been considered mostly as it occurs in the performance of proattitudinal behavior. When counterattitudinal group actions are involved, one might expect to observe an additional decrease in involvement and effort (motivated social loafing?), since this kind of foot dragging might allow group members to conclude that they did not (much) engage in the behavior.

On the other hand, there may be instances in which individuals are more involved and expend more effort as members of groups than when alone. For instance, there may exist pressures to pull together and work hard on difficult group tasks, such as making decisions with impactful and potentially aversive consequences. When individuals engage in personally distasteful collective actions, such as counterattitudinal and/or counternormative behaviors, the result may be a feeling of separation from outsiders, greater in-group solidarity, and less social loafing. In addition, when a group is engaged in difficult or counterattitudinal actions loafing may be especially taboo, and each group member may feel that the others are monitoring his or her contribution. The result is, in effect, that one engages in more counterattitudinal behavior in a group and may therefore experience more postbehavioral dissonance than one may experience when acting alone.

Evidence gathered by Zanna and Sande (in press, Study 1) indicates that, at least in some circumstances, individuals' perceived effort and involvement are greater in collective counterattitudinal activities than when each acts alone. In that experiment, subjects, alone or in groups of three, wrote counterattitudinal essays. Subjects engaging in collective counterattitudinal actions under conditions of high choice did not engage in social loafing in order to avoid the experience of dissonance. Their essays were equal in quality to those written by subjects in the other conditions. Measures of *perceived* effort and involvement show that these subjects (in the High-Choice/Group condition) loafed less than subjects in the High-Choice/Alone condition and the Low-Choice/Group condition.

Consequences. As previously discussed, the perception that one's actions will have aversive consequences is a necessary prerequisite for the arousal of dissonance (cf. Nel, Helmreich, & Aronson, 1969; Cooper & Worchel, 1970). One's perceptions of the effectiveness of collective action, compared to individual action, might be expected to influence the perceived aversiveness of the consequences of those behaviors. If group performance is seen as inferior to individual performance (e.g., "too many cooks spoil the broth"), collective behavior can be expected to lead to less aversive consequences. For example, in an experiment where groups and individuals are induced to write essays that support a position inconsistent with their beliefs, group members may perceive that their essays are less likely to persuade a third party than individual subjects perceive. However, if the belief that "three heads are better than one" prevails, group members may believe that their efforts will have more aversive consequences than individual actions (i.e., their essays will be more persuasive). In the latter case, there ought to be more dissonance aroused as the result of collective actions. In the previously mentioned Zanna and Sande (in press) experiment, subjects in the High-Choice/Group condition did, in fact, rate their essays as more persuasive than did the High-choice subjects acting alone.

Personal responsibility.[1] Research using individual subjects has demonstrated that only when people perceive that they have a high degree of choice about whether or not to perform some behavior do they assume personal responsibility for their actions and experience dissonance. In one sense, collective actions provide information that ought to decrease the probability of high-choice attributions. The fact that everyone in the group is participating in a given behavior, especially one that is counterattitudinal, carries information about the pressures to conform. If a group member were sensitive to such information, perceptions of choice (and the experience of dissonance) might be attenuated. However, influences such as peer pressure and role constraints can be very subtle and difficult to identify. For example, subjects in conformity studies are often unaware that their behavior has been influenced by the responses of others (Hood & Sherif, 1962). This may lead one to overestimate the extent of one's freedom of action. This overestimation may be exacerbated by a motivational tendency to see oneself as being in control of one's own behavior (Langer, 1975). It appears, then, that although evidence is available to suggest that the action has, at least to some extent, been coerced, people engaging in collective actions may still perceive a high degree of personal choice. This was confirmed in the

---

[1]At this point our discussion is limited to the effects of perceived choice and foreseeability on the assumption of personal responsibility. Diffusion of responsibility is discussed as a means of coping with or resolving dissonance after it has been aroused. It is possible, however, that people may avoid dissonance by diffusing responsibility before or during the performance of counterattitudinal behavior.

Zanna and Sande (in press) group dissonance study. Subjects performing counterattitudinal behaviors in groups perceived no less choice than those acting alone. The result of this may be a relatively unusual situation, i.e., one in which coercion leads to private attitude change. Because group members underestimate the extent to which their behavior has been coerced, cognitive dissonance may cause them to change their attitudes to correspond with, and justify, their actions.

The group context may also influence whether or not the aversive consequences of an action are foreseen. In his analysis of the groupthink syndrome, Janis (1972) proposes that disastrous collective actions may result when group members convince each other that negative consequences are improbable. Especially in very cohesive groups, a reluctance to assess the group's strategy critically (and, in particular, to consider the possibility and costs of failure) may cause an illusion of invulnerability to develop. One might expect, then, that because aversive consequences are not foreseen in groups, actions producing such consequences are all the more likely. Furthermore, after those consequences occur, it may become obvious that they ought to have been foreseen. In retrospect those aversive consequences are judged to have been foreseeable. After the Bay of Pigs fiasco, this process of retrospective foreseeability led John F. Kennedy and his colleagues to feel responsible for an outcome that, due to groupthink, they had not foreseen. As a result, Kennedy took deliberate steps to avoid groupthink during the Cuban missile crisis in 1962 (Janis, 1972). In the context of collective counterattitudinal action, an after the fact invocation of foreseeability may lead to the arousal of dissonance where none initially occurred.

In summary, there are a number of characteristics of group settings that determine whether collective actions produce more or less dissonance than solitary actions. We have argued that because of group norms and pressures one may be more likely to engage in counterattitudinal behaviors in groups than when alone. Whether or not dissonance is aroused as the result of those actions depends on whether the situation leads to social loafing, assumptions about the impact or effectiveness of group action, the subtlety of compliance pressures operating in the group and the resulting perceptions of one's freedom to act, and group dynamics, which influence whether potential aversive consequences are foreseen or are subsequently judged to have been foreseeable.

The Resolution of Group Dissonance

At this point we shall focus primarily on two means of reducing the dissonance that is aroused by collective actions: attitude change and diffusion of responsibility. In cases where neither of these options is viable, a third course of action, seeking social support from within or from outside of the group, may be taken. Discussion of this latter alternative is reserved for later, when we talk about group dissonance in religious organizations.

Psychologists have been primarily interested in studying the conditions in which dissonance has been resolved by means of attitude change. Since it is generally accepted that attitude change is one of the more effortful and "costly" means of coping with dissonance (Zanna & Aziza, 1976), researchers have usually closed off all other avenues of dissonance reduction in order to get subjects to change their attitudes. For example, the procedures of these studies usually make it very difficult for subjects to deny that they have engaged in counterattitudinal behavior of their own free will and that those actions have had foreseeable aversive consequences.

However, group members have a viable avenue of dissonance reduction not available to individuals acting alone. They have an opportunity to diffuse responsibility for the group's behavior and its aversive consequences to the other group members. To the extent that an interactive process leading to a group product is not systematic, i.e., it is relatively free flowing and unmonitored and particular group members are not assigned responsibility for certain ideas, the contributions of individual members are difficult to identify. Group members may then be able to underestimate or downplay their own role in the interaction and thereby avoid having to change their attitudes in order to resolve dissonance.

It has been demonstrated, in a number of situations, that group members diffuse responsibility for behaviors with potentially aversive or costly consequences. In the domain of helping behavior, it has been shown that people in groups are less likely than solitary individuals to help a dependent person (Berkowitz, 1978) or a victim of illness or accident (Latané & Darley, 1970). In these kinds of helping contexts, diffusion of responsibility is an excuse for inaction, a decision to let someone else render aid. Blaming of others after the fact for the aversive consequences of action [e.g., when "teachers" in Milgram's (1974) studies blamed the experimenter for the pain inflicted on innocent "learners"], is a different, but probably related, form of responsibility diffusion.[2] It is this sort of diffusion that we consider, for the most part, in our discussion of group dissonance. This kind of diffusion has been demonstrated by Mynatt and Sherman (1975), who induced subjects, alone or in groups, to give advice to a target person. When this advice turned out to be helpful to the target, group members took no less personal responsibility than did individuals. However, when the advice had negative

---

[2]It may be considerably more difficult to diffuse responsibility for action than for inaction. Since events have a greater impact on our judgments than nonevents (Fazio, Sherman, & Herr, 1982), actions may cause us to attribute more responsibility to a target than the failure to act (even when the target is oneself). In addition, the consequences of inaction may be ambiguous (e.g., we may conclude that someone else helped the victim), whereas the consequences of action may be much more clear and undeniable.

consequences for the target, group members diffused responsibility, taking less than individual subjects. In light of the evidence that attitude change may be the least preferred avenue of dissonance reduction, one might expect that group members would be more likely to engage in postbehavioral diffusion of responsibility rather than attitude change. However, there may be characteristics of the group setting that make a person less willing or less able to diffuse. In those circumstances, attitude change may be a more likely avenue of dissonance reduction.

The central proposition in this discussion is that attitude change and diffusion of responsibility are inversely related avenues of dissonance reduction. That is, the tendency to resist changing one's attitude may be opposed by a tendency to avoid diffusing responsibility in group settings. In Lewinian terms, following dissonance-arousing collective actions, the group member may experience a kind of "avoidance–avoidance" conflict (Lewin, 1935). So, for example, the more difficult it is to diffuse responsibility, the more likely is the resolution of dissonance to be accomplished by means of attitude change, and vice versa. The following discussion considers factors affecting the probability that each of these means of dissonance reduction will be used. Of course, because of the inverse relation between attitude change and diffusion of responsibility, a factor that affects one means of dissonance reduction indirectly affects the probability of using the other means.

Attitude change. One of the critical factors that influences the tendency to avoid attitude change is the individual's commitment to his or her initial attitude; the greater this commitment the stronger the motive to avoid attitude change. Commitment may be a function of the salience of the initial attitude, or of the centrality of that attitude to one's value system or self-concept. Researchers have found that when subjects are induced to perform behaviors inconsistent with highly salient or central attitudes, they employ avenues of dissonance reduction other than attitude change, such as downplaying the aversiveness of the consequences (Scheier & Carver, 1980) or attitude bolstering (Sherman & Gorkin, 1980). In group contexts, researchers have found that when the attitude violated is central to one's group membership, subjects may cope with dissonance by misattributing their arousal to external sources, such as the presence of rival outgroups (Cooper & Mackie, 1983) or aversive environmental stimuli (Gonzalez & Cooper, reported in Zanna and Cooper, 1976). We might then expect collective actions that are inconsistent with a highly salient or central attitude to be less likely to lead to attitude change and more likely to lead to diffusion of responsibility.

Diffusion of responsibility. Whether or not a group member will diffuse responsibility is a function of (at least) two factors. The first concerns the motivation to diffuse or avoid diffusing; the second concerns the opportunity to diffuse. Just as commitment to one's initial attitude may increase resistance to attitude change, one's commitment to the group may increase the tendency to avoid diffusing responsibility. That is, one may be less likely to blame others for one's action and its consequences when group interdependence or cohesiveness is high or when one's emotional ties to the other group members are strong. For example, diffusion of responsibility in a bystander intervention situation is less likely to occur in groups composed of friends than in groups composed of strangers (Latané & Rodin, 1969).

A second motivational factor influencing responsibility diffusion is "the individual tendency to accept rationales for denying responsibility for the consequences of one's behavior" (Schwartz, 1977, p. 230). Schwartz developed a method to assess this predisposition using a scale that includes items, "which mention or allude to actions with interpersonal consequences and provide rationales for ascribing (some) responsibility for the actions and/or their consequences away from the actor" (Schwartz, 1977, p. 257). It has been demonstrated that "Responsibility Deniers" are less likely than "Responsibility Ascribers" to help a person in need, presumably because Deniers diffuse responsibility to the other people present (Schwartz & Clausen, 1970).

Given the motivation to diffuse responsibility, whether or not one does must be, in part, a function of the opportunity to diffuse. There are a number of factors that influence that extent to which "reality constraints" allow group members to convince themselves that they were not responsible for the dissonance-producing behavior. We will consider four of these factors: group size, group homogeneity, group structure, and public accountability.

The first factor is group size. Members of large groups ought to have more opportunity to diffuse responsibility than members of small groups because the extent of one's relative contributions to a group product is less easy to trace in larger groups.

Group homogeneity may also determine the opportunity a group member has to diffuse responsibility.[3] When a group has a heterogeneous composition, one may blame the "different" members for an aversive consequence. For instance, when an organizational strategy goes awry, management can blame the bad advice of the consultants, while the consultants can blame the inability of management to operationalize sound advice. When military plans fail, as in the case of the Bay of Pigs invasion or the Viet Nam war, members of the military blame civilian policy makers, while the civilians blame the professioinal soldiers, intelligence agencies, etc.

The structure of the group also influences the opportunity to diffuse. This factor is interesting, not only because different positions in a hierarchy are naturally associated with different levels of responsibility, but also because

---

[3]Increased heterogeneity may also be associated with decreased group cohesiveness and therefore with a decreased motive to avoid diffusing responsibility.

it may be easier to diffuse responsibility from some positions than others. That is, one's position may be associated with the amount of dissonance aroused by a collective action and the manner or ease with which dissonance can be resolved. Since group leaders have more control over the course of the collective action, they are more likely to feel responsible for the consequences and may therefore experience greater dissonance. In addition, since "authorities are held to more stringent standards of accountability" (Hamilton, 1978, p. 326), it is usually difficult for them to diffuse responsibility to their subordinates as a means of dissonance reduction.

At the other end of the hierarchy, low-status subordinates usually have little control over the collective action and ought to experience less dissonance. These people may easily cope with what little dissonance may be aroused by diffusing responsibility to their superiors, claiming that they have been simply following orders.

Those who occupy middle-level positions in an organization, e.g., consultants or advisors, may react differently depending on the outcome of the collective action. When collective actions have positive, nondissonant outcomes, these individuals may exaggerate their control or responsibility for the group's action, claiming to be the "power behind the throne." However, when the collective actions are counterattitudinal, they ought to experience a moderate amount of dissonance, which they may resolve by emphasizing the constraints of their subordinate position and diffusing responsibility to their superiors.

The above discussion suggests that one's position or role in the group affects one's opportunity to diffuse responsibility for collective counter-attitudinal actions. In general, the greater one's authority or status, the less the opportunity to diffuse, and the more we may expect to see attitude change employed as a means of reducing dissonance. This argument becomes more complicated when one introduces the notion of public accountability. In many cases, an individual group member may be called upon to account publicly for or justify the group's actions. In general, to the extent that one is or expects to be held publicly and personally accountable for a group's behavior, diffusion of responsiblity is less available as an avenue of dissonance reduction. This is because observers, to whom accounts are given, are more likely to make attributions holding the actor responsible. The actor in turn will be influenced by the observers' attributions.

Jones and Nisbett (1971) have shown that actors and observers often differ in the extent to which they attribute the causes of the actor's behavior to internal and external factors, with observers perceiving greater internal causation. When collective actions have aversive consequences, there may be considerable disagreement between actors and observers over the extent to which an actor is responsible for the group's behavior and its consequences. This disagreement may develop because of the following processes.

1. Observers may use different rules to determine responsibility. For example, an actor may hold himself or herself personally responsible only for consequences that were foreseeable and intended. However, observers may hold the actor responsible for any act that was committed by, or even simply associated with the actor (see Heider, 1958, pp. 113–114; Hamilton, 1978, for a discussion of these different stages of responsibility attribution).

2. Actors and observers may focus on different aspects of the collective action when they assess responsibility. While the actor, in an attempt to deny responsibility for the consequences may focus on his or her motive for acting, the observer may focus on the aversive consequences themselves (Hamilton, 1978). The actor may see his or her good intentions, for example, to be an obedient employee, a loyal group member, or a "team player," as the primary consideration in determining personal responsibility. For the observer, the outcome of the collective action may be the most salient and the most relevant determinant.

3. Observers and actors may differ in their perceptions of the amount of choice the actor had and the foreseeability of the aversive consequences. Compared to the actor, observers may perceive greater choice of action within the role, greater freedom to defy role prescriptions, and greater freedom to leave the role rather than act in a counterattitudinal manner. That is, the observer may underestimate role constraints, or the sanctions for breaking group norms, or the costs to the actor of leaving the group. We suggested earlier that, before dissonance is aroused, the actor may underestimate situational constraints on his or her behavior, and that this, in fact, contributes to the arousal of dissonance. We suggest that, once dissonance is aroused, the actor searches for and attends to information about external constraints in an effort to resolve the conflict.

For the reasons listed above, observers and actors may differ in their attributions of how responsible an individual actor is for a group's behavior. The consequence of these divergent perceptions is that observers may hold an actor personally responsible for behaviors and consequences for which the actor would not ordinarily hold himself or herself responsible. In cases where an individual is made to publicly account for or justify a group's behavior, that individual may find it difficult to convince observers that he or she ought to bear little responsibility for that behavior. This individual will then find it difficult to reduce dissonance by diffusing responsibility to the other group members and may be more likely to resolve dissonance by means of attitude change.

To relate the above discussion to the effect of group structure, for the reasons listed above observers may hold even low-status subordinates to be responsible for a group's actions. This kind of post hoc induction of accountability may lead the subordinate to feel responsible for a behavior for which he or she did not initially take responsibility. This may lead to a retroactive arousal of dissonance and the possibility of delayed attitude change, where none was initially observed.

To summarize this section of the chapter: It has been proposed that, following dissonance-arousing collective actions, group members have available inversely related avenues of dissonance reduction. We have discussed a number of factors that influence the probability of employing each mode of dissonance reduction. The probability of using attitude change to reduce dissonance is a function of such factors as the salience of the initial attitude and the centrality of that attitude to the person's value system and self-concept. Employment of an alternate avenue, diffusion of responsibility, varies according to motivational factors, such as commitment to the group and the predisposition to deny or ascribe responsibility to the self, and opportunity factors, which are influenced by such considerations as group size and structure and public accountability.

In two experiments, Zanna and Sande (in press) found evidence consistent with the notion that diffusion of responsibility is a viable alternative to attitude change as a means of resolving dissonance following collective actions. In the first study, subjects who freely wrote counter-attitudinal essays as members of a three-person group showed subsequent attitude change if they were egocentrically biased (i.e., if they took more responsibility for the collective action than the other group members attributed to them; see Ross & Sicoly, 1979). Altercentrically biased subjects (who took less responsibility than others gave them) did not change their attitudes. In a second experiment which employed the free-choice paradigm, individuals with a predisposition to deny responsibility (as measured by Schwartz's Responsibility Denial Scale, 1960) did not change their attitudes following a group decision. In contrast, following a group decision, Responsibility Ascribers did spread apart their evaluations of the chosen and rejected alternatives.

What follows is a brief discussion of how dissonance processes may operate in a number of specific social contexts. We shall consider how a dissonance analysis may help us to understand the effects of interpersonal processes, such as attributions of responsibility or attitude change.

Applications

Antisocial Behavior

Earlier in this chapter we stated that people do things in groups that they are not normally likely to do alone.[4] Milgram's (1963) classic study of obedience

---

[4]We do not mean to imply that collective actions are typically or always less desirable than individual actions. We simply contend that certain characteristics of the group, e.g., collective norms, relative anonymity, etc., may sometimes overcome individual inhibitions against engaging in antisocial behavior (see also Wheeler, 1966, on behavioral contagion).

demonstrated the coercive power of authority figures. In that experiment, ordinary people were induced to shock an innocent and defenseless individual. Zimbardo (1970) showed that simple deindividuation, without the presence of a coercive authority, could produce the same kind of behavior. Under conditions of deindividuation, "sweet, normally mild-mannered college girls shocked another girl almost everytime they had an opportunity to, sometimes for as long as they were allowed, and it did not matter whether or not that fellow student was a nice girl who didn't deserve to be hurt" (Zimbardo, 1970, p. 270). Other research has shown that deindividuation may produce antisocial behaviors such as administering aversive noise to others (Prentice-Dunn & Rogers, 1980), suicide baiting (Mann, 1981), and lynching atrocities (Mullen, 1986).

The literature on conformity clearly demonstrates that groups exert pressures on their members to comply with the group's wishes (cf., Sherif, 1935; Asch, 1958). Most of us have experienced pressures to "go along" with the group. Adolescents may experience peer pressure to engage in antisocial behaviors such as vandalism, using drugs, etc. Adult members of business organizations may find themselves participating in actions that harm society in order to help the organization, such as price fixing, polluting the environment, cheating on tax laws, etc.

When an action is induced by a clearly identifiable coercive agent, compliant behavior does not normally produce the internalization of behavior-congruent attitudes (Kiesler & Kiesler, 1969; Kelman, 1958). In dissonance terms, behavior induced under conditions of low choice does not cause the actor to make attributions of personal responsibility, cognitive dissonance is not aroused, and attitude change does not ensue. However, the coercive power of groups is often very subtle. As we noted earlier, group members may underestimate the influence of peer pressure on their behaviors and may then overestimate their freedom of choice. Thus, the subtle power of group pressure may produce dissonance. If this dissonance is resolved by means of attitude change, collective antisocial behavior may result in individual antisocial attitudes.

As we have suggested, diffusing responsibility to other members of the group is an alternative avenue of dissonance reduction. This is precisely what one would want to bring about if one wanted to prevent the postbehavioral formation of antisocial attitudes. However, diffusion of responsibility may be a very difficult thing for the actor to do, in that it may be associated with profound psychological costs. As we suggested earlier, the higher the level of commitment or cohesiveness in a group, the less willing a group member is likely to be to blame his or her colleagues for the action. In fact, in highly cohesive groups there may be a tendency to do the opposite, to "take the rap" for the others and assume more responsibility than one ought to.

Diffusing responsibility, or blaming the others, is an act of distancing or disassociating oneself from the group. However, one's membership in the group may constitute a significant part of one's own identity (Tajfel & Turner, 1979). We often look to peer groups as sources of support and approval. In addition, withdrawal from a group such as a business organization means a loss of income. The prospect of high psychological costs (loss of identity and support) and physical costs (employment and income) may preclude the diffusion of responsibility.

As we previously mentioned, in addition to these motivational factors, one's opportunity to diffuse responsibility may be limited. If, for example, the behavior becomes public knowledge, one may be held accountable for the actions of the group. To try to diffuse responsibility in such circumstances leaves the actor open to considerable costs. In a society that holds that individuals ought to be in control of their own actions, admitting to others (and to oneself) that one has been pressured into acting in a counterattitudinal manner is likely to prove embarrassing and may lead one to incur sanctions over and above what one might incur for the behavior itself.

To the extent, then, that the actor is unwilling or unable to diffuse responsibility for a collective antisocial action, individual antisocial attitudes become more likely, which, in turn, may lead to further antisocial behavior even when the group is not present.

Worker Productivity

In most North American corporations, decision-making power is concentrated at the top of the hierarchy, while those at the lower levels of the organization have little or no control over their behavior on the job. Probably the most extreme example of this is the assembly line, where a worker's behavior is precisely specified and regulated. In some foreign companies, and a few domestic companies (e.g., the new "Saturn" project by General Motors), there has been a relatively recent trend toward involving all employees in making decisions about at least some aspects of the production process. Notably in Scandinavia and Japan, the trend toward "participative management" has resulted in workers deciding about work design, pace, and quality control. In these countries, participative management has been credited with stimulating productivity increases (see Gyllenhammar, 1977; Ouchi, 1981).

Early work by Kurt Lewin and his colleagues, directed at changing the eating habits of Americans during wartime food shortages, showed that group decision-making processes were more effective in altering behavior than were lectures by an authority (Lewin, 1947a). Subsequent studies in industrial settings demonstrated that allowing employees to participate in work-related decisions led to reduced conflict and absenteeism, faster adaptation to procedural changes, and greater productivity (Fleishman, 1965; Zander & Armstrong, 1972). A dissonance analysis of this phenomenon would suggest that postdecisional cognitive dissonance leads members of the group to evaluate the chosen course of action more positively, which has the effect of committing the person to the chosen behavior [or, in Lewin's (1947a, b) terms, "refreezing" the new attitude].

Our analysis of the effects of collective actions would suggest several necessary conditions to bring about postdecisional attitude change in these situations. First, group members must perceive a high degree of choice. It may require a highly skilled leader to help group members to arrive at a decision without coercion (Lewin, 1947a). In addition, the workers must see that the company is actually instituting their decisions, that their choice is not just an illusion. Pseudo-participation, or the failed attempt to create the mere illusion of choice, can have disastrous effects on employee satisfaction and performance (Luthans, 1977). Finally, if group members diffuse responsibility for the decision, postdecisional attitude change and commitment will be reduced, a concern voiced by Yukl (1981). For participative decision making to be effective, the opportunity to diffuse responsibility must be decreased, for instance, by increasing the public nature (and accountability) of the collective decision.

The increased commitment produced by postdecisional attitude change may, at times, have unfortunate consequences for the organization. People become committed to bad decisions as well as good ones. As Staw (1976) has shown, there is a tendency in such cases to escalate one's commitment to a potentially disastrous course of action. Janis' (1972) analysis of the escalation of the war in Viet Nam and other situations suggests that decision-making groups are also vulnerable to the tendency to "throw good money after bad." In fact, Janis suggests that highly cohesive groups (in which, we have proposed, there is a motivation to avoid diffusing responsibility for failures) are especially likely to fall victim to this tendency. This is because postdecisional attitude change becomes more likely as diffusion of responsibility becomes less likely. Thus, we would expect escalation to be more common in groups than when individuals act alone, especially if the groups are cohesive.

Participation in Religious Organizations

In the 1950s, a religious sect called the "Seekers" published a prophecy of a catastrophic flood that would inundate the west coast of North and South America. The leader of the Seekers, Mrs. Keech, had supposedly received a warning about the flood from beings on another planet. She further asserted that those beings would come to the earth in flying saucers to rescue the faithful (the Seekers). Several members of the group gathered at the critical time to await their rescuers. As one might expect, when Mrs. Keech's predictions failed to materialize, some of the Seekers abandoned their beliefs and the group. Suprisingly, several of the members not only maintained their beliefs, but seemed to intensify them.

These events provided Leon Festinger and his colleagues with the opportunity to study how members of a religious group would react when confronted with unequivocal evidence that a strongly held belief is wrong (Festinger, Riecken, & Schachter, 1956). Such evidence would certainly arouse cognitive dissonance. As we noted earlier, the more central a belief is to one's value system, the more difficult it will be to change that attitude when one is confronted with dissonant information. Since religious beliefs are often very important to one's understanding of the world and of oneself, they may be particularly resistant to disconfirmation. Feather (1964) demonstrated that individuals' judgments about the truth or falsity of information were consistent with their religious beliefs. Batson (1975) showed that disconfirming information may not undermine basic religious beliefs and, in fact, may lead to belief intensification. In short, attitude change may not be a viable response to the disconfirmation of religious beliefs.

Perhaps we would expect members of the Seekers to cope with dissonance arising from disconfirmation by diffusing responsibility for the group's actions to the other group members. However, religious beliefs are closely tied to, and are in fact the reason for, membership in the religious group. In this case, commitment to the attitude implies commitment to the group. Blaming the other group members may be tantamount to denying one's faith. Diffusion of responsibility is difficult for other reasons. Entering a religious sect may be a costly process. One has to change old attitudes and habits and may well suffer disapproval and rejection from family and friends. Through the process of justification of effort, the group may come to be seen as particularly attractive (Aronson & Mills, 1959). As we mentioned earlier, group membership may be a significant part of one's sense of identity, and the other group members may be an important source of approval and affection. For these reasons, a group member may be unwilling to cope with dissonance by diffusing responsibility.

Festinger and Aronson (1962) suggested another way in which the group context provides an opportunity to reduce dissonance. Social support from other people allows the individual to add new cognitive elements that are consonant with the initial belief, i.e., "other people agree with me." This reduces dissonance by increasing the proportion of consonant cognitive elements (Festinger, 1957). If immediately following disconfirmation of a strongly held belief support from the other members of the group is available, belief intensification may occur. This was dramatically demonstrated in the case of the Seekers. Those members who waited together to be rescued emerged from the disconfirmation even more firmly convinced of the truth of their beliefs than before. However, those members of the group who waited alone for the fulfillment of the prophecy discarded their beliefs and left the group (Festinger et al., 1956).

Group members may seek additional social support by trying to convince others of the validity of their beliefs. Festinger et al. (1956) observed that immediately following the disconfirmation, there was a dramatic increase in proselytizing by the Seekers. However, a study by Hardyck and Braden (1962) of a similar situation involving disconfirmed prophecy showed that when the level of within-group support is sufficiently high, dissonance can be resolved without seeking outside support.

These two studies demonstrate an additional avenue for the resolution of dissonance that is aroused by collective actions. If attitude change and diffusion of responsibility are difficult, the support provided by other group members helps the individual to reduce the magnitude of dissonance. A series of studies by Stroebe and Diehl (1981) confirmed the notion that social support reduces the probability of attitude change following counter-attitudinal behavior. Intensified commitment to the initial belief (and perhaps to the group) may result. Although members of most religious groups may not experience such dramatic and unequivocal disconfirmation of their beliefs, they may often have to deal with potentially disconfirming information such as belief-inconsistent results of scientific research, etc. Support from their fellow group members may play an important role in helping them resolve the resultant cognitive dissonance.

Conclusion

In this chapter we have considered some of the effects of collective action on the attributions and attitudes of individual group members. Our approach has been to extend cognitive dissonance theory into the realm of group processes. Obviously, there are many processes besides dissonance that operate in groups and that affect attitude change and attributions of responsibility. In conducting our research (Zanna & Sande, in press) we have considered some of these processes, such as social comparison, persuasion, and self-presentation. The other chapters in this volume contribute additional perspectives on these issues.

In general, our approach to these issues seems justified by the existing literature on group dynamics and by the results of our research to date. In addition, these ideas seem directly applicable to an analysis of specific social settings.

Acknowledgments. The original research reported in the present chapter was supported by a grant from the Social Sciences and Humanities Research Council of Canada to both authors. In addition to the editors we wish to thank Robert Croyle for comments on an earlier draft. Correspondence may be sent to G.N. Sande, now at the Department of Psychology, University of Manitoba, Winnipeg, Manitoba, Canada R3T 2N2.

References

Aronson, G., & Mills, J. (1959). The effects of severity of initiation on liking for a group. *Journal of Abnormal and Social Psychology, 59,* 177–181.

Asch, S. (1958). Effects of group pressure upon modification and distortion of judgments. In E. Maccoby, T. Newcomb, & E. Hartley (Eds.), *Readings in Social Psychology* (3rd ed. pp. 174–83). New York: Holt.

Batson, C. (1975). Rational processing or rationalization?: The effect of disconfirming information on a stated religious belief. *Journal of Personality and Social Psychology, 32,* 176–184.

Berkowitz, L. (1978). Decreased helpfulness with increased group size through lessening the effects of the needy individual's dependency. *Journal of Personality, 46,* 299–310.

Brehm, J. (1956). Post-decision changes in desirability of alternatives. *Journal of Abnormal and Social Psychology, 52,* 384–389.

Cooper, J., & Fazio, R. (1984). A new look at dissonance theory. In L. Berkowitz (Ed.), *Advances in experimental social psychology* (Vol. 17 pp. 229–266). New York: Academic Press.

Cooper, J., & Mackie, D. (1983). Cognitive dissonance in an intergroup context. *Journal of Personality and Social Psychology, 44,* 536–544.

Cooper, J., & Worchel, S. (1970). Role of undesired consequences in arousing cognitive dissonance. *Journal of Personality and Social Psychology, 16,* 199–206.

Davis, K., & Jones, E. (1960). Changes in interpersonal perception as a means of reducing cognitive dissonance. *Journal of Abnormal and Social Psychology, 61,* 402–410.

Fazio, R., Sherman, S., & Herr, P. (1982). The feature-positive effect in the self-perception process: Does not doing matter as much as doing? *Journal of Personality and Social Psychology, 42,* 404–411.

Feather, N. (1964). Acceptance and rejection of arguments in relation to attitude strength, critical ability, and intolerance of inconsistency. *Journal of Abnormal and Social Psychology, 69,* 127–136.

Festinger, L. (1957). *A theory of cognitive dissonance.* Stanford, CA: Stanford University Press.

Festinger, L. (1964). *Conflict, decision and dissonance.* Stanford, CA: Stanford University Press.

Festinger, L., & Aronson, E. (1962). The arousal and reduction of dissonance in social contexts. In D. Cartwright & A. Zander (Eds.), *Group dynamics* (2nd ed. pp. 214–231). Evanston, IL: Row, Peterson and Company.

Festinger, L., & Carlsmith, J. (1959). Cognitive consequences of forced compliance. *Journal of Abnormal and Social Psychology, 58,* 203–210.

Festinger, L., Pepitone, A., & Newcomb, T. (1952). Some consequences of de-individuation in a group. *Journal of Abnormal and Social Psychology, 47,* 382–389.

Festinger, L., Riecken, H., & Schachter, S. (1956). *When prophecy fails.* Minneapolis, MN: University of Minnesota Press.

Fleishman, E. (1965). Attitude versus skill factors in work group productivity. *Personnel Psychology, 18,* 253–266.

Gerard, H., & Mathewson, G. (1966). The effects of severity of initiation on liking for a group: A replication. *Journal of Experimental Social Psychology, 2,* 278–287.

Goethals, G., Cooper, J., & Naficy, A. (1979). Role of foreseen, foreseeable and unforeseeable behavioral consequences in the arousal of cognitive dissonance. *Journal of Personality and Social Psychology, 37,* 1179–1185.

Gyllenhammar, P. (1977). How Volvo adapts work to people. *Harvard Business Review, 55,* 102–113.

Hamilton, V. (1978). Who is responsible? Toward a social psychology of responsibility attribution. *Social Psychology, 41,* 316–328.

Hardyck, J., & Braden, M. (1962). Prophecy fails again: A report of a failure to replicate. *Journal of Abnormal and Social Psychology, 65,* 136–141.

Heider, F. (1958). *The psychology of interpersonal relations.* New York: Wiley.

Hood, W., & Sherif, M. (1962). Verbal report and judgment of an unstructured stimulus. *Journal of Psychology, 54*, 121–130.

Janis, I. (1972). *Victims of groupthink: A psychological study of foreign-policy decisions and fiascos*. Boston: Houghton Mifflin.

Jones, E. E., & Nisbett, R. (1971). *The actor and the observer: Divergent perceptions of the causes of behavior*. Morristown, NJ: General Learning Press.

Kelman, H. (1958). Compliance, identification, and internalization: Three processes of attitude change. *Journal of Conflict Resolution, 2*, 51–60.

Kiesler, C., & Corbin, L. (1965). Commitment, attraction and conformity. *Journal of Personality and Social Psychology, 2*, 890–895.

Kiesler, C., & De Salvo, J. (1967). The group as an influencing agent in a forced compliance paradigm. *Journal of Experimental Social Psychology, 3*, 160–171.

Kiesler, C., & Kiesler, S. (1969). *Conformity*. Reading, MA: Addison-Wesley.

Kiesler, C., & Munson, P. (1975). Attitudes and Opinions. In M. Rosenzweig & L. Porter (Eds.), *Annual review of psychology* (Vol. 26 pp. 415–456). Palo alto, CA: Annual Reviews Inc.

Knox, R., & Inkster, J. (1968). Postdecision dissonance at post time. *Journal of Personality and Social Psychology, 8*, 319–323.

Langer, E. (1975). The illusion of control. *Journal of Personality and Social Psychology, 32*, 311–328.

Latané, B., & Darley, J. (1970). *The unresponsive bystander: Why doesn't he help?* Englewood Cliffs, NJ: Prentice-Hall.

Latané, B., & Rodin, J. (1969). A lady in distress: Inhibiting effects of friends and strangers on bystander intervention. *Journal of Experimental Social Psychology, 5*, 189–202.

Latané, B., Williams, K., & Harkins, S. (1979). Many hands make light work: The causes and consequences of social loafing. *Journal of Personality and Social Psychology, 37*, 822–832.

LeBon, G. (1896). *The crowd: A study of the popular mind*. London: Ernest Benn.

Lewin, K. (1935). *A dynamic theory of personality*. New York: McGraw-Hill.

Lewin, K. (1947a). Group decision and social change. In T. Newcomb & E. Hartley (Eds.), *Readings in social psychology* (pp. 330–344). New York: Holt.

Lewin, K. (1947b). Frontiers in group dynamics. *Journal of Human Relations, 1*, 5–40.

Linder, D., Cooper, J., & Jones, E. (1967). Decision freedom as a determinant of the role of incentive magnitude in attitude change. *Journal of Personality and Social Psychology, 6*, 245–254.

Luthans, F. (1977). *Organizational behavior* (2nd ed.). New York: McGraw-Hill.

Mann, L. (1981). The baiting crowd in episodes of threatened suicide. *Journal of Personality and Social Psychology, 41*, 703–709.

Milgram, S. (1963). Behavioral study of obedience. *Journal of Abnormal and Social Psychology, 67*, 371–378.

Milgram, S. (1974). *Obedience to authority*. New York: Harper & Row.

Mullen, B. (1986). Atrocity as a function of lynch mob composition: A self-attention perspective. *Personality and Social Psychology Bulletin, 12*, 187–197.

Mynatt, C., & Sherman, S. (1975). Responsibility attribution in groups and individuals: A direct test of the diffusion of responsibility hypothesis. *Journal of Personality and Social Psychology, 32*, 1111–1118.

Nel, E., Helmreich, R., & Aronson, E. (1969). Opinion change in the advocate as a function of the persuasibility of his audience: A clarification of the meaning of dissonance. *Journal of Personality and Social Psychology, 12*, 117–124.

Ouchi, W. (1981). *Theory Z: How American business can meet the Japanese challenge*. Reading, MA: Addison-Wesley.

Petty, R., Harkins, S., & Williams, K. (1980). The effects of group diffusion of cognitive effort on attitudes: An information-processing view. *Journal of Personality and Social Psychology, 38,* 81–92.

Prentice-Dunn, S., & Rogers, R. (1980). Effects of deindividuating situational cues and aggressive models on subject deindividuation and aggression. *Journal of Personality and Social Psychology, 39,* 104–113.

Ross, M., & Sicoly, F. (1979). Egocentric biases in availability and attribution. *Journal of Personality and Social Psychology, 37,* 322–336.

Scheier, M., & Carver, C. (1980). Private and public self-attention, resistance to change, and dissonance reduction. *Journal of Personality and Social Psychology, 39,* 390–405.

Schwartz, S. (1968). Words, deeds, and the perception of consequences and responsibility in action situations. *Journal of Personality and Social Psychology, 10,* 232–242.

Schwartz, S. (1977). Normative influences on altruism. In L. Berkowitz (Ed.), *Advances in experimental social psychology* (Vol. 10 pp. 222–279). New York: Academic Press.

Schwartz, S., & Clausen, G. (1970). Responsibility, norms, and helping in an emergency. *Journal of Personality and Social Psychology, 16,* 299–310.

Sherif, M. (1935). A study of some social factors in perception. *Archives of Psychology, 27,* 1–60.

Sherman, S., & Gorkin, L. (1980). Attitude bolstering when behavior is inconsistent with central attitudes. *Journal of Experimental Social Psychology, 16,* 388–403.

Singer, J., Brush, C., & Lublin, S. (1965). Some aspects of deindividuation: Identification and conformity. *Journal of Experimental Social Psychology, 1,* 365–378.

Staw, B. (1976). Knee-deep in the big muddy: A study of escalating commitment to a chosen course of action. *Organizational Behavior and Human Performance, 16,* 27–44.

Stroebe, W., & Diehl, M. (1981). Conformity and counter attitudinal behaviour: The effect of social support on attitude change. *Journal of Personality and Social Psychology, 41,* 876–889.

Tajfel, H., & Turner, J. (1979). An integrative theory of intergroup conflict. In W. Austin & S. Worchel (Eds.), *The social psychology of intergroup relations* (pp. 33–47). Monterey, CA: Brooks/Cole.

Wheeler, L. (1966). Toward a theory of behavioral contagion. *Psychological Review, 73,* 179–192.

Yukl, G. (1981). *Leadership in organizations.* Englewood Cliffs, NJ: Prentice-Hall.

Zander, A., & Armstrong, W. (1972). Working for group pride in a slipper factory. *Journal of Applied Social Psychology, 2,* 160–168.

Zanna, M., & Aziza, C. (1976). On the interaction of repression-sensitization and attention in resolving cognitive dissonance. *Journal of Personality, 44,* 577–593.

Zanna, M., & Cooper, J. (1976). Dissonance and the attribution process. In J. Harvey, W. Ickes, & R. Kidd (Eds.), *New directions in attribution research* (pp. 199–217). Hillsdale, NJ: Erlbaum.

Zanna, M., & Sande, G. (in press). The effects of collective actions on the attitudes of individual group members: A dissonance analysis. In M. Zanna, J. Olson, & C. Herman (Eds.), *Social influence: The Ontario symposium on personality and social psychology* (Vol. 5). Hillsdale, NJ: Erlbaum.

Zimbardo, P. (1970, April). *Symposium on social and developmental issues in moral research.* Paper presented at the meeting of the western Psychological Association, Los Angeles, CA, April.

Zimbardo, P., Weisenberg, M., Firestone, I., & Levy, B. (1965). Communicator effectiveness in producing public conformity and private attitude change. *Journal of Personality, 33,* 233–255.

Chapter 4

Self-Presentation Theory: Self-Construction and Audience Pleasing

Roy F. Baumeister and Debra G. Hutton

General Principles

Self-presentation is behavior that attempts to convey some information about oneself or some image of oneself to other people. It denotes a class of *motivations* in human behavior. These motivations are in part stable dispositions of individuals but they depend on situational factors to elicit them. Specifically, self-presentational motivations are activated by the evaluative presence of other people and by others' (even potential) knowledge of one's behavior.

Two types of self-presentational motivations can be distinguished (Baumeister, 1982a). One (pleasing the audience) is to match one's self-presentation to the audience's expectations and preferences. The other (self-construction) is to match one's self-presentation to one's own ideal self.

The expression of the audience-pleasing motive varies across situations, especially since different audiences have different preferences; one presents oneself differently when attending church with one's parents than when attending a party with one's sorority or fraternity mates. The audience-pleasing motives can even produce inconsistent or contradictory self-presentations with different audiences. Additionally, audience-pleasing self-presentational motivations vary in strength as a function of the audience's power and importance, particularly with regard to how much the self-presenter is dependent on the audience.

The self-construction motive is presumably a fairly stable disposition and therefore it should lead to self-presentations that are essentially consistent across different situations and different audiences. The strength of the self-construction motive may vary as a function of the desire to claim a certain trait and with uncertainty about whether one has it.

Important refinements of the audience-pleasing concept were introduced by Jones and Pittman (1982). These authors pointed out that self-presentation can be geared toward the audience yet not toward making a favorable impression. Instead of pleasing the audience, someone may desire to present himself or herself as dangerous (strategy of intimidation), as morally virtuous (strategy of exemplification), or as helpless and needy (strategy of supplication). The general principle behind all these self-presentations, then, is that people present themselves so as to create a particular and useful impression on the audience, in order to influence or manipulate the audience to benefit the self-presenter. Often this is accomplished by impressing the audience as likable and competent; but sometimes it can be most useful to appear dangerous or helpless.

Some further general principles regarding self-presentation were articulated by Hogan (1982). He notes that self-presentation is structured both by the immediate peer group and by the larger, partly internalized reference group, and individuals vary in whether their main orientation is toward the peer group or the reference group. He says that the images of self that guide self-presentation can sometimes be *defensive*—that is, self-presentation can be a matter of *denying* some image of self rather than claiming it. He emphasizes that the entire process of self-presentation gradually becomes overlearned, automatic, and hence unconscious. Lastly, he says self-presentational motivations and skills derive from and two fundamental needs of human social life, namely the needs for status and for popularity.

Operation of the Theory in Group Contexts

Self-presentational motivations are produced by the presence of other people, who represent a potential audience. Thus, group settings by definition raise self-presentational motivations, although to various degrees and in various ways. The main contribution of self-presentation theory to understanding group processes is to raise and answer the following question: How is the behavior of each group member determined by his or her concern with how he or she is perceived by the other group members? A second issue is plausible but has received negligible research attention. That issue is how groups present themselves to other groups. This topic encompasses everything from the public relations effort of giant corporations to a married couple's public misrepresentation of their level of mutual contentment. As we said, though, research has focused so far on the self-presentational dynamics of individuals, and that is what we shall emphasize here.

Why should individuals care about how other members of the group regard them? There are several reasons. First, human social interactions are structured and shaped by mutual interpersonal evaluations, and so group members are affected by these evaluations as long as the group continues to exist and to meet. In simple terms, it is difficult and unpleasant to continue to meet with someone who regards you as asinine, incompetent, or obnoxious. Second, groups may control rewards and punishments for their members, and so making a good impression on the rest of the group is an important means of obtaining rewards and avoiding punishments. Third, every audience represents an opportunity to pursue the process of constructing and completing the public self (cf. Gollwitzer, 1986). Thus, group contexts may give rise to both the audience-pleasing and the self-construction motivations for self-presentation.

The presence of multiple motives raises the possibility of conflict between different motives. Audience-pleasing motives may conflict with self-construction motives, such as when the group tries to influence one to behave contrary to one's own ideals or inclinations. Behavior then is a compromise between the desire to meet the group's standards and expectations and the desire to create the desired public image of self. Subjectively, making such compromises may feel like diplomacy, hypocrisy, or conformity. Objectively, the balance between audience-pleasing and self-construction motives is presumably altered by several variables, including one's status and power within the group and one's attraction to or dependency on the group.

In general, differences between public and confidential behavior are taken as evidence of the operation of self-presentational factors. Such differences signify that the behavior is partly a response to the presence and the attention of others, which is the essence of self-presentation. Thus, to study self-presentation in groups, one looks for changes in behavior that are caused by whether the individual's actions are known to the other members of the group.

Applications

Classroom

In the classroom, the students perform against relatively explicit standards of success and failure. The primary self-presentational concern of the student is to appear intelligent and well prepared—that is, to show both ability and effort. The teacher is the main audience but the rest of the class may be an influential second audience, especially if feedback in class is public. One's grades and classroom exploits also affect one's self-presentation to friends and to one's parents who may be paying the tuition bills. Failing a test has many sorts of consequences, but one of them is the dilemma of self-presentation. Failure makes it hard to maintain a public self (reputation) as competent, bright, and hard working. To handle the self-presentational damage of test failure or course failure—and even getting a C may be a terrible failure if you expected an A—one may use accounts (Schlenker, 1980; also Scott & Lyman, 1968), that is, making excuses, such as lost notebooks or inadequate sleep.

Some people start to use these self-presentational strategies in advance, making sure their excuse is all ready before the performance. The goal is to protect at all costs the image of self as competent and intelligent. Indeed, in our culture most people would rather be considered lazy than stupid. Jones and Berglas (1978) suggested that underachievement is a strategy for preserving the image of self as capable and smart by never putting forth maximum effort. Failure can then always be attributed to lack of effort, not lack of ability. The pupil can then continue to believe in his or her innate high abilities. If he/she gets Cs in school, he/she can tell friends and family, "I could get As if I'd apply myself more, but I'd rather have a good time while I'm young," instead of saying, "I try my best but still get mainly Cs probably because I'm just plain dumb." Recent research has shown that such *self-handicapping* strategies are often self-presentational (Kolditz & Arkin, 1982; Tice & Baumeister, 1985).

Appearing to be intelligent is not the only self-presentational goal in the classroom. This may be particularly true in the primary and secondary schools, where the student population may have norms of antiintellectuality (cf. Kett, 1977). The good student may have to confront a self-presentational problem caused by having simultaneous audiences with incompatible values. Optimal impression management toward the teacher may consist of doing good work, being polite and well behaved in class, and responding with alacrity to the teacher's exertions. However, if the student does that, the other pupils may regard him or her as a "teacher's pet." Optimal impression management toward the rest of the class may involve adequate but not outstanding work and a detached, cool, vaguely antiauthoritarian attitude toward the teacher. It may be impossible to satisfy both audiences—thus, a self-presentational dilemma.

Reticence about volunteering answers to a teacher's questions during class discussion, then, even in a prointellectual environment, is not always attributable to student ignorance. Probably every teacher has known students who say nothing in class for months but, after one has given up on them as hopelessly incompetent, turn in stellar work on written assignments or tests. Nonparticipation or passivity in the classroom can arise from a variety of self-presentational factors, such as reluctance to seem ostentatious about one's knowledge, or even shyness, which can be considered a self-presentational pathology. A teacher who is aware of these self-presentational patterns may want to deal with them by attempting to minimize the audience. For example a teacher may want to schedule a one-on-one conference with such a student to assess the specific motives of the strategy without the group pressure present. In this environment the teacher may be able to ascertain whether the student is not performing well due to shyness, peer pressure, or lack of ability.

The student is not the only self-presentationally motivated participant in the classroom. The teacher has self-presentational concerns, too. For example, in the attempt to appear competent and knowledgeable, a teacher could become reluctant to answer "I don't know" to any student questions. Such an attitude could lead a teacher to misrepresent speculation as established fact or even to discourage students in general from asking questions.

Group Psychotherapy

Group psychotherapy provides an interesting setting for the study of self-presentation. Indeed, the role of self-presentation accounts for much of the difference between group therapy and individual therapy. In individual therapy, the goal is often to set up a relationship that is nearly devoid of self-presentational influences. This is in order that the client can discuss his or her problems more freely than is possible in other relationships. A client's concern with impressing the therapist is often regarded as a problem or obstacle in individual therapy.

In group therapy, the group constitutes a real audience for self-presentation in a way that the individual therapist tries to avoid. The advantages and disadvantages of group therapy can be understood in relation to this presence of the group as audience. On the positive side, self-presentation is an important part of human life, so group therapy *can* claim to involve the whole person more than individual therapy does. Another advantage is that the audience function of the group confers what Wicklund and Gollwitzer (1982) call *social reality* on the events. Simply put, social reality means that something matters only if other people know about it. Thus, successfully expressing something in front of a group audience may be a much more powerful experience than expressing the same thing in private, individual therapy. The enhanced experiential power may enhance the therapeutic value of the experience. For example, getting a shy person to talk in group therapy seems a greater and more promising victory than getting that same person to talk the same amount in individual therapy. On the negative side, though, self-presentational concerns may make it harder to discuss certain things in group therapy than in individual therapy. It is one thing to admit embarrassing problems such as sexual perversions or inadequacies in private with one's doctor; it is something else to discuss them with a large group of new acquaintances.

A further issue in applying self-presentation theory to group therapy is the distinction between ongoing groups and single-session (including marathon) groups. Certain patterns of self-presentation occur only in the context of continuing interactions (cf. Baumeister, 1982a, b), and it is probably safe to say that the expectation of further interaction greatly enhances self-presentational motivations. A good example might be the hypothesis that public resolutions and commitments will be more effective when made in ongoing group therapy than in single-session therapy. Making such a resolution in group therapy constitutes a self-presentational act. The value of the group is that if you fail to carry out that resolution you suffer self-presentational humiliation—you owe the group an accounting for why you have failed. If the group will not meet again, however, the backslider will not have to confront the disappointed audience, and the self-presentational dilemma is avoided. Consequently, part of the motivation for carrying out the resolution is lost. On the other hand, self-presentation in individual therapy can hinder therapy. If the person is worried about presenting himself in a certain way to his therapist, he may avoid discussing areas of his personality or behaviors which are an embarrassment to him. Unfortunately it is most probably these areas which brought him to psychotherapy in the first place.

In sum, self-presentation in individual insight therapy would be considered by most to be detrimental, yet in a behavior modification program it might prove to be beneficial by keeping the individual committed to the program.

Religious Groups

Participation in religious groups is a complex, multifaceted set of phenomena, so we shall offer only a few observations about how self-presentation theory could be applied to some types of participation. One feature is that public displays of piety and belief are likely to strengthen private or inner faith. Historically, one might contrast the emphasis on public ritual such as in medieval Catholic Christianity with the emphatic internality of Protestant and especially Puritan Christianity. It is worth noting, though, that despite the ideological intentions of the founders, Protestantism has hardly succeeded in erasing self-presentational motivations from that religion.

Research on attitude change has confirmed the power of public statements or actions for producing changes in attitudes (e.g., Baumeister & Tice, 1984). There has been some controversy about whether such public behavior produces real or merely superficial attitude change. One view is that people merely act as if their attitudes and behaviors are consistent (e.g., Tedeschi, Schlenker, & Bonoma, 1971). The other view is that public behavior does produce real attitude change in private attitudes (e.g., Schlenker, 1982; Baumeister, 1982a). Probably both processes are valid in different contexts. For present purposes, we are interested in the occurrence of real attitude change following self-presentation (this real attitude change may be a result of cognitive dissonance mechanisms; see Sande & Zanna, Chapter 3, this volume).

The Catholic ritual of confession deserves some comment. In this ritual, the individual Christian describes his own recent sins to a priest. The priest normally assigns some ritual penance which presumably expiates the guilt and thus nullifies the spiritual consequences of those sins. This practice became common during the 12th century in medieval Europe (e.g., Morris, 1972), as part of a general revision which put Christian faith and practice on a newly individualistic basis (Aries, 1981; Baumeister, 1986). Issues of self-presentation have been central to the confession rite for centuries. People are more willing to discuss their sins and misdeeds confidentially and anonymously than publicly, but the psychological values of confession seems to depend on the act of making the sins public. The church rite has evolved a kind of compromise strategy that blends confidentiality with disclosure. The penitent confesses in a dark booth to a priest in an adjoining cubicle, so it seems as if the confession is anonymous. In practice, however, the priest often may know who is confessing.

Some recent experiments shed new light on the idea that making one's private guilts and regrets public, by means of confession, has psychological or therapeutic value. Pennebaker (1984, in press) has used a procedure in which subjects are asked to discuss the worst things they ever did, either orally or in writing. Clinic records indicate that these people have better physical health records in the months following the confession than the health of a control group of subjects who do not confess. The implication is that carrying around a "guilty secret" may be bad for your health. Opening up and presenting one's personal tragedies and regrets to others, on the other hand, may be good for you.

On a more sinister note, cult indoctrination seems to include a heavy dose of public advocacy of the cult's doctrines, first to the controlled audience of other cult members, but later perhaps to unsympathetic strangers on the streets and in airports. Underlying these cult practices is the psychological principle that a person's private attitudes can be shaped and altered by his or her public statements. A person may not believe some doctrine, but if that person can be induced to make public statements favoring that doctrine, his or her private belief will soon follow. This principle has been demonstrated in work on cognitive dissonance. Numerous studies have shown that when people are induced to say things they do not initially believe, their expressions of attitudes change to conform to their behavior (e.g., Festinger & Carlsmith, 1959). Tedeschi et al. (1971) proposed that self-presentation is an essential part of such effects. That is, people express attitudes consistent with their recent behavior because they want to make a good impression on others, and self-contradiction or inconsistency makes a bad impression. Current evidence indicates that not all dissonance effects can be reduced to self-presentation, but self-presentation is one of the central and most powerful causes of dissonance effects (Baumeister & Tice, 1984; Paulhus, 1982; Schlenker, 1982).

The importance of self-presentation for religious faith was dramatized in a different way by the Victorian crisis of faith. According to Houghton (1957), many Victorians believed that religion was necessary for decent society but were unable to sustain their own personal beliefs in Christian doctrine. Their self-presentational dilemma was whether to voice their doubts candidly, thus further undermining religion in society at large, or to pretend to believe, thus being in a sense hypocritical. Houghton says many Victorians felt justified in espousing sentiments (Christian belief) they wished they had, but did not have.

Mysticism is another form of religious participation. A comparative study of mysticisms suggests that most have waged serious attacks on self-presentational motivations. Mystical novices are often required to shave their heads, wear drab and uniform clothing, perform anonymous acts of charity and dedication, separate themselves from most or all self-presentational audiences, and remain constantly and abjectly humble. It seems important to learn why self-presentational motivations are regarded as being so bad for mystical advancement. One reason may be that one's reputation or public self constitutes a constraint on one's behavior (Baumeister & Jones, 1978), and such constraints are an impediment to spiritual advancement (cf. Castaneda, 1972). People expect other people to be consistent, and so the more that people know about you, the more they expect you to behave in certain ways. Such expectations can limit your opportunities for freedom, spontaneity, and growth, for they constitute social pressure to remain the same. If you do change, you have to explain your behavior to others so they can "understand" why you deviate from their expectations.

The broader implication is that the stability and consistency of the self may depend heavily on the public self. Being surrounded by people who know you well may cause you to remain stable and constant across a long period of time. Personality change, on the other hand, may be most likely to occur following a drastic change in a person's social environment. Studies of brainwashing (e.g., Hinkle, 1957; Lifton, 1957) provide support for this view. Brainwashing is the attempt to cause basic and far-reaching changes in a person's beliefs, values, and opinions. To accomplish this, one almost universal feature of brainwashing techniques is to separate the person from those who know him from the past, for those people's expectations constitute social support for the old identity. Deprived of such contact, people become much more malleable (see Baumeister, 1986). Cults often seem to apply this principle effectively. New members of a cult are often systematically deprived of contact with parents, relatives, and other former acquaintances, even to the extent where a member's letters home are written for him by other cult members.

Health

We have already described one effect of self-presentational factors on health, namely Pennebaker's evidence that keeping intimate personal secrets about guilts and regrets may contribute to physical illness. In this section we shall focus on the presentation of self as healthy or sick.

That self-presentation can include one's health status is evident from the way some people misrepresent the state of their health. Sometimes people may present themselves as ill despite being healthy, and sometimes it is the other way around. This pattern may begin in childhood. Probably most parents have noticed the medically suspect syndrome in which a child is far too ill to attend school in the morning but miraculously feels well enough to play outside by midafternoon! The implication is that self-presentation may distort one's physical condition in either direction, for ulterior motives. Faced with school or household chores, the child may exaggerate feelings of illness in presenting himself or herself. However, faced with the prospect of missing a daytrip to the amusement park or a long-awaited chance to perform in the school play or swim meet, the child's self-presentation may minimize symptoms.

The idea that some adults may be motivated to present themselves as ill, and that they may become very skilled at doing so, goes back at least to Alfred Adler (1921). It is hard to determine at what point deceptive self-presentation shades into genuine illness, but Adler observed that many of these people do eventually end up having physical problems that prevent them from achieving certain goals. This may be a tragic instance of the principle we discussed earlier, in which public or self-presentational behavior leads to changes.

Why would people want to present themselves as sick? Two ulterior motives in particular deserve mention. First, becoming ill may be another instance of self-handicapping (e.g., Smith, Snyder, & Perkins, 1983). Illness provides a convenient excuse for various possible failures, so that failures will be attributed to the illness rather than to lack of competence. In other words, being sick is a kind of insurance policy for performance: Whatever happens, you cannot be proved incompetent if you are sick. Second, sick people often receive special attention and consideration from others, which can be gratifying. Family members may pamper and care for the sick person, and important people (e.g., physicians) may devote substantial interest and concern to him or her. The group thus provides strong reinforcements for presenting oneself as ill. For some chronic hypochondriacs, such reinforcements may become the dominant motivation in their lives. Smith *et al.* found that hypochondriacs report more physical ailments and illnesses, in an evaluative setting when these ailments could be used as an excuse for poor performance, than they did in a nonevaluative setting, or a setting where physical ailments were not an excuse for poor performance. People who were not hypochondriacs, however, reported the same level of ailments and illness in every condition. In other words, they did not inflate their reporting of illnesses to justify their poor performance.

Symptoms of mental illness are also affected by self-presentation (Sacco & Hokanson, 1982). For example Braginsky, Braginsky, and Ring (1969) theorized that institutionalized mental patients would manage their symptoms in order to serve their goals of remaining on the reasonably comfortable and secure open wards. Such a goal requires one to steer an intermediate course between seeming too healthy, which would result in being released into the threatening and uncertain world outside the hospital, and seeming too ill, which would result in being transferred to a locked ward with dangerous, seriously disturbed inmates. Braginsky and his colleagues conducted an ingenious experiment in which each patient was assigned an appointment with a visiting psychiatrist. On the way to the interview, the patient was given one of three messages about the alleged purpose of the interview. One third of the mental patients, chosen at random, were told that the psychiatrist was evaluating them to see whether they should be dismissed from the hospital. The second third were told that the psychiatrist's evaluation concerned whether they should be transferred to a locked ward, and the final third were told they were merely having an evaluation. Although the three groups did not differ in terms of actual degree of illness, their behavior in the interview was different. Those worried about being released from the hospital came across as quite ill, in comparison with those who worried about being transferred to a locked ward—the latter came across as relatively sane!

Antisocial Behavior

The study of deviant groups is perhaps the best place to discern the power of peers to produce antisocial behavior by means of self-presentational pressures. Emmler (1984) has provided a self-presentational analysis of juvenile delinquency that emphasizes the difference in group expectations and norms between mainstream and delinquent groups.

In Emmler's analysis, the occasional temptation to cheat or steal is not peculiar to juvenile delinquents but is a common part of human nature in modern life. Everyone experiences such temptations, but most people refrain from acting them out because they wish to be perceived as morally good. The general community values honest, fair, and law-abiding behavior, and so most people seek to present themselves consistent with that image. Thus, the reason most people do not deface or despoil public property is not some inner trait or virtue but rather a matter of self-presentation. Emmler points out that such self-presentation has substantial practical advantages. If an established citizen were to lose his reputation as an honest, law-abiding member of the community, his job and even his family relationships might be jeopardized.

Delinquents, however, do not have established jobs and families to worry about, and Emmler concludes from this that they have much less need to engage in virtuous self-presentation than other citizens. The critical point is that the adolescent's peer group does not place high value on being a good citizen by community standards, so efforts to present oneself according to that model will go unrewarded. Instead, the adolescent peer group may develop a quite different set of values and expectations. Status and popularity in a group of adolescent troublemakers may depend on having a reputation of being tough, strong, daring or reckless, and hostile toward established authority. Aggressive or delinquent behavior may often be a matter of trying to present oneself to fit such expectations (Toch, 1969), perhaps in response to the threat of being labeled weak or cowardly (Felson, 1978).

Thus, the deviant or antisocial behavior of juvenile delinquents can be understood in terms of self-presentation. Emmler's analysis does not depend on innate traits or acquired characteristics that cause some adolescents to become delinquent. Instead, antisocial behavior is seen as a plausible and even rational response to the norms and expectations of the peer group. Once an individual is labeled or categorized by the school system as a troublemaker, he tends to get placed with other slow learners or troublemakers. Such groups evolve their own norms, often perhaps as a deliberate reaction against the normal community that has rejected or stigmatized them. The individual then engages in aggressive or defiant behavior in order to impress peers and friends.

Hogan *et al.* (1970, 1982) have applied a self-presentational analysis to drug abuse. Although drug abuse is common in criminal populations, criminal addicts differ from other criminals—in much the same way that drug users in the general population differ from nonusers. Drug users have a strong self-presentational motivation to be known as different and unconventional, and their drug use fills that need. Hogan *et al.* go on to say that drug addicts in the criminal population often are using drugs to some extent in order to achieve a reputation for deviancy. In self-presentational terms, the criminal's public image of being tough is augmented by drug abuse, which confers the public image of being deviant.

Courtroom

Self-presentation theory has little that is new to say about jury decision processes. The value of anonymity (i.e., lack of self-presentation) for promoting fair and honest judgment has been recognized for a long time, even without the benefit of experimental studies. On the other hand, defendants and plaintiffs have strong presentational concerns, especially in the case of a jury trial. Self-presentation strategies may vary from trying to show oneself as mentally unstable to the more common strategy of presenting oneself as sincere, honest, and believable. Some plaintiffs and defendants may need to learn new self-presentational strategies to appeal to a specific audience, such as in the Errol Flynn case.

In 1943 Flynn was accused of statutory rape. The girl in question was 17 at the time but worked in a chorus line. Her working attire was brief, to say the least. On the day of the trial, however, she arrived wearing pigtails, bobby sox, and flat shoes. Obviously both outfits and self-presentational strategies were geared toward different audiences. (In spite of this new attire, Flynn was not convicted.)

In the Flynn case the defendant was presenting herself in a certain manner to the jury, but this is only a small part of the self-presenting occurring in the courtroom. For instance, the attorneys not only have to present themselves as knowledgeable to the jury, but they must also seem compassionate to their clients and distinguished to the other attorneys and the judge. The judge also must present himself as knowledgeable and distinguished, yet his presentation may change as a function of whether a jury is present, such as if he becomes more authoritarian or even autocratic with a jury present. The jury also has self-presentational concerns. They need to present themselves as responsible, intelligent individuals. As the jury becomes larger and each individual juror feels more anonymity, one would expect each juror's perception for the need to self-present to decrease. Saul Kassin's (1984) work has shown though that low publicly self-conscious jurors behave more like high publicly self-conscious jurors in front of a video camera. We might infer their that while a large jury might decrease self-consciousness, a video camera increases self-consciousness. A large jury being videotaped may therefore behave the same way a small jury would.

Worker Productivity

Self-presentation can be an important determinant of worker productivity. The central idea is that workers are motivated by a desire to make a favorable impression on their superiors, and quite likely on their co-workers and subordinates too. The quality and quantity of one's work thus become not an end in themselves but a means for conveying information about the self.

Worker motivation varies both with workers' personal values and traits and with level and type of supervisor surveillance. Two experiments by Tang and Baumeister (1984) explored the effects of personal endorsement of the Protestant work ethic. In the first experiment, subjects performed the task and then were left alone during a period with the task materials and other possible activities. When the task had been presented as a "work" task, people who believed in the work ethic spent the most free time on that task. When the same task was presented as a game or leisure pastime, however, those people did not devote their free time to it. The second experiment added an important qualification. Half the subjects were told that the experimenter would ask them how they spent their free time, whereas the others were led to believe that no one would know what they did. The task was always presented as work. Many people who claimed high endorsement of the work ethic showed little interest in the activity unless someone was watching. In other words, many people claim to be highly motivated and to place high personal value on work; but often these claims are purely self-presentational, for the choices they make in private do not emphasize work.

Another personality trait that affects the motivation and performance of workers is self-esteem. Although a comprehensive treatment of the relation between trait self-esteem and self-presentation is not available, the evidence suggests the following picture. People with high self-esteem are motivated to make very positive impressions on others, while people with low self-esteem simply want to get by and avoid failure or embarrassment. People with high self-esteem thus may often draw attention to themselves, whereas people with low self-esteem do the opposite. People with high self-esteem tend to be quite sophisticated and ambitious in their use of self-presentational strategies, unlike people with low self-esteem (e.g., Baumeister, 1982b).

A public, humiliating failure appears to cause people with high self-esteem to exert maximum effort to avoid another such failure (e.g., McFarlin, Baumeister, & Blascovich, 1984). If required to perform again, they often show dramatic improvement. Their motivation behind such improvement appears, however, to be mainly due to self-presentation (that is, to their reluctance to have other people see them fail), for their private inclination would be to abandon the task rather than to work for improvement. According to a recent model, the primary orientation of people with high self-esteem is to maximize their talents in order to excel, so they tend to be most interested in pursuing tasks on which they initially succeed. People with low self-esteem, in contrast, are primarily motivated to reach adequate or passable levels, so they have the highest intrinsic motivation for tasks on which they initially fail (Baumeister & Tice, 1985; also Silverman, 1964).

It has long been known that performance is affected by working near other people. Although some of these social facilitation effects derive from the mere presence of others (Zajonc, 1965), other effects are clearly self-presentational. Bond (1982) has argued that many social facilitation effects are due to concern over potential evaluation by others—in other words, to self-presentational motivations and processes that arise from having an audience (see also Bond & Titus, 1983). The general pattern is that the threat of evaluation and the presence of others causes people to perform simple tasks better but complex tasks worse than when working alone.

Working together with others can cause individuals to reduce the effort they invest, as in "social loafing" (Latané, Williams, & Harkins, 1979). Self-presentation is a critical mediator of social loafing. When anonymous, people will loaf and thus take free rides on the group effort. Latané et al. asked experimental subjects involved to clap or shout as loudly as they could. The subjects wore headphones so that they could not hear themselves or the other individuals, and they were also blindfolded. Subjects were told that they would be clapping or yelling individually, in groups of two, or in groups of six. Latane found that when individuals thought that one other person was shouting with them they shouted only 82% as loudly as when they were alone, and when they thought that five people were shouting with them the performed at only 74% of capacity.

Sweeney (1973) conducted an experiment that showed that when each member's contribution to the group product is identified, the pattern of social loafing disappears. Individuals in Sweeney's experiment were asked to pump air with a bicycle tire. When individuals were led to believe that only the group's output was being monitored they pumped less than when they were told that each person's individual contribution to the group whole would also be monitored. Thus, self-presentation can lead to improvement in effort and performance.

In some cases, having an audience or an evaluative supervisor can create performance pressure, which can harm skilled performance (Baumeister, 1984, 1985). In one study, the work performance of professional athletes was evaluated. The pressure of having an audience with high expectations, combined with the pressure of having a chance to win the championship, caused athletes to choke. Thus, the home field switches from an advantage to a disadvantage in the final game of a championship series (Baumeister & Steinhilber, 1984), and the decline in performance is seen in the increased number of errors and misplays by the home team. In cognitive performance too, an audience with high expectations can create pressure and harm performance (Baumeister, Hamilton, & Tice, 1985). Thus, self-presentational factors can raise *or* lower quality of work.

Finally, self-presentational factors can affect what workers say is fair compensation for their work (Greenberg, 1983). In particular, gender differences in perceived fairness have attracted some study, based on evidence that women tend to claim less payment than men for the same work (Deaux & Major 1977). Major and Adams (1983) and Major, McFarlin, and Gagnon (1984) found also that women only pay themselves less when pay norms are not made salient. Women claim equal compensation as men, however, when pay norms are available. Kidder, Bellettirie, and Cohn (1977) found that these gender differences are substantially attributable to self-presentational factors, for different patterns are found in private and public judgments. When men and women had to award extra credit points to themselves and a co-worker, women gave equal points in the public condition and men gave equitable points. In the private condition, however, the patterns were *reversed*: women divided the points equitably and men divided the points equally. Kidder *et al.* hypothesized that the reason for the differences was that men and women had to fulfill traditional sex-linked roles in the public condition but were freed from the restraints in the private condition. It would seem that the operation of self-presentation in salary negotiations of collective bargaining is ripe for study.

Conclusion

Self-presentation is an influential cause of group processes. The behavior of group members is often powerfully affected by their concerns with how they are regarded by the rest of the group. The variety of effects of self-presentation is remarkable, and there is little doubt that research will continue to discover ways that group behavior is shaped by self-presentation.

There are several major holes in the present mass of knowledge about self-presentation. More research is needed on conflicts among various self-presentational motives, and between conflicting audience expectations in complex groups with multiple subgroups. The self-presentational strategies of intimidation and supplication—which entail presenting oneself in a strategic but not necessarily likable fashion—have scarcely been studied at all. Many applications of self-presentation to specific types of group contexts need further study, as we have noted in the preceding pages. Last, it is time to begin applying self-presentation theory to the group as a whole, instead of applying it only to the individual members of the group. How do groups present themselves to other groups?

Self-presentation theory does not pretend to offer a complete account of group processes. There are other things in groups beside self-presentation. Still, it seems safe to say that any account of group processes that neglects self-presentation is incomplete and inadequate. Meanwhile, the operation of self-presentational processes and motivations in group settings is a promising area for research.

References

Adler, A. (1921). *The neurotic constitution: Outlines of a comparative individualistic psychology and psychotherapy*. New York: Moffat Yard.

Aries, P. (1981). *The hour of our death*. New York: Knopf.

Baumeister, R. F. (1982a). A self-presentational view of social phenomena. *Psychological Bulletin, 91,* 3–26.

Baumeister, R. F. (1982b). Self-esteem, self-presentation, and future interaction: A dilemma of reputation. *Journal of Personality, 50,* 29–45.

Baumeister, R. F. (1984). Choking under pressure: Self-consciousness and paradoxical effects of incentives on skillful performance. *Journal of Personality and Social Psychology, 46,* 610–620.

Baumeister, R. F. (1985). The championship choke. *Psychology Today, 19*(4:April), 48–52.

Baumeister, R. F. (1986). *Identity*. New York: Oxford University Press.

Baumeister, R. F., Hamilton, J. C., & Tice, D. M. (1985). Public versus private expectancy of success: Confidence booster or performance pressure? *Journal of Personality and Social Psychology, 48,* 1447–1457.

Baumeister, R. F., & Jones, E. E. (1978). When self-presentation is constrained by the target's prior knowledge: Consistency and compensation. *Journal of Personality and Social Psychology, 36,* 608–618.

Baumeister, R. F., & Steinhilber, A. (1984). Paradoxical effects of supportive audiences on performance under pressure: The home field disadvantage in sports championships. *Journal of Personality and Social Psychology, 47,* 85–93.

Baumeister, R. F., & Tice, D. M. (1984). Role of self-presentation and choice in cognitive dissonance under forced compliance: Necessary or sufficient causes? *Journal of Personality and Social Psychology, 46,* 5–13.

Baumeister, R. F., & Tice, D. M. (1985). Self-esteem and responses to success and failure: Subsequent performance and intrinsic motivation. *Journal of Personality, 53,* 450–467.

Bond, C. F. (1982). Social facilitation: A self-presentational view. *Journal of Personality and Social Psychology, 42,* 1042–1050.

Bond, C. F., & Titus, L. J. (1983). Social facilitation: A meta-analysis of 241 studies. *Psychological Bulletin, 94,* 265–292.

Braginsky, B. M., Braginsky, D. D., & Ring, K. (1969). *Methods of madness: The mental hospital as a last resort.* New York: Holt, Rinehart & Winston.

Castaneda, C. (1972). *Journey to Ixtlan: The lessons of Don Juan.* New York: Simon & Schuster.

Deaux, K., & Major, B. (1977). Sex-related patterns in the unit of perception. *Personality and Social Psychology Bulletin, 3,* 297–300.

Emmler, N. (1984). Differential involvement in delinquency: Toward an interpretation in terms of reputation management. *Progress in Experimental Personality Research, 13,* 174–239.

Festinger, L., & Carlsmith, J. M. (1959). Cognitive consequences of forced compliance. *Journal of Abnormal and Social Psychology, 58,* 203–210.

Felson, R. (1978). Aggression as impression management. *Social Psychology Quarterly, 41,* 205–213.

Gollwitzer, P. M. (1986). Striving for specific identities: The social reality of self-symbolizing. In R. Baumeister (Ed.), *Public self and private self.* New York: Springer-Verlag.

Greenberg, J. (1983). Self-image versus impression management in adherence to distributive justice standards: The influence of self-awareness and self-consciousness. *Journal of Personality and Social Psychology, 44,* 5–19.

Hinkle, L. (1957). [Untitled.] In *Methods of forceful indoctrination: Observations and interviews.* New York.

Hogan, R. (1982). A socioanalytic theory of personality. In M. Page (Ed.), *Nebraska symposium on motivation* (pp. 55–89). Lincoln, NE: University of Nebraska Press.

Hogan, R., Mankin, D., Conway, J., & Fox, S. (1970). Personality correlates of undergraduate marijuana use. *Journal of Consulting and Clinical Psychology, 35,* 58–63.

Houghton, W. E. (1957). *The Victorian frame of mind: 1830–1870.* New Haven: Yale University Press.

Jones, E. E., & Berglas, S. C. (1978). Control of attributions about the self through self-handicapping strategies: The appeal of alcohol and the role of underachievement. *Personality and Social Psychology Bulletin, 4,* 200–206.

Jones, E. E., & Pittman, T. S. (1982). Toward a general theory of strategic self-presentation. In J. Suls (Ed.), *Psychological perspectives on the self* (Vol. 1, pp. 231–262). Hillsdale, NJ: Erlbaum.

Kassin, S. M. (1984) T. V. Cameras, public self-consciousness and mock juror performance. *Journal of Experimental Social Psychology, 20,* 336–349.

Kett, J. F. (1977). *Rites of passage: Adolescence in America 1790 to the present.* New York: Basic.

Kidder, L. H., Bellettirie, G., & Cohn, E. S. (1977). Secret ambitions and public performances: The effects of anonymity on reward allocations made by men and women. *Journal of Experimental Social Psychology, 13,* 70–80.

Kolditz, T. A., & Arkin, R. M. (1982). An impression management interpretation of the self-handicapping strategy. *Journal of Personality and Social Psychology, 43,* 492–502.

Latané, B., Williams, K., & Harkins, S. (1979). Many hands make light the work: The causes and consequences of social loafing. *Journal of Personality and Social Psychology, 37,* 822–832.

Lifton, R. J. (1957). [Untitled.] In *Methods of forceful indoctrination: Observations and interviews.* New York.

Major, B., & Adams, J. B. (1983). Role of gender, interpersonal orientation, and self-presentation in distributive-justice behavior. *Journal of Personality and Social Psychology, 45,* 598–608.

Major, B., McFarlin, D. B., & Gagnon, D. (1984). Overworked and underpaid: On the nature of gender differences in personal entitlement. *Journal of Personality and Social Psychology, 47,* 1399–1412.

McFarlin, D. B., Baumeister, R. F., & Blascovich, J. (1984). On knowing when to quit: Task failure, self-esteem, advice, and nonproductive persistence. *Journal of Personality, 52,* 138–155.

Morris, C. (1972). *The discovery of the individual: 1050–1200.* New York: Harper & Row.

Paulhus, D. (1982). Individual differences, self-presentation, and cognitive dissonance: Their concurrent operation in forced compliance. *Journal of Personality and Social Psychology, 43,* 838–852.

Pennebaker, J. W. (1984). Confiding, ruminating, and psychosomatic disease. In J. W. Pennebaker (Chair), *New paradigms in psychology.* Symposium conducted at the annual convention of the American Psychological Association, Toronto, Canada, August 1984.

Pennebaker, J. W. (in press). Traumatic experience and psychosomatic disease: Exploring the roles of behavioral inhibition, obsession, and confiding. *Canadian Psychology.*

Sacco, W. P., & Hokanson, J. E. (1982). Depression and self-reinforcement in a public and private setting. *Journal of Personality and Social Psychology, 42,* 377–385.

Schlenker, B. R. (1980). *Impression management: The self-concept, social identity, and interpersonal relations.* Monterey, CA: Brooks/Cole.

Schlenker, B. R. (1982). Translating actions into attitudes: An identity-analytic approach to the explanation of social conduct. In L. Berkowitz (Ed.), *Advances in experimental social psychology* (Vol. 15 pp. 194–247). New York: Academic Press.

Scott, M. B., & Lyman, S. M. (1968). Accounts. *American Sociological Review, 33,* 46–62.

Silverman, I. (1964). Self-esteem and differential responsiveness to success and failure. *Journal of Abnormal and Social Psychology, 69,* 115–119.

Smith, T. W., Snyder, C. R., & Perkins, S. C. (1983). The self-serving function of hypochondriacal complaints: Physical symptoms as self-handicapping strategies. *Journal of Personality and Social Psychology, 44,* 787–797.

Sweeney, J. (1973). An experimental investigation of the free rider problem. *Social Science Research, 2,* 277–292.

Tang, T. L. P., & Baumeister, R. F. (1984). Effects of personal values, perceived surveillance, and task labels on task preference: The ideology of turning play into work. *Journal of Applied Psychology, 69,* 99–105.

Tedeschi, J. T., Schlenker, B. R., & Bonoma, T. V. (1971). Cognitive dissonance: Private ratiocination or public spectacle? *American Psychologist, 26,* 685–695.

Tice, D. M., & Baumeister, R. F. (1985). Self-esteem, self-handicapping, and self-presentation: The benefits of not practicing. Unpublished manuscript, Case Western Reserve University.

Toch, H. (1969). *Violent men.* Chicago: Aldine.

Wicklund, R. A., & Gollwitzer, P. M. (1982). *Symbolic self-completion.* Hillsdale, NJ: Erlbaum.

Zajonc, R. (1965). Social facilitation. *Science, 149,* 269–274.

Chapter 5

Drive Theory: Effects of Socially Engendered Arousal

Russell G. Geen and Brad J. Bushman

Presentation of the Theory

Early Viewpoints

The idea that motivation has an intensive component independent of the direction of behavior goes back to Woodworth (1918), who defined drive as "the power applied to make ... mechanism(s) go" (p. 36). Actually, drive was only one of several constructs invented by motivation theorists during the 1920s and early 1930s to take the place of the recently abandoned concept of instinct (Herrnstein, 1972). As such, its theoretical status was at first unclear. Cannon (1934) used the term to describe local sensations arising from specific tissue deficits; hence, for example, the hunger drive was defined as pangs caused by gastric contractions. Others believed that drives consist of more than stimuli. Richter (1922), like Cannon, linked drives to deficits. Unlike Cannon, he treated drive as an internal state of the organism that produces random and diffuse activity. Meanwhile Warden (1931) identified a multiplicity of specific drive states, each elicited by a specific type of deprivation and each manifested not in random activity, but in specific goal-directed action. These early studies were important in that they laid the groundwork for a more developed theory of drive by raising several important questions (Bolles, 1975). These were:

1. Is drive unitary, or may we speak of several different drives?
2. Does drive arise from central processes, or does it consist of peripheral events, such as local stimuli?
3. Is drive an antecedent of behavior or a dimension of behavior?
4. Does drive influence the direction or the intensity of behavior?

Each of these questions was answered by Hull (1943), whose theory of drive constituted the dominant viewpoint on motivation within American psychology for the better part of two decades.

Hull's Theory of Drive

Hull began by reducing the several "drives" studied by the earlier investigators to a single generalized state; this state was considered to be central and not directly observable. For Hull, drive was a construct that could be defined only by reference to its position within a large and comprehensive network of similar constructs. For this reason, it could not be considered an observable property of behavior but had instead to be an antecedent condition that exerted some influence on behavior. Finally, that influence was defined by Hull as being intensive only. The direction of behavior (i.e., *what* the organism does as opposed to *how vigorously* it behaves) was defined as a function not of drive, but of learned responses.

In his original version of drive theory, Hull (1943) linked generalized drive (*D*) to an animal's biological needs. Following Richter (1922), Hull proposed that drive accumulated as a direct function of the amount of time the animal had been deprived of some commodity necessary to survival, such as food or water. As a result the animal engages in restless activity of gradually increasing intensity. At the same time, the conditions that produce the drive state are also generating localized reactions, such as dryness in the mouth following water deprivation, which act as "goads" (the term is Cannon's) to specific behaviors. These local conditions, called *drive stimuli*, supply the initial direction to behavior while drive is furnishing the intensive component.

The other important construct in Hull's system is habit strength (*H*), which also fulfills a directional role in behavior. Habit strength is the immediate result of drive reduction. In its activated state, the animal eventually is able to make a consummatory response (e.g., eating, drinking) that removes or attenuates the original condition of deprivation. The resulting drop in the strength of the drive state is a primary reinforcement for the behavior that preceded it. Hence, when the animal next finds itself in the same state of drive the reinforced response will be more likely to occur than it had been prior to reinforcement. It has acquired an increase in habit strength as a result of drive reduction. As a response acquires habit strength it takes on increasing directional control of behavior.

In any situation, then, the likelihood that a given response will occur is a function of its habit strength relative to that of all other possible responses. A response that has the highest relative level of H in a situation is called the dominant response and all others are called subordinate responses. Because drive is a generalized condition it energizes all responses in a situation, whether or not the response is relevant to the condition producing the drive. The motive state, called "irrelevant drive," is thus a broadly based activator of behavior (Brown, 1961). The potential strength of a response (called excitatory potential, or E) is equal to the habit strength for that response multiplied by the drive level ($E = D \times H$). Because of the multiplicative relationship of D to H, the rate at which E grows for a dominant response as

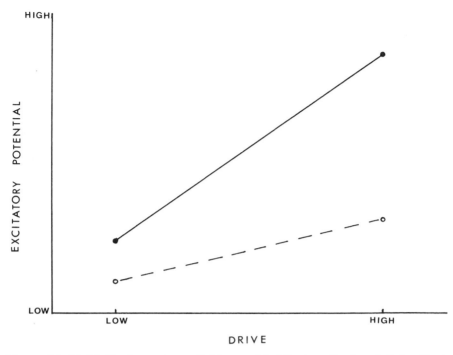

Figure 5.1. Multiplicative nature of drive and habit strength. (- - -) Subordinate responses; (—) dominant responses.

D increases is greater than the corresponding rate for subordinate responses (see Figure 5.1).

Modifications of Hullian Theory

Subsequent versions of Hullian drive theory modified the strongly biological flavor of the original. Both Hull (1952) himself and several of his students and younger colleagues broadened and liberalized the drive construct in later years (e.g., Miller, 1959). The latter group, known collectively as the Neo-Hullians, was especially active in redefining drive in ways that made the idea more applicable to human behavior. Miller and Dollard (1941), for example, proposed that drive be characterized simply in terms of stimulation:

> A drive is a strong stimulus which impels action. Any stimulus can become a drive if it is made strong enough. The stronger the stimulus, the more drive function it possesses. The faint murmur of distant music has but little primary drive function; the infernal blare of the neighbor's radio has considerably more. (p. 18)

By describing drive in such terms the Neo-Hullians opened the construct to still further elaboration through the medium of acquired drives. Hull

(1943) had written of secondary or acquired drives as neutral stimuli that assume drive properties through association with primary (i.e, biological) drive states. If primary drives are now to be thought of only as arousing conditions in the environment, then secondary drives can arise from any of a host of associated conditions. This is especially important for social psychology, because it indicates that any social situation can be a source of arousal if it bears some association with other arousing situations. Thus, for example, an audience can be a condition giving rise to increased drive if audiences have been associated with some strong primary aversive condition in the past, such as social punishment. The drive produced by an audience may energize behaviors that have nothing to do with the audience. This premise forms the basis for the drive-theoretical approach to social facilitation, which represents the most important contribution of the theory to contemporary social psychology.

Another important modification of drive theory was made by Broen and Storms (1961), who proposed the existence of a hypothetical ceiling on excitatory potential for any response. This ceiling is set by the physiological capacity of the nervous system to respond, and its effect is to limit the extent to which dominant responses are energized at the expense of subordinate ones by increased drive. Figure 5.2 illustrates the Broen-Storms hypothesis. The left-hand portion of the figure shows the multiplicative relationship

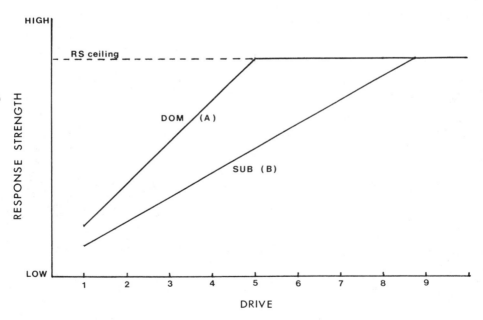

Figure 5.2. Effects of response-strength ceiling on development of response potential. (Adapted from Broen & Storms, 1961.)

between D and H (cf. Figure 5.1). The dominant response (A) reaches the ceiling for E sooner than does a subordinate response (B). When drive level is increased beyond level (5), the differences in E for the two responses begin to diminish until at drive level (9) the two responses have equal potential. The effect of this process is that as D increases beyond level (5), the strength of response A, *relative* to that of response B, begins to diminish. The significance of the Broen-Storms model for processes of social arousal is discussed in the third section of this chapter.

Operation of the Theory in Group Contexts

The Problem of Social Facilitation

The term *social facilitation* is usually used to describe both the enhancement and inhibition of performance by the presence of an audience or group of coactors. The problem is among social psychology's oldest, with its roots in the pioneer work of Triplett (1898) on the effects of a single coactor on speed of a simple motor response. Although many studies of audience and coactor effects were reported during the early decades of this century (Dashiell, 1935), no single theory was advanced that could account for both enhancement and inhibition effects in terms of a single set of constructs. By the early 1960s, interest in the problem had virtually died out.

The modern revival of interest in social facilitation began with the publication of a paper by Zajonc (1965). Zajonc based his argument on two premises. The first is that an individual experiences arousal in the presence of other people; social settings produce an increase in the level of generalized drive. The second premise derives directly from Hullian drive theory: socially generated arousal energizes dominant responses more than subordinate ones according to the equation $E = D \times H$. Hence, the presence of others, either as an audience or as a group of coactors, facilitates performance on an easy task (in which the dominant response is the correct one) but inhibits performance on a more difficult task, in which the dominant response is one of many possible incorrect ones. In addition, drive enhances performance of a well-learned response but hinders acquisition of a new one.

The response energization paradigm requires that dominant and subordinate responses be specified in any given situation. Two methods have been used for making habit strength operational. Some studies have included the creation of implicit hierarchies through manipulation of the amount of practice allowed subjects across a number of different responses. This is followed by measurement of the frequency of occurrence of each response to ambiguous stimulus conditions, with subjects responding either before an audience or alone. In the first experiment designed in this way, Zajonc and Sales (1966) found that well-learned responses were more likely

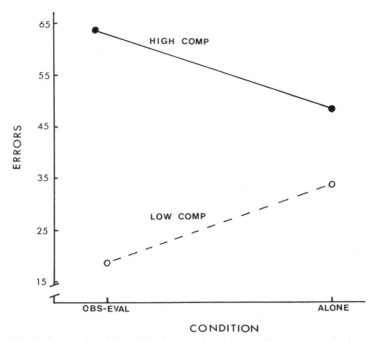

Figure 5.3. Effects of social evaluation on learning of lists varying in interresponse competition. (Drawn from data reported by Geen, 1983a.)

to be elicited than less well-learned ones, with the effect being stronger in the presence of an audience than among subjects who worked alone. This finding, which is consistent with the Hullian prediction of a multiplicative relationship between habit strength and drive, supports the claim that the audience increased drive level.

Other investigators have assumed that habit strength hierarchies are reflected in differing levels of performance across variations in a task. An example of the assumption of differential habit strengths in an experimental setting is shown in an experiment by Geen (1983a) in which subjects learned a paired-associates list made of items with a either a high or a low degree of interresponse competition. It was predicted that the presence of an observer who judged the subject's performance would facilitate learning of the low competition (i.e., easy) list but hamper the learning of the high competition (i.e., difficult) list. As Figure 5.3 shows, subjects who worked in the presence of an evaluating observer made more errors on the difficult list than those who worked alone, but fewer errors on the easy list.

Theories of Socially Engendered Drive

The question of why the presence of others produces increased drive has been answered in several ways.

Mere presence. In his original formulation of the drive theory of social facilitation, Zajonc (1965) stated that the *mere presence* of conspecific organisms produced increased drive. In the years that followed, this hypothesis came under attack from those who insisted that the presence of others raises drive only when those others are perceived as potential judges or evaluators. We review this viewpoint below. Some studies have shown evidence of the social facilitation effect with evaluation cues controlled, however, and these studies are usually cited as evidence of the mere presence hypothesis (e.g., Markus, 1978). Nevertheless, the notion of mere presence is at best a statement of an empirical observation. By itself it is not an explanation for social facilitation.

Evaluation apprehension. We have already noted the argument that the the presence of others elicits arousal because the others are regarded as possible evaluators and dispensers of rewards and punishments. Cottrell, Wack, Sekerak, and Rittle (1968) introduced this hypothesis in a study in which the presence of others was shown to energize dominant responses when the others constituted an observing audience but not when they were blindfolded and obviously inattentive. Further evidence was provided by Henchy and Glass (1968), who showed that socially engendered drive varied with the status of the observer. This finding would be expected if the observer were regarded as a judge, but not if mere presence were the sole cause of arousal.

The reason an evaluating audience elicits apprehension has been the subject of some controversy. Cottrell (1972) proposed that the presence of others is a learned source of activation that acquires its arousal potential by serving as a conditioned stimulus for anticipation of positive or negative outcomes. The evidence from most studies on evaluation apprehension supports Cottrell's hypothesis only in part (Geen & Gange, 1977). Evaluation apprehension has been shown to be related to expectation of negative outcomes, but, with one exception (Good, 1973) to be unrelated to anticipation of positive effects (Geen, 1979; Seta & Hassan, 1980; Weiss & Miller, 1971). Recently Geen (1980) has extended the evaluation apprehension hypothesis to the study of coaction effects. The coaction setting, by introducing implicit feelings of competitiveness among subjects, fosters fears of losing in competition.

Distraction/conflict. A third drive-related explanation of social facilitation has been proposed in a series of studies by Baron and his associates, who have attributed the effects to attentional conflict. Baron and his colleagues first demonstrated that distraction by a nonsocial stimulus can elevate drive (Sanders & Baron, 1975). In subsequent studies they showed that an audience has a distracting effect on the subject similar to that of nonsocial stimuli (Baron, Moore, & Sanders, 1978; Sanders, Baron, and Moore, 1978), and that the overall effect of this increased drive is the energization of dominant responses at the expense of subordinate ones. In addition, an experiment by Groff, Baron, and Moore (1983) showed that the drive-inducing effects of distraction could not be attributed to any evaluation apprehension that the subject may have been experiencing.

Uncertainty and social monitoring. As we noted earlier, the explanation for socially produced drive originally given by Zajonc (1965) was that other people, merely through their presence, exerted an arousing influence. In a later paper, Zajonc (1980) elaborated on his earlier position by linking social drive to uncertainty. Because the presence of others always implies interaction, the person must be constantly prepared to respond to changes in the social environment that cannot be entirely anticipated.

Guerin and Innes (1982) have extended Zajonc's views to a process that they call *social monitoring.* Because others, by their presence, create uncertainty and a readiness to respond, the individual must periodically observe them in an attempt to anticipate what they may do. In general, Guerin and Innes (1982) conclude that "the more predictable the future behavior of the other, the less attention is needed" (p. 12). The purpose of social monitoring is to reduce uncertainty regarding the possible behavior of others. The presence of others should therefore elicit less arousal when those others can be monitored than when they cannot. However, an audience elicits arousal, even though it can be monitored, when it is paying close attention to the individual, because the individual is relatively uncertain as to what the audience may do. The greatest amount of uncertainty should be elicited by an audience that is nearby, attentive to the subject, and outside the subject's range of monitoring. An experiment by Guerin (1983) has reported findings that support the social monitoring hypothesis.

Attention overload. In this review, we have often used the terms *drive* and *arousal* as if they were equivalent. In a strictly theoretical sense, they are, of course, quite different from each other in several ways (Geen, Beatty, & Arkin, 1984, pp. 185–188). Nevertheless, many who work in the social facilitation area tend to use drive and arousal as similar, if not identical terms. This merging of the two terms is done at the level of the intervening variables: arousal theory is used to explain the relationship between the social situation and some intermediate process of activation, and drive theory is invoked to link this intermediate state to performance. This process was in fact suggested in Zajonc's (1965) original paper. Zajonc cited as evidence of the arousing properties of the social setting a number of studies indicating increased physiological reactions among animals under conditions of crowding. He then went on to propose that the resulting state of activation affected performance along lines laid down by Hullian theory.

Recently, however, Baron and his associates have challenged the assumption that social facilitation is best explained in terms of response energization, as Hullian theory states. Although they accept the idea of socially engendered arousal, they argue that the main effect of such arousal is selective attention (Baron, 1986; Moore & Baron, 1983). An idea similar to this may be found in the current literature on cognitive processes in attention. One of the main premises of this approach is that individuals possess a limited capacity for processing information (Kahneman, 1973), and that as environmental demands increase, greater and greater demands are made on this limited capacity. Attention is an effortful process, so that when environmental demands become too great for capacity the person restricts attention and allocates effort to only certain features of the environment (Hockey, 1979). Typically, the person focuses attention on stimuli that are most relevant to the task and stops attending to those that are irrelevant or less relevant to performance (Cohen, 1978).

How may this approach explain social facilitation? Baron and his colleagues (Baron, 1986) have suggested that there is a link between social settings, arousal, and cognitive–attentional overload. Thus, social facilitation may represent a process by which the aroused person narrows the range of attention and cue utilization. The relationship between drive and the range of cue utilization has been described by Easterbrook (1959). As drive increases, the range of stimuli or cues to which the person attends becomes narrowed. Low levels of drive produce an elimination of attention to stimuli peripheral to the task, i.e., largely irrelevant ones, whereas higher levels of arousal lead to elimination of attention to central cues needed for problem solving. Easy tasks require attention to a relatively small number of central cues, whereas more complex tasks have a larger range of relevant stimuli to which attention must be paid. If we assume that high arousal causes elimination of attention to a given range of cues regardless of whether the task is easy or hard, then it should be most likely to terminate attention to irrelevant distractors when the task is easy but cause interference with attention to important central stimuli when the task is difficult.

Geen (1976a) has reported findings that support the viewpoint outlined here. Subjects were given a serial learning task either in its original form or with additional cues. The latter were either relevant or irrelevant to the task. The critical group in the study was made up of highly test-anxious subjects who were observed and evaluated by the experimenter. These subjects were helped less than were high-anxious subjects who worked alone by the addition of relevant information but were also harmed less by the provision of irrelevant cues. High-anxious evaluated subjects apparently restricted their attention to the task cues and not to the ones that were added.

Applications

Worker Productivity

Despite the obvious relevance of the drive theory of social facilitation for the study of worker productivity we have little evidence from controlled studies.

One prediction that we might make would be that working as part of a team would increase drive and hence facilitate or hinder performance depending on the difficulty of the task. Similar results would be predicted in cases where workers performed under strict supervision. Another prediction would follow from the cue utilization hypothesis discussed in the preceding section. On a task requiring attention to signals, in which attention would be fostered by any condition that restricts distraction by peripheral stimuli, close supervision should facilitate performance. Bergum and Lehr (1963) did report findings consistent with this hypothesis. National Guardsmen served as subjects in a study in which reports had to be made each time one of a series of visual signals occurred over a period of more than 2 hours. Some of the subjects worked alone, whereas others were observed from time to time by an officer. Those subjects who worked under occasional surveillance made fewer errors of omission in reporting signals than did those who were not observed. This finding suggests that persons who work at tasks requiring attention to brief and infrequent signals over a long period of time, such as air-traffic controllers or naval radar operators, are likely to function better with occasional observation.

Classroom Participation

Drive is an aversive condition that animates attempts at escape and avoidance. Even though students of social facilitation have done little to test the possibility that being observed by an audience may promote both active and passive avoidance, that premise is a logical deduction from the theory (Weiss & Miller, 1971). A recent study (Geen, 1985) showed that subjects who were high in test anxiety and who also worked before an evaluating experimenter were more likely to withhold reporting solutions of anagrams than similarly test-anxious subjects who worked at the anagrams alone. In another experiment that involved the same anagrams task, Thomas and Geen (1985) found that subjects who worked in coacting groups of four withheld reporting solutions more than those who performed alone. In both studies negative correlations were found between the number of anagram solutions reported and the subjects' level of state anxiety. The findings were interpreted as showing that subjects became cautious and conservative in responding under conditions of evaluation apprehension. Response withholding was considered to be evidence of passive avoidance motivated by fear of failure.

Classroom participation that requires recitation or other forms of public action may represent a source of anxiety to students, especially those who are prone to experience test anxiety. Some studies reported by Paivio (1965) support this line of reasoning. Paivio found that children who scored high on the audience anxiety subscale of his Children's Audience Sensitivity Scale showed evidence of being more aroused while speaking to an audience than those scoring low on the subscale. These children also spoke for shorter lengths of time than did less anxious children, possibly because of a desire to escape from the aversive situation. In another study, highly anxious children expressed a stronger desire than less anxious ones to keep the ambient lighting at a low level, possibly to avoid being as clearly visible as they would have been in a bright room.

A study by Geen (1977) indicates that even in highly evaluative settings, steps may be taken that can reduce a student's anxiety over performance. In this experiment subjects were given difficult anagrams under one of four conditions. Some subjects worked alone. Others worked before an experimenter who casually observed. Still others worked before an experimenter who not only carefully observed and made notes of the subject's performance, but also announced that the purpose of the observation was evaluation. In a fourth condition the experimenter evaluated the subject but explained that the evaluation was "diagnostic" rather than judgmental. Subjects in this condition were told that on the basis of the observations, the experimenter would later advise the subject on how to improve anagram performance. The results of the study showed that when testing was couched in "diagnostic" terms, it elicited less evaluation apprehension and associated performance decrements than when it was described in purely judgmental terms.

Other studies indicate that arousal in evaluative social settings may be mitigated by preceding experiences of success. Prior success may reduce the perceived probability of failing at the task, so that being observed does not engender as strong a feeling of evaluation apprehension as it normally would. Both Geen (1979) and Seta and Hassan (1980) showed that when subjects were first led to believe that they had done well on a preliminary task, they performed no worse on a difficult problem before observers than they did when working alone. The expected social inhibition of performance before an audience occurred only after prior failure. We might expect that in realistic educational settings at least some of the evaluative arousal that attends task performance would be alleviated through providing a climate of success for the student. The natural tendencies of highly anxious students to participate may be somewhat offset in this way.

Antisocial Behavior

The relationship of social arousal to aggressive behavior would seem at first to be a fairly simple and straightforward one. Even though the social facilitation of aggression, in the sense that we have defined social facilitation, has not been shown, we do have evidence from other research suggesting that arousal may be an antecedent of aggressive behavior. High ambient temperature (Anderson & Anderson, 1984) and crowding (Griffitt & Veitch, 1971), both of which could be stimuli for increased arousal, have been shown to produce high levels of aggression or hostility toward others. Some of the clearest evidence of a connection between arousal and aggression is found in studies of the effects of media violence on emotions and behavior. Several studies of media violence have shown that presentations of violence elicit both increased autonomic activation and heightened aggressive behavior (for reviews, see Geen, 1983b; Geen & Thomas, in press; Tannenbaum & Zillmann, 1975).

Although noise is a stimulus that is often used to create arousal in the laboratory, and has been shown to bring about aggression (Geen, 1978; Geen & McCown, 1984), only one study has been designed to treat noise as an antecedent of increased drive. Geen and O'Neal (1969) stimulated subjects with white noise of moderate intensity immediately after showing them a movie of a violent prize fight and found that this treatment led to higher levels of aggression than a combination of noise and a nonviolent film. The violent film made aggressive responses prepotent in the observers' response hierarchy; these responses were then energized by increased drive caused by the noise.

The Geen and O'Neal findings prompted O'Neal, McDonald, Hori, and McClinton (1977) to carry out an experiment in which arousal was elevated in a social setting. Boys aged 5–6 years viewed either an aggressive or a nonaggressive film and were tested immediately for imitative aggression. One day later the children were again tested for imitative aggression without being shown the film again. Prior to being tested, half the children engaged in vigorous play with the experimenter and half in quiet play. O'Neal and his associates found that when nonvigorous play preceded testing, the children were considerably less likely to imitate the film on the second day than they had been on the first. However, when vigorous play preceded the second day's testing, the children came closer to reaching the previous day's level of imitation. This was true whether or not the film had been violent. The conclusion drawn from these data is that vigorous social interaction facilitates the expression of responses learned through observation, including aggressive ones, and that the facilitation may result from play-induced arousal energizing dominant imitative responses. Unfortunately the study did not include a condition in which children engaged in nonsocial play. We are not able, therefore, to determine to what extent the social setting per se affected arousal.

Health Behavior

The evaluation apprehension produced by an audience or coactors is usually within the tolerance range of most people. We seldom undergo serious evaluation by others, such as is encountered in public performances, without feeling some anxiety, but most of the time we manage to get through the experience without suffering any serious consequences for physical or mental wellbeing. The social facilitation/inhibition effect thus has few direct implications for health for most people. When we take individual differences into account, however, the picture changes somewhat. For one thing, social settings may not cause undue stress in general yet be relatively stressful for people who are characterized by high levels of general anxiety. As we observed earier in this review, being prone to experience test anxiety, for example, exacerbates the state of anxiety experienced in an audience setting (cf. Geen, 1976b).

Another variable that moderates the effects of social settings is the Type A behavior pattern. Type As are defined as intense and hard-driving individuals who have strong motives to succeed in competition and an exaggerated sense of time pressures (Glass, 1977). When placed in situations calling for achievement and mastery, Type As typically react with intense behavior aimed at gaining control over the situation and with increased physiological arousal. In an experiment that is relevant to our discussion, Gastorf, Suls, and Sanders (1980) found that Type As differed from their more relaxed Type B counterparts in situations involving coaction with one other person. Subjects did either a difficult or easy form of a task while either alone or with the coactor. Type A subjects performed in a way predictable from the drive theory of social facilitation. They performed better on the simple task when coacting than when working alone, but less well on the complex one. Type B subjects showed no such effects for either task. Type As may have been more susceptible to evaluation apprehension in the coaction setting than Type Bs, seeing that setting as an occasion for competition. This conclusion is supported by the evidence of another study showing that Type As reveal a higher incidence of fear of failure on a projective test than do Type Bs (Gastorf & Teevan, 1980).

These findings may establish a link between arousing social conditions and health. Type A people show higher levels of blood pressure during competition than Type Bs (Pittner & Houston, 1980). The coaction setting, by fostering feelings of competitiveness, may therefore elicit unhealthy physiological arousal in the Type A to a greater degree than in the Type B. We also have evidence of a positive correlation between the Type A pattern and incidence of coronary heart disease (Jenkins, 1971). These data therefore suggest that the Type A person may be at greater risk of cardiovascular problems in social settings than the Type B.

Areas of Special Interest

Counselor training. In one specialized area of education we have data that support the Hullian analysis of response energization by drive. In a recent review of the effects of evaluative observation on counselor training, Schauer, Seymour, and Geen (1985) concluded that the drive model might accounted for some of the anxiety and performance shortcomings seen in beginning counselor trainees. Specifically, Schauer *et al.* (1985) assumed that experienced students have acquired and learned well the appropriate techniques, whereas novices were more likely to emit responses that were not indicative of good counseling. They further assumed that the experience of being observed during counseling would raise the anxiety level of all students. It follows, then, that whereas experienced counseling students may react to the presence of live supervisors, video cameras, or tape recorders by showing more effective counseling behavior, novices should respond to those conditions with increased inappropriate behaviors. Schauer *et al.* assumed that the experience level of counseling students affected only habit strength, and that evaluation apprehension was approximately equal in beginning and experienced students. The latter finding has been reported in several studies (Bowman & Roberts, 1978; Bowman, Roberts, & Giesen, 1978; Monke, 1971).

A study by Amos (1984) was designed to test some of these possibilities. Subjects consisted of 11 beginning students and 11 advanced students in a counseling practicum. Each subject carried out an actual counseling session with a student client in full knowledge that the session was being audiorecorded. Some subjects were told that the recording of the session would be evaluated in the near future by a member of the counseling psychology faculty, whereas others were not informed that they would be evaluated in this way. Anxiety was assessed by means of the state form of the Spielberger State-Trait Anxiety Inventory before experimental instructions had been given and again just after the subject was told that his/her performance would be recorded on tape. Finally, the effectiveness of the counseling given to the client was measured by means of a rating scale, filled out by independent judges who listened to the recordings of the sessions.

The findings of the study showed that experienced and beginning counselors did not differ in state anxiety either before or after instructions were given, and that both groups showed a significant increase in anxiety from the preinstruction to the postinstruction measurement. Thus, as Schauer *et al.* (1985) had assumed, experience level did not contribute to differential drive levels. Subjects who believed that they would be evaluated were more anxious than those who had not been given instructions that evaluation would follow. Finally, the prediction of differentially effective counseling in the two groups was supported, as Table 5.1 shows. As expected, beginning students were less effective when they thought that they were to be evaluated than when they did not, whereas experienced students showed the reverse. Overall, therefore, the findings support the analysis proposed by Schauer *et al.* (1985).

Athletic events. Sports events are rarely if ever performed in isolation. The number of observers may range from a small crowd at a Little League game to millions of spectators at the Olympic Games, but in most cases there is an audience of some size. In addition, sports competition often involves playing in the company of others doing more or less the same thing. Athletics is therefore an activity that lends itself well to study in terms of the social facilitation/inhibition of behavior. In fact, the original experimental

Table 5.1. Mean Scale Ratings of Counseling Effectiveness

	Condition	
Experience level	No evaluation	Evaluation
Advanced	89.1	103.3
Beginning	70.9	60.2

Source: Data from Amos (1984).

study of social facilitation (Triplett, 1898), which was mentioned earlier in this review, grew out of an interest on the part of the investigator in sports bicycling. Triplett noted that cyclists attained faster times when accompanied by another rider than when performing alone.

A few studies give direct support to the hypothesis that the presence of an audience creates evaluation apprehension. In one such study Strube, Miles, and Finch (1981) examined the effect of an audience on jogging speed. Runners selected for study were males and females running in a university fieldhouse, with any given runner chosen for observation only if s(he) were running alone at least 30 m from another runner. Possible coaction effects were obviated by this procedure. Three conditions were compared. In a *no spectator* condition an observer timed the runner unobtrusively. In an *inattentive spectator* condition the observer made brief eye contact with the runner but then pretended to attend to other matters. In an *attentive spectator* condition the observer gazed at the runner and attempted to maintain prolonged eye contact; subsequent questioning established that eye contact was maintained in almost every case. The results showed that subjects who were observed by an attentive spectator increased running speed significantly over that of subjects who were not observed. Running before an inattentive spectator did not affect speed. These findings in a natural setting are similar to those obtained by Cottrell *et al.* (1968) in the laboratory and support the evaluation apprehension hypothesis.

Similar findings have been reported by Worringham and Messick (1983). People were surreptitiously photographed by means of a hidden movie camera as they ran along two 45-yard segments of a footpath. All subjects ran the first section alone. Upon reaching a bend in the path, two-thirds of the runners encountered a confederate of the experimenter seated near the path. The confederate faced some of the subjects but was turned away from the others. Compared to a group of control subjects who did not encounter the confederate, those who came upon the confederate facing them increased their running speed over the second segment of the path significantly. Those who saw an inattentive confederate did not differ from the controls.

Other studies of audience effects on athletic performance do not support the simple drive theoretical model. In a series of studies, Paulus and his associates (Paulus & Cornelius, 1974; Paulus, Shannon, Wilson, & Boone, 1972) investigated the influence of observers on the performance of novice and advanced gymnasts. The general finding of the studies was that performance before an audience was less damaging to the performance of beginners (for whom the complicated routines should have represented nondominant responses) than to the performance of advanced practitioners (for whom the routines should have been relatively easy). In the initial study, beginning gymnasts showed slight but nonsignificant improvement from a session in which they performed alone to one in which an audience was on hand. In a second study, advanced gymnasts showed a decrement in performance from the first (alone) session to the second (in which an audience was present). A third study showed that among beginners, the ones who showed the largest performance decrement before an audience were the ones who were originally the most skilled at the routines. A final study reaffirmed the conclusions of the preceding one, showing overall decrements in performance before an audience, especially among skilled students and more so when specific forewarning of the audience presence was given.

Clearly, these findings are inconsistent with simple predictions drawn from the premise that audience-induced drive energizes dominant responses more than subordinate ones. How, then, can we interpret them? One possible way is by invoking the Broen-Storms (1961) hypothesis of response-strength ceilings. For example, subjects who received prior warning that they would be observed may have been more apprehensive than those given no warning. Their overall drive level, therefore, may have been higher than the level at which the excitatory potential for dominant responses reached the ceiling. Further increases in drive caused by the audience would therefore lead to enhancement of subordinate responses which, for the advanced performer, would probably be incorrect ones. The most interesting of the findings of Paulus and his associates was that audience presence brought about performance decrements in advanced gymnasts. The dominant responses of these performers (which were relatively likely to be correct ones) may have been close to the response strength ceiling at low drive levels. Higher drive levels would thus be expected to increase the relative strength of subordinate *incorrect* responses. The same drive levels, however, would be leading to a progressive *weakening* of the response strength of dominant (incorrect) responses ones among beginners. Hence the paradox that increased drive helps beginners but hurts advanced performers.

The response-ceiling hypothesis may also explain the findings of Forgas, Brennan, Howe, Kane, and Sweet (1980) in a study of the effects of an audience on squash players. The study was unobtrusive. Players in action were first identified as being relatively superior or inferior. Some were then watched surreptitiously by observers who pretended to pay no attention to the players. Others were watched by highly visible observers who made clear the fact that they were attending closely to the play. The results clearly showed that the presence of the visible observers led to improvement of the play of inferior participants and to worse play among the superior performers. The reasoning used to interpret the results of Paulus and his colleagues could also explain this finding. We are well aware that such an argument is post hoc and speculative only. Invoking the response ceiling hypothesis to explain findings that run counter to the usual drive theoretical explanation has a "can't-miss" label attached to it. We are merely arguing here that the results discussed in the latter part of this section *can* be interpreted in ways that are not entirely inconsistent with drive theory.

Conclusion

Research on social facilitation has come far since Zajonc revived interest in the problem two decades ago. As we have shown in this review, the approach based on drive-arousal theory has generated a considerable body of research evidence in both laboratory and field studies. Although the bulk of the earlier evidence for the theory involved simple and highly controlled tasks, more recent studies show that the theory can account for such diverse phenomena as classroom participation, stress-related behaviors, and performance in athletic events. Indeed, it seems safe to conclude that one of the few areas of research in which Hullian drive theory is still viable today is that of social facilitation (Geen & Gange, 1977).

As we have also shown, however, the original simplified Hullian hypothesis proposed by Zajonc (1965) has been subjected to considerable modification. What was once thought to be a simple matter of response energization due to the mere physical presence of others has been shown to involve other processes at both the stimulus and response ends. The antecedents of social arousal are now described in such terms as uncertainty, social monitoring, evaluation apprehension, and distraction from the task. The connection between social arousal and performance may also involve more than energization of dominant responses at the expense of subordinate ones. As we have observed, the assumption that response energization was the outcome of socially engendered arousal originated with Zajonc (1965) and was followed by most researchers thereafter. It was this assumption that lead to the tendency of those working on social facilitation to treat drive and arousal as being virtually identical. However, more recent approaches suggest that social arousal may have cognitive and attentional effects that can also explain the main outcomes of the typical social facilitation experiment. If further theorizing continues to relate social facilitation to both arousal and cognitive processes, the future for research on this phenomenon appears bright.

References

Amos, J.G. (1984). The performance level effects of anxiety in low and high experience counselor trainees predicted by social facilitation theory. Unpublished Ph.D. dissertation, University of Missouri, Columbia, MO.

Anderson, C.A., & Anderson, D.C. (1984). Ambient temperature and violent crime: Tests of the linear and curvilinear hypotheses. *Journal of Personality and Social Psychology, 46*, 91–97.

Baron, R.S. (1986). Distraction-conflict theory: Progress and problems. In L. Berkowitz (Ed.), *Advances in Experimental Social Psychology*. (Vol. 19, pp. 1–40). New York: Academic Press.

Baron, R.S., Moore, D.L., & Sanders, G.S. (1978). Distraction as a source of drive in social facilitation research. *Journal of Personality and Social Psychology, 36*, 816–824.

Bergum, B.O., & Lehr, D. (1963). Effects of authoritarianism on vigilance performance. *Journal of Applied Psychology, 47*, 75–77.

Bolles, R.C. (1975). *Theory of motivation* (2nd Ed.). New York: Harper & Row.

Bowman, J.T., & Roberts, G.T. (1978). Counselor anxiety during a counseling interview. *Counselor Education and Supervision, 18*, 205–217.

Bowman, J.T., Roberts, G.T., & Giesen, J. (1978). Counselor trainee anxiety during the initial counseling interview. *Journal of Counseling Psychology, 25*, 137–143.

Broen, W.E., & Storms, L.H. (1961). A reaction potential ceiling and response decrements in complex situations. *Psychological Review, 68*, 405–415.

Brown, J.S. (1961). *The motivation of behavior*. New York: McGraw-Hill.

Cannon, W.B. (1934). Hunger and thirst. In C. Murchison (Ed.), *Handbook of general experimental psychology* (pp. 558–634). Worcester, MA: Clark University Press.

Cohen, S. (1978). Environmental load and the allocation of attention. In A. Baum & S. Valins (Eds.), *Advances in environmental research* (pp. 1–29). Hillsdale, NJ: Erlbaum.

Cottrell, N.B. (1972). Social facilitation. In C.G. McClintock (Ed.), *Experimental social psychology*. New York: Holt.

Cottrell, N.B., Wack, D.L., Sekerak, G.J., & Rittle, R.H. (1968). Social facilitation of dominant responses by the presence of an audience and the mere presence of others. *Journal of Personality and Social Psychology, 9*, 245–250.

Dashiell, J.F. (1935). Experimental studies of the influence of social situations on the behavior of individual human adults. In C. Murchison (Ed.), *Handbook of social psychology*. (pp. 1097–1158). Worcester, MA: Clark University Press.

Easterbrook, J.A. (1959). The effect of emotion on cue utilization and organization of behavior. *Psychological Review, 66*, 187–201.

Forgas, J.P., Brennan, G., Howe, S., Kane, J.F., & Sweet, S. (1980). Audience effects on squash players' performance. *Journal of Social Psychology, 111*, 41–47.

Gastorf, J.W., Suls, J., & Sanders, G.S. (1980). Type A coronary-prone behavior pattern and social facilitation. *Journal of Personality and Social Psychology, 38*, 773–780.

Gastorf, J.W., & Teevan, R.C. (1980). Type A coronary-prone behavior pattern and fear of failure. *Motivation and Emotion, 4*, 71–76.

Geen, R.G. (1976a). Test anxiety, observation, and range of cue utilization. *British Journal of Social and Clinical Psychology, 15*, 253–259.

Geen, R.G. (1976b). The role of the social environment in the induction and reduction of anxiety. In C.D. Spielberger & I.G. Sarason (Eds.), *Stress and anxiety* (Vol. 3, pp. 105–126). Washington, DC: Hemisphere.

Geen, R.G. (1977). The effects of anticipation of positive and negative outcomes on audience anxiety. *Journal of Consulting and Clinical Psychology, 45*, 715–716.

Geen, R.G. (1978). Effects of attack and uncontrollable noise on aggression. *Journal of Research in Personality, 12*, 15–29.

Geen, R.G. (1979). Effects of being observed on learning following success and failure experiences. *Motivation and Emotion, 3*, 355–371.

Geen, R.G. (1980). The effects of being observed on performance. In P. Paulus (Ed.), *Psychology of group influence* (pp. 61–97). Hillsdale, NJ: Erlbaum.

Geen, R.G. (1983a). Evaluation apprehension and the social facilitation/inhibition of learning. *Motivation and Emotion, 7*, 203–212.

Geen, R.G. (1983b). Aggression and television violence. In R.G. Geen & E.I. Donnerstein (Eds.), *Aggression: Theoretical and empirical reviews,* Vol. 2, *Issues in research* pp. 103–125). New York: Academic Press.

Geen, R.G. (1985). Evaluation apprehension and response withholding in solution of anagrams. *Personality and Individual Differences, 6*, 293–298.

Geen, R.G., Beatty, W.W., & Arkin, R.M. (1984). *Human motivation: Physiologcal, behavioral and social approaches.* Boston: Allyn & Bacon.

Geen, R.G., & Gange, J.J. (1977). Drive theory of social facilitation: Twelve years of theory and research. *Psychological Bulletin, 84*, 1267–1288.

Geen, R.G, & McCown, E.J. (1984). Effects of noise and attack on aggression and physiologiocal arousal. *Motivation and Emotion, 8*, 231–241.

Geen, R.G., & O'Neal, E.C. (1969). Activation of cue-elicited aggression by general arousal. *Journal of Personality and Social Psychology, 11*, 289–292.

Geen, R.G., & Thomas, S.L. (in press). The immediate effects of media violence on behavior. *Journal of Social Issues.*

Glass, D. (1977). *Behavior patterns, stress, and coronary disease.* Hillsdale, NJ: Erlbaum.

Good, K.J. (1973). Social facilitation: Effects of performance anticipation, evaluation, and response competition on free association. *Journal of Personality and Social Psychology, 28*, 270–275.

Griffitt, W., & Veitch, R. (1971). Hot and crowded: Influences of population density and temperature on interpersonal affective behavior. *Journal of Personality and Social Psychology, 17*, 92–98.

Groff, B.D., Baron, R.S., & Moore, D.L. (1983). Distraction, attentional conflict, and drivelike behavior. *Journal of Experimental Social Psychology, 19*, 359–380.

Guerin, B. (1983). Social facilitation and social monitoring: A test of three models. *British Journal of Social Psychology, 22*, 203–214.

Guerin, B., & Innes, J.M. (1982). Social facilitation and social monitoring: A new look at Zajonc's mere presence hypothesis. *British Journal of Social Psychology, 21*, 7–18.

Henchy, T., & Glass, D.C. (1968). Evaluation apprehension and the social facilitation of dominant and subordinate responses. *Journal of Personality and Social Psychology, 10*, 446–454.

Herrnstein, R.S. (1972). Nature as nurture: Behaviorism and the instinct doctrine. *Behaviorism, 1*, 23–52.

Hockey, R. (1979). Stress and cognitive components of skilled performance. In V. Hamilton & D.M. Warburton (Eds.), *Human stress and cognition: An information-processing approach.* (pp. 141–177). New York: Wiley.

Hull, C.L. (1943). *Principles of behavior.* New York: Appleton Century.

Hull, C.L. (1952). *A behavior system.* New Haven: Yale University Press.

Jenkins, C.D. (1971). Physiologic and social precursors of coronary disease, *New England Journal of Medicine, 284*, 244–255, 307–317.

Kahneman, D. (1973). *Attention and effort.* Englewood Cliffs, NJ: Prentice-Hall.

Malmo, R.B. (1958). Measurement of drive: An unsolved problem. In M. Jones (Ed.), *Nebraska Symposium on Motivation, 1958* (pp. 229–265). Lincoln, NE: University of Nebraska Press.

Markus, H. (1978). The effect of mere presence on social facilitation: An unobtrusive test. *Journal of Experimental Social Psychology, 14*, 389–397.

Miller, N.E. (1959). Liberalization of basic S-R concepts: Extensions to conflict behavior, motivation, and social learning. In S. Koch (Ed.), *Psychology: A study of a science* (Vol. 2, pp. 196–292). New York: McGraw-Hill.

Miller, N.E., & Dollard, J. (1941). *Social learning and imitation*. New Haven: Yale University Press.

Monke, R. (1971). Effect of systematic desensitization on the training of counselors. *Journal of Counseling Psychology, 18*, 320–323.

Moore, D.L., & Baron, R.S. (1983). Social facilitation: A psychophysiological analysis. In J. Cacioppo & R. Petty (Eds.), *Social psychophysiology: A sourcebook* (pp. 434–466). New York: Guilford Press.

O'Neal, E.C., McDonald, P., Hori, R., & McClinton, B. (1977). Arousal and imitation of aggression. *Motivation and Emotion, 1*, 95–102.

Paivio, A. (1965). Personality and audience influence. In B. Maher (Ed.), *Progress in experimental personality research* (Vol. 2, pp. 127–173). New York: Academic Press.

Paulus, P.B., & Cornelius, W.L. (1974). An analysis of gymnastic performance under conditions of practice and spectator observation. *Research Quarterly, 45*, 56–63.

Paulus, P.B, Shannon, J.C., Wilson, D.L., & Boone, T.D. (1972). The effect of spectator presence on gymnastic performance in a field situation. *Psychonomic Science, 29*, 88–90.

Pittner, M.S., & Houston, B.K. (1980). Response to stress, cognitive coping strategies, and the Type A behavior pattern. *Journal of Personality and Social Psychology, 39*, 147–157.

Richter, C.P. (1922). A behavioristic study of the activity of the rat. *Comparative Psychology Monographs, 1*, 1–55.

Sanders, G., & Baron, R.S. (1975). The motivating effects of distraction on task performance. *Journal of Personality and Social Psychology, 32*, 956–963.

Sanders, G., Baron, R.S., & Moore, D.L. (1978). Distraction and social comparison as mediators of social facilitation effects. *Journal of Personality and Social Psychology, 14*, 291–303.

Schauer, A.H., Seymour, W.R., & Geen, R.G. (1985). Effects of observation and evaluation on anxiety in beginning counselors: A social facilitation analysis. *Journal of Counseling and Development, 63*, 279–285.

Seta, J.J., & Hassan, R.K. (1980). Awareness of prior success and failure: A critical factor in task performance. *Journal of Personality and Social Psychology, 39*, 70–76.

Strube, M.J., Miles, M.E., & Finch, W.H. (1981). The social facilitation of a simple task: Field tests of alternative explanations. *Personality and Social Psychology Bulletin, 7*, 701–707.

Tannenbaum, P., & Zillmann, D. (1975). Emotional arousal in the facilitation of aggression through communication. In L. Berkowitz (Ed.), *Advances in experimental social psychology* (Vol. 8, pp. 149–192). New York: Academic Press.

Thomas, S., & Geen, R.G. (1985). Effects of observer presence on coaction. Paper presented at annual convention of the Midwest Psychological Association, Chicago, May.

Triplett, N. (1898). The dynamogenic factors in pacemaking and competition. *American Journal of Psychology, 9*, 507–533.

Warden, C.J. (1931). *Animal motivation: Experimental studies on the albino rat*. New York: Columbia University Press.

Weiss, R.F., & Miller, F.G. (1971). The drive theory of social facilitation. *Psychological Review, 78*, 44–57.

Woodworth, R.S. (1918). *Dynamic psychology*. New York: Columbia University Press.

Worringham, C.J., & Messick, D.M. (1983). Social facilitation of running: An unobtrusive study. *Journal of Social Psychology, 121*, 23–29.

Zajonc, R.B. (1965). Social facilitation. *Science, 149*, 269–274.

Zajonc, R.B. (1980). Compresence. In P. Paulus (Ed.), *Psychology of group influence* (pp. 35–60). Hillsdale, NJ: Erlbaum.

Zajonc, R.B., & Sales, S. (1966). Social facilitation of dominant and subordinate responses. *Journal of Experimental Social Psychology, 2*, 160–168.

Chapter 6

Social Impact Theory: A Social Forces Model of Influence

Jeffrey M. Jackson

General Principles

A recent theory of social impact (Latané, 1981; Latané & Nida, 1980) has been shown to be increasingly important in the fields of interpersonal influence and group behavior. Social impact is defined as

> any of the great variety of changes in physiological states and subjective feelings, motives and emotions, cognitions and beliefs, values and behavior, that occur in an individual, human, or animal, as a result of the real, implied or imagined presence or actions of other individuals. (Latané, 1981, p. 343)

This theory describes social impact in terms of social force fields that impinge upon us, pushing us to think or behave in a particular way. These social forces have been equated to physical forces that govern the transmission of light, sound, gravity, magnetism, etc. For example, the amount of light that falls on a table top is a function of the strength of the lights that shine on the table, their distance from the table, and the number of lights that are present. In an analogous way, the social impact felt by an individual should be a function of the strength, immediacy, and number of source persons that are present. Thus, these three elements, or descriptions, of source persons should all directly effect the social force felt by a target person. Mathematically, the elements are related multiplicatively in the following form, $I = f(SIN)$, where I is the social impact on the target person and S, I, and N, are the strength, immediacy, and number of the source persons. As the strength (status, power, ability, etc.), immediacy (equal to the inverse of the distance between the source and target), or the number of source persons increase, impact on the target person should also increase. In a more complex set of predictions, social impact theory's multiplicativity predicts that the effect of any one variable will be greater when the value of the other variables is large. For example, if a target person is being persuaded to donate money to a charity by strangers (low-strength sources), a large number of strangers will be somewhat more effective than a small number of strangers. However, if the persuaders are high in strength (e.g., Jerry Lewis, Michael Jackson, etc.) a large number of familiar people will be extremely effective compared to a small number of familiar people.

Another tenet of social impact theory specifies that impact is diffused across other target persons (co-workers, other team members, etc.). Again, this is analogous to physical forces. Picture a stand of trees bending under the force of a strong wind. The force experienced by a particular tree will be reduced as the other trees around it become larger, more immediate to the target tree, and greater in number. Similarly, social impact theory states that social forces from outside of a group will be reduced as the strength, immediacy, and number of others in the group increases. That is, high-strength cotargets should absorb most of the source's impact, leaving little to affect the low-strength sources; a physically or psychologically close cotarget should absorb more of the target's impact than should a distant cotarget; and large numbers of targets should divide up the source's impact to a greater degree than small numbers of targets. That is, there is only a limited amount of social impact that source persons emit and this is divided up among the target persons present. These factors are related divisively in the form $I = f(1/SIN)$. As the strength, immediacy, or number of coactors increases, less impact is felt by the target person, and the effect of any one variable will be greater when the value of the other variables is small. For example, if a group of medically unsophisticated bystanders (low coactor strength) were asked for help by an accident victim, an individual in a small bystanding group would be considerably more likely to help than an individual in a large group. However, if that same individual was surrounded by bystanding doctors and paramedics (high coactor strength), he would be relatively unaffected by the number of bystanders (i.e., he would be unlikely to help regardless of group size).

Social impact theory further suggests that as the number of sources or targets increases each additional person has less effect upon the impact than the previous person. That is, the first few people in a situation should be extremely important in determining the degree of impact. As more people are added, they should change the social impact, but the amount of this change should become increasingly minor. When the number of people involved is large, the addition of others should be negligible. This concept is similar to that of marginally decreasing utility in economics. Specifically, the marginally decreasing impact produces a power function relating the number of persons present and impact: for sources, $I = sN^t$, where s is a scaling constant, N is the number of sources, and t is the exponent (which is always less than one); and for the targets, $I = sN^{-t}$, where N is the number of targets. Unlike the previous tenets of social impact theory, these last equations are somewhat descriptive, rather than predictive, in nature. Social impact theory does not specify the value of the exponent, t, except that it is less than one, positive for sources, and negative for targets. This allows the theory to "fit" a wide variety of results, since the value of t is determined post hoc. However, this fact does not impugn the predictiveness of the general form of the expected relationships (i.e., marginally decreasing impact).

It should also be noted that number of sources and number of targets are not the only factors that should have marginally decreasing impact. Although little or no attention has yet been focused on the marginally decreasing nature of strength and immediacy, social impact theory predicts that they should also be power functions like number. Indeed, the general equation for social impact theory is

$$I = k(S^a T^b N^c_{\text{sources}}/S^d I^e N^f_{\text{targets}}),$$

where k is a scaling constant, and a, b, c, d, e, and f are all less than one.

Operations of the Theory in Group Contexts

Considerable evidence is available that demonstrates the effectiveness of producing impact with each of the source person elements: strength, immediacy, and number. Communicator characteristics (strength) have often been shown to effect persuasion (e.g., Hass, 1981). Typically high-status, high-expertise, and highly credible sources have more impact on their audiences (are more persuasive) than are low-status sources. Similarly, research in the area of personal space is supportive of the effectiveness of the immediacy element. Typically, strangers who move very close to a target person produce a high level of impact on the target (high discomfort, attempts to move away, etc.) (Knowles, 1980). The number of source persons has also been shown to be a potent variable in producing impact. In conformity studies, as the number of members of a faction increases, so does the conformity exhibited by the target person (Asch, 1951; Gerard, Wilhelmy, & Conolley, 1968; Moscovici, 1980). Target passersby are more likely to crane and gawk at a window in a large building when there is a large number of gawkers already looking (Milgram, Bickman, & Berkowitz, 1969). And stutterers have more speech disfluencies as the number of listeners grows (Porter, 1939).

The multiplicative set of predictions involving the interaction between the elements has also received support. Specifically, this multiplicativity posits that the higher in value any one of the elements is, the more pronounced will be the effects of the other variables. In one study (Jackson & Latané, 1982), participants were asked to shout as loud as they could by either a low-strength source or by a high-strength source. For half of the participants' shouts the source was physically immediate and for half he was out of the room. Not surprisingly, both the source's strength and immediacy affected the loudness of the participants' shouts, with louder shouts in the high-strength and high-immediacy conditions. However, a multiplicative interaction was obtained; the source's immediacy mattered most when the source was high in strength, and the source's strength mattered most when the source was immediate. In another study (Bassett & Latané, 1976), the relationship between immediacy and number was investigated. Participants read descriptions of hypothetically newsworthy events and editorialized about how much space should be allotted to the story in a newspaper. The events varied in terms of how far away they occurred and how many people were involved in the event. Participants gave more space to close rather than far events and to events involving many rather than few people. In addition, the predicted multiplicative interaction was obtained; the number of people involved was a more important variable when the events occurred nearby (high immediacy). Finally, the third combination of these elements, source strength, and number, has also been investigated (Jackson & Latané, 1981a). Experimenters canvassed a neighborhood asking for donations to charity. Experimenters were either high strength (nicely dressed, middle-aged women) or low strength (casually dressed college girls) and approached doors either alone or in pairs. Again, each variable affected responding individually; more money was given in the high-strength and pair conditions. Again, a multiplicative interaction occurred, with the number of solicitors variable being most effective when the solicitors were high in strength (Figure 6.1).

While research involving target variables is sparse compared to source variables research, a number of studies have focused on the target number variable. Latané and Darley's (1970) influential work on bystander intervention is one such example. These authors demonstrated that whether the participant was given the opportunity to report a fire or theft or help an injured lady or a student experiencing an epileptic seizure, that participant was less likely to intervene as the number of other bystanders grew. Latané and Darley interpret this as resulting, in part, from a diffusion of responsibility across the potential helpers (targets). In another study, Freeman, Walker, Borden, and Latané (1975) assessed the relationship between the number of diners at a table and tip size. The results indicated that as the size of the party grew, the percentage of the bill left as a tip correspondingly dropped. These authors also describe these results in terms of diffusion of responsibility—in this case the responsibility to the waiter.

Again, the coactor variables are combined in a multiplicative (or more precisely divisive) function. In fact, a general equation that includes both the source and target variables is of the form:

$$I = f(SIN_{\text{sources}}/SIN_{\text{targets}}).$$

Social impact would thus be a result of a multiplicative relationship of all six variables. Evidence supportive of this relationship was supplied by Jackson and Latané (1981b). Participants were asked to role play as singers in front of an audience and estimate their stagefright in various situations. Audiences consisted of either one, three, or nine high-status or low-status

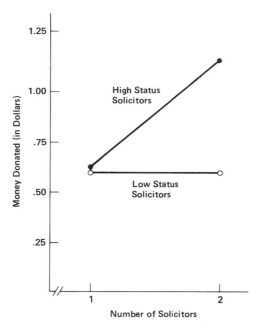

Figure 6.1. Multiplicative interation between source (solicitor) strength and number demonstrated with results from a door-to-door charity collection experiment. (From "Strength and number of solicitors and the urge toward altruism" by J.M. Jackson and B. Latané, 1981, *Personality and Social Psychology Bulletin, 7*, p. 420. Copyright 1981 by the Society for Personality and Social Psychology, Inc. Reprinted by permission.)

people, while the participant sang either alone, with two, or with eight other singers. As predicted, participants reported more stagefright in front of large audience, in front of high-status audiences, and when performing alone. In addition, multiplicative interactions were obtained involving all three of these variables. For example, as the number of coactors variable decreased the manipulations of audience size and status became more effective in producing stagefright.

In Gerard's *et al.* (1968) conformity study, for example, each successive source had less ability to produce conformity in the target. Figure 6.2 represents this marginally decreasing relationship and the impact power function that quite accurately describes it. Jackson and Latané (1981b) demonstrated a similar relationship between the number of audience member sources and stagefright in performers. This study also provides evidence supporting the marginally decreasing effect of adding coactors. Talent show participants rated their stagefright just before and just after walking on stage. As expected, the number of performers in an act was

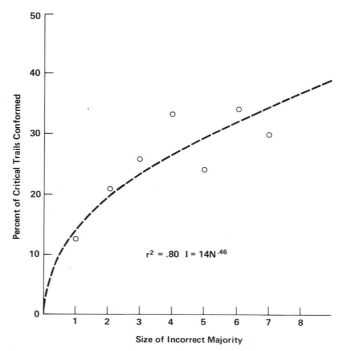

Figure 6.2. Marginally decreasing impact of sources (majority members) demon-strated with results from a conformity experiment. (From "The psychology of social impact" by B. Latané, 1981, *American psychology, 36*, p. 345. Copyright 1981 by the American Psychological Association, Inc. Reprinted by permission.)

negatively related to stagefright and this negative relationship is well described by social impact theory's marginally decreasing function (Figure 6.3).

It should be noted that social impact theory is not the only theory that deals with many of these issues. Knowles (1978, 1983) has developed a proximity model to explain the effects of crowding. Specifically, he states that others' influence is a result of the combination of their number and distance from the target person. Mathematically, this is demonstrated by

$$E = kN^n/D^d,$$

where the potential influence of others (E) is a function (k) of the number of people (N) to some power (n) divided by their distance (D) raised to some power (d). Knowles (1983) has suggested that the most likely values for n and d are 0.5. This model is quite consistent with social impact theory wherein Knowles' distance, D, appears to be identical to the inverse of impact's immediacy.

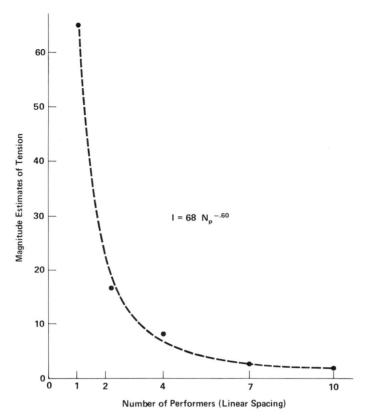

Figure 6.3. Marginally decreasing impact of cotargets (performers) demonstrated with results from a talent show stagefright experiment. (From "All alone in front of all those people: Stage-fright as a function of number and type of co-performers and audience" by J.M. Jackson and B. Latané, 1981, *Journal of Personality and Social Psychology, 40*, p. 81. Copyright 1981 by the American Psychology Association, Inc. Reprinted by permission.)

A second relevant model has recently been suggested by Tanford and Penrod (1984) for conformity, minority influence, and deviate rejection. These authors attempt to explain the influence process in terms of a mathematical combination of the number of sources and number of targets. Based upon a mathematical Gompertz growth model as well as fitting the model to computer simulation results, Tanford and Penrod proposed that

$$I = e^{-4e^{-(S^{1.75})/T}},$$

where I is the amount of growth of the function, S is the number of sources, T is the number of targets and e is the natural antilog of 1 (2.7183 . . .). The model applies quite well to conformity situations in which some maximum level of influence exists (e.g., complete agreement with one faction in a two-sided argument). While the shape of the Gompertz growth function differs somewhat from that predicted by social impact's functions, both models are related to power functions and both are based upon the number of sources divided by the number of targets. Social impact's main advantage over Tanford and Penrod's (1984) Social Influence model and Knowles' (1978) Proximity model is its inclusion of many more factors in the same general formulation (e.g., strength of sources, etc.).

In sum, social impact theory has received considerable support as a social forces model of human interaction. This support includes not only evidence of the power of the individual elements to produce impact, but in addition evidence for the complex multiplicative and marginally decreasing nature of these elements. Thus, given the strong empirical support for social impact theory, its application to "real world" group phenomena may be especially useful.

Applications

Worker Productivity

An undeniable characteristic of manager–worker situations is that the workers almost always outnumber managers. In social impact terms, a relatively small number of managers (sources) attempt to exert impact upon a large number of workers (targets) to work hard and to make few mistakes. Thus, the managers' impact is diffused across the workers, each experiencing only a small fraction of the impact to work hard. Experimental research has investigated this phenomenon, which has been termed "social loafing" (Latané, Williams, & Harkins, 1979). In a typical social loafing experiment, participants were asked to shout or clap their hands as loud as they could individually as well as in various sized groups. Since the experimenter's request was diffused across the participants when they performed in groups, the authors expected effort in groups to be low, whereas individual effort (when no diffusion occurs) should have been high. As predicted, participants shouted and clapped their hands loudest when they performed individually and as the number of coactors grew, participants produced less noise in a marginally decreasing manner: That is, they loafed in groups. Further research has attested to the generalizability of this phenomenon, demonstrating social loafing in various tasks; typing, evaluating the quality of poems, songwriting, thought generation, computer game playing, and maraca shaking (Jackson & Williams, 1985). Thus, this social loafing derivation of social impact theory appears to be quite generalizable and applicable to work settings.

Williams, Harkins, and Latané (1981) provide evidence for one solution to the social loafing problem: identifiability. Specifically, if managers individually monitor workers' output, even when they work in groups, social loafing disappears. In social impact terms, identifiability of individual workers' performances changes a group situation (large number of targets) into functionally an individual situation. The workers can no longer "hide in the crowd" and so do not divide up the manager's impact to work hard. Thus, piecework systems or systems that directly evaluate outputs of the workers should result in better productivity.

Classroom Settings

Overcrowding in classrooms seems to have increasingly become a strategy to stretch small school budgets; thus the effectiveness of teachers in these large classes has become a crucial issue. Since typical classes consist of one teacher and many students, as the class size increases, each student should feel less of the teacher's social impact. Social impact theory predicts that students in overcrowded classes will receive less attention from the teacher, pay less attention to the instruction, be less obedient in class, and consequently learn less. All of these predictions follow from the division of impact, in which the teacher's influence is divided up among the students. These predictions picture large classes as quite detrimental to the students; however, the situation is not that bleak. Since social impact theory postulates a marginally decreasing effect for adding coactors (students), each additional student added to the class should reduce the teacher's impact by less than the previous student. Indeed, a recent metaanalysis of studies investigating class size (Smith & Glass, 1980) demonstrated exactly this relationship. For both achievement and attitude scores, increasing class size had large effects when classes were small but began leveling off in large class sizes. Social impact's power function, with $t = -.31$, fits these data extremely well, accounting for 98% of the variance in the means. Thus, adding a few students to an already large class has only a minute detrimental effect on the rest of the students. This suggests that while overcrowding has some negative effects, the strength of these effects has probably been overestimated.

Social impact theory also predicts that students sitting in the front of the room (high source immediacy) will be most affected by the teacher. Not surprisingly, an educational truism is that good students tend to be those who sit in front. This is reasonable because, as suggested by Koneya (1976), students who like sitting in front have learned the most from the immediate teacher and because, aware of this relationship, the able students choose to sit in front. Unfortunately, it is these good students that should suffer most by overcrowded classrooms. Teacher immediacy, a source characteristic should be divisively related to student number, a target characteristic, as demonstrated by the general equation in the previous section. Thus, social impact theory predicts that when teacher immediacy is high, the number of students should have its most powerful detrimental effects. Thought of another way, the students in the front have the most to lose by the divisive increase in class size.

Jury Decision Processes

Recent U.S. Supreme Court decisions have allowed many states to reduce the size of juries from 12 to 9, or even 6. While some debate has centered around the fact that 6 or 9 jurors may not be as representative of the population as 12, social impact theory predicts that the 9 (or especially 6) jurors will experience more of the judge's impact to reach a fair decision. Each of the members of small juries should be more involved in the decision, remember more of the facts of the case, and follow the judge's instructions better. This may or may not make up for the loss of representativeness of the 12 person jury, but it should at least mitigate the problem.

In addition, social impact theory predicts that the foreman of the jury (who has high target strength) should feel more personally responsible, more involved, etc., than the rest of the jury. He or she will diffuse the judge's impact only to a small degree in that the other jury members have relatively small target strengths. Not surprisingly, then, the foreman will benefit to a large degree by reduced jury size (mutiplicative interaction). On the other hand, the nonforeman members of the jury will benefit the least from a reduction in jury size.

Within the jury, subgroups of jurors spend most of their time influencing each other with reason, logic, and sometimes even threats. To be sure, these direct attempts at attitude change or compliance are often successful. However a model of jury decision making based solely on persuasive arguments fails to account for a common finding: the original distribution of votes almost always determines the final verdict. Considerable evidence demonstrates the extremely low probability of a minority faction changing the votes of a majority (e.g., Davis, Kerr, Atkin, Holt, & Meek, 1975; Penrod & Hastie, 1980).[1] If, indeed, a simple persuasive model were operative, these reversals would not be so rare; forceful, persuasive jurors would often convince the majority. Instead it seems likely that, in addition to direct

---

[1]Tanford and Penrod (1983) provide some suggestive evidence that minorities can have some effect on majorities, especially when the jury size is small. However, this conclusion is based on a computer simulation of juror decision making in which the minority faction was not persuadable (i.e., unswerving). While this situation may occur infrequently in real life, almost everyone is somewhat persuadable even when they are positive they are correct (Asch, 1951).

persuasive appeals, indirect influence involving the other jurors' characteristics (e.g., strength, number, etc.) should affect decision making. In order to explain the dearth of jury reversals, social impact theory need only propose that the number of jurors in one faction (number of sources) is directly related to their impact. That is, large factions are more persuasive than small factions, with little importance accruing to what they actually say.

The above analysis demonstrates the dynamic nature of social impact theory. Jurors are simultaneously the targets of the judge's instructions, as well as targets and sources of persuasive attempts involving other jurors. Research, however, has yet to capture and investigate this complex interplay of simultaneous impact.

Group Psychotherapy

Comparing individual with group psychotherapy is especially difficult given the wide diversity of practices that take place in both the individual and the group areas. In the group area alone these approaches include psychoanalytic groups, psychodrama groups, crisis groups, Alcoholics Anonymous, marital couples groups, family therapy groups, traditional T groups, personal growth T groups, nude therapy groups, transactional analysis groups, and Gestalt groups, to name just a few (Yalom, 1975). To complicate matters further many of these approaches do not have direct counterparts in individual therapy, making comparison difficult. Nonetheless, a common feature shared by all these approaches is the inclusion of more, and in some cases many more people. At issue for social impact theory is the role of the other people; sources or targets.

It is likely that in many group psychotherapies, the other patients act as sources of impact. Yalom (1975) states that

> The curative factors in group therapy are primarily mediated not by the therapist but by the other members, who provide the acceptance and support, the hope, the experience of universality, the opportunities for altruistic behavior, and the interpersonal feedback, testing, and learning. (p. 83)

With all of these extra sources, then, it should be that members of groups experience more impact than if they are in individual therapy. If the therapist can direct the group toward curative actions, this greater impact would be evidenced in greater commitment to therapy, greater understanding and acceptance of insight, and greater desire to change behavior. Of course, this clear prediction is muddied to some degree by the inequality of the situations and therapeutic techniques used in individual and group psychotherapy.

An important distinction should be made between traditional group therapy and one of its special cases, family therapy. In family therapy, intact or nearly intact nuclear families are treated together with the emphasis placed on the relationships or system between them. That is, therapists usually attempt to direct focus away from particular family members and onto the reactions to and relationships between them (i.e., the family system). In social impact terms this pictures the family as the patient and the individual family members as cotargets of the therapist's influence. Consequently, they should be less committed, less accepting of insight, and less willing to change than members of traditional groups or individuals. Indeed, consistent with this, Nichols (1984) comments that family systems are especially difficult to change since people become set in disfunctional roles and are not very willing to change.

Conclusions

Social impact theory has been shown to apply easily to a variety of social influence situations. One of the most appealing aspects of this theory is its applicability to a wide scope of arenas, while at the same time it makes quite specific predictions. Indeed the small number of "real world" areas presented here, as well as the small number of predictions made within each area has only scratched the surface of the applicability of social impact theory.

However, social impact theory is not without a few problems. First, there has been no definition (empirical or theoretical) presented that distinguishes between sources and targets. Latané (1981) simply defines targets as "people who stand with the individual as the targets of forces coming from outside the group" (p. 349). The typical situation used to demonstrate the difference is a performer on stage in front of an audience. The performer is the source of impact and with his or her words, music, etc., he or she affects the audience members (targets of impact) who listen and watch. However, it is clear that a particular audience member is affected by his or her neighbors' reactions (cheering, booing, boredom, etc.). Are the other audience members cotargets, sources, or both? If they are both, no formulations of social impact theory can, as yet, deal with them. Second, no clues have been offered as how impact from one source group combines with impact from another source group that pushes the target in another direction. For example, in a jury setting picture the hapless undecided juror who is beset by arguments from a not guilty faction, a guilty of Murder I faction, and a guilty of second degree murder faction. Social impact might be able to predict the amount of force from each faction, but does not specify how these combine or cancel. Neither of these problems is critical to the viability of social impact theory, but they point out its limitations. Very likely, both deficiencies will be empirically solved in the future with studies that address them directly.

A third potential problem with the theory is not one that can be addressed empirically to reach resolution. Social impact theory never specifies a psychological process that underlies its predictions, which can lead to some ambiguities. For example, in the social loafing/shouting paradigm there are at least two possible processes that might be predicted a priori; attempts to get away from loafing, or embarrassment at shouting in front of strangers. If the first were operative, the theory would predict that as group size grew, shouting would drop off in a marginally decreasing manner (which is, in fact, the actual result). If, however, the embarrassment process were operative, the theory would predict the opposite; as group size grows shouting should increase in a marginally decreasing manner, since shouting alone is highly embarrassing. Thus, the theory's nonspecification of process could predict two opposite results. There are, however, two arguments that can be made in defense of social impact theory. First, social impact theory relies on other theories for specifying processes, and once a process is known, this theory can predict quite accurately how much certain social characteristics of the situation will affect the outcome. Thus, in the above example, once it is known that people are attempting to get away with loafing in groups, social impact theory correctly predicts the marginally decreasing shape of the results as well as the effects of other variables (e.g., experimenter strength) on shouting. A second argument in favor of the nonspecification of process is the immense applicability of theory. Indeed, the lack of a focus to one particular process allows social impact theory to be virtually unlimited in its usefulness.

References

Asch, S.E. (1951). Effects of group pressure upon the modification and distortion of judgements. In H. Guetzkow (Ed.), *Groups, Leadership, and Men* (pp. 177-190). Pittsburgh: Carnegie Press.

Bassett, R.L., & Latané, B. (1976). *Social influences and news stories.* Paper presented at the meeting of the American Psychological Association, Washington, DC, September.

Davis, J.H., Kerr, N.L., Atkin, R.S., Holt, R., & Meek, D. (1975). The decision processes of 6- and 12-person mock juries assigned unanimous and two-thirds majority rules. *Journal of Personality and Social Psychology, 32,* 1-14.

Freeman, S., Walker, M.R., Borden, R., & Latané, B. (1975). Diffusion of responsibility and restaurant tipping: Cheaper by the bunch. *Personality and Social Psychology Bulletin, 1,* 584-587.

Gerard, H.B., Wilhelmy, R.A., & Conolley, E.S. (1968). Conformity and group size. *Journal of Personality and Social Psychology, 8,* 79-82.

Hass, R.G. (1981). Effects of source characteristics on cognitive responses and persuasion. In R.E. Petty, T.M. Ostrom, & T.C. Brock (Eds.), *Cognitive responses in persuasion* (pp. 141-172). Hillsdale, NJ: Erlbaum.

Jackson, J.M., & Latané, B. (1981a). Strength and number of solicitors and the urge toward altruism. *Personality and Social Psychology Bulletin, 7,* 415-422.

Jackson, J.M., & Latané, B. (1981b). All alone in front of all those people: Stage-fright as a function of number and type of coperformers and audience. *Journal of Personality and Social Psychology, 40,* 73-85.

Jackson, J.M., & Latané, B. (1982). *Experimenter immediacy and social loafing.* Paper presented at the Midwestern Psychological Association, Minneapolis, MN, May.

Jackson, J.M., & Williams, K.D. (1985). Social loafing: A theoretical and meta-analytic review of literature. Manuscript in preparation.

Knowles, E.S. (1978). The gravity of crowding. Applications of social physics to the effects of others. In A. Baum & Y. Epstein (Eds.), *Human response to crowding.* Hillsdale, NJ: Erlbaum.

Knowles, E.S. (1980). An affiliative conflict theory of personal and group spatial behavior. In P. Paulus (Ed.), *The psychology of group influence* (pp. 133–188). Hillsdale, NJ: Erlbaum.

Knowles, E.S. (1983). Social physics and the effects of others: Tests of the effects of audience size and distance on social judgments and behavior. *Journal of Personality and Social Psychology, 45,* 1263–1279.

Koneya, M. (1976). Location and interaction in row-and-column seating arrangements. *Environment and Behavior, 8,* 265–277.

Latané, B. (1981). The psychology of social impact. *American Psychologist, 36,* 343–356.

Latané, B., & Darley, J.M. (1970). *The unresponsive bystander: Why doesn't he help?* New York: Appleton-Century-Crofts.

Latané, B., and Nida, S. (1980). Social impact theory and group influence: A social engineering perspective. In P. Paulus (Ed.), *The psychology of group influence* (pp. 3–34). Hillsdale, NJ: Erlbaum.

Latané, B., Williams, K., & Harkins, S. (1979). Many hands make light the work: The causes and consequences of social loafing. *Journal of Personality and Social Psychology, 37,* 822–832.

Milgram, S., Bickman, L., & Berkowitz, L. (1969). Note on the drawing power of crowds of different size. *Journal of Personality and Social Psychology, 13,* 79–82.

Moscovici, S. (1980). Toward a theory of conversion behavior. In L. Berkowitz (Ed.), *Advances in Experimental Social Psychology, 13,* 209–239.

Nichols, M. (1984). *Family therapy: Concept and methods.* New York: Gardner Press.

Penrod, S., & Hastie, R. (1980). A computer simulation of jury decision making. *Psychological Review, 87,* 133–159.

Porter, H. (1939). Studies in the psychology of stuttering. XIV. Stuttering phenomena in relation to size and personnel of audience. *Journal of Speech Disorders, 4,* 323–333.

Smith, M.L., & Glass, G.V. (1980). Meta-analysis of research on class size and its relationship to attitudes and instruction. *American Educational Research Journal, 17,* 419–433.

Tanford, S., & Penrod, S. (1983). Computer modeling of influence on the jury: The role of the consistent juror. *Social Psychology Quarterly, 46,* 200–212.

Tanford, S., & Penrod, S. (1984). Social influence model: A formal integration of research on majority and minority influence processes. *Psychological Bulletin, 95,* 189–225.

Williams, K., Harkin, S., & Latané, B. (1981). Identifiability as a deterrent to social loafing: Two cheering experiments. *Journal of Personality and Social Psychology, 40,* 303–311.

Yalom, I.D. (1975). *The theory and practice of group psychotherapy.* New York: Basic Books.

Chapter 7

Self-Attention Theory: The Effects of Group Composition on the Individual

Brian Mullen

The self is the *Summum Genus* of the psychologist, the theoretical concept which expresses the necessity he finds for a common reference in all the phenomena he considers.

(MacDougall, 1916)

Presentation of the Theory

Self-attention theory (Carver, 1979, 1984; Carver & Scheier, 1981; Duval & Wicklund, 1972; Mullen, 1983) is concerned with self-regulation processes that occur as a result of becoming the figure of one's attentional focus. According to self-attention theory, there are three fundamental require-ments for any self-regulation of behavior to occur. These requirements are: self-focused attention, a salient behavioral standard, and a sufficiently good outcome expectancy to warrent continued efforts. We will begin by delineating each of these three elements of self-attention theory.

Self-attention refers to the process of taking oneself as the focus of one's own attention, or becoming aware of oneself. Self-focused attention might result from situational induction of self-awareness or from an enduring predisposition for self-consciousness. For example, self-awareness might be situationally induced by the presence of an audience, a mirror, a video camera, the tape-recorded sound of one's voice, or minority status in a group setting. The states of self-awareness induced by these manipulations have been measured using the proportion of self-focused responses on Exner's (1973) Self-Focus Sentence Completion Blank (Carver & Scheier, 1981; Mullen, 1983) and by the proportionate use of first person singular pronouns, either in spontaneous speech (Mullen, 1985a; Mullen & Peaugh, 1985), or on Wegner and Guiliano's (1980, 1983) Linguistic Implications Form. Predispositional levels of self-consciousness have been operationalized in terms of Fenigstein, Scheier, and Buss's (1975) Self-Consciousness Scale, a 23-item self-report measure.

Behavioral standards define appropriate behavior. Some behavioral standards are made salient by the environment. For example, a university library may evoke behavioral standards of quiet, slow, and scholarly behaviors, whereas a university rathskellar may evoke behavioral standards of loud, boisterous, and gregarious behaviors. Some behavioral standards are more or less accepted by members of a given culture or subculture and constitute "norms" for that group of people. For example, in our society, it is generally accepted that one should help the needy, be respectful to one's elders, and refrain from arbitrarily inflicting harm upon others. Although there are certainly exceptions to the general acceptance of these standards of behavior, they are common enough to have been characterized as norms. Finally, some behavioral standards are purely idiosyncratic to the individual. For example, in spite of cultural norms, a convicted "serial murderer" might indicate that his intentional, methodical slaying of a dozen innocent youths was appropriate and legitimate behavior for him.

Self-attention in conjunction with some salient behavioral standard may lead the individual to begin a matching to standard process (Carver, 1979; Carver & Scheier, 1981). That is, if one is sufficiently aware of oneself, one may more readily come to recognize a discrepency between one's present behavior and the standard of behavior which is salient in that setting. However, whether or not the individual begins to try to reduce this discrepency depends on the third element of the theory: outcome expectancy. This refers to the subjective probability of success. A good outcome expectancy means that one believes that one can successfully reduce the discrepency between what one has intended to be doing and what one is currently doing. Assuming that the individual is self-attentive and that there is a salient standard of behavior, then a good outcome expectancy leads the individual to attempt to match his or her behavior to the salient standard of behavior. A poor outcome expectancy means that one believes that one cannot sucessfully reduce the discrepency between what one should be doing and what one is currently doing. Assuming self-focused attention and a salient standard of behavior, a poor outcome expectancy will lead the individual to withdraw from attempts to match his or her current behavior to the salient standard of behavior. A number of recent studies have demonstrated that good outcome expectancies enhance, and poor outcome experiences impair, attempts by self-attentive individuals to match to salient standards of behavior (Carver & Blaney, 1977; Carver, Blaney, & Scheier, 1979, 1980; Duval, Wicklund, & Fine, 1972; Feinberg, Miller, Mathews, & Denig, 1979; Steenbarger & Aderman, 1979).

Carver and Scheier (1981) have noted that self-attention, behavioral standards, and outcome expectancy can interact to produce three distinct processes. *Self-regulation* refers to the intentional matching of one's behavior to some salient behavioral standard. Self-regulation is most likely to occur under conditions of high self-attention and a salient behavioral standard in conjunction with a good outcome expectancy. It is in this type of setting that an increase in self-attention will bring about an increase in the behavior defined by the behavioral standard.

Withdrawal refers to a breakdown in normal, intentional matching of one's behavior to salient behavioral standards. Withdrawal from attempts to match to standards is most likely to occur under conditions of relatively high self-attention and a salient behavioral standard in conjunction with a poor outcome expectancy. It is in this type of setting that an increase in self-attention will bring about an a decrease in the behavior defined by the standard.

Finally, *absence of regulation* refers to the failure to even begin to consider the discrepency between present states and salient standards. The absence of regulation occurs under conditions of relatively low self-attention, regardless of behavioral standards or outcome expectancy. With low self-attention, the individual is unlikely to attend to his or her own behavior, and so salient behavioral standards are not relevant (and outcome expectancy is never evaluated). Since the matching to standard process never even begins, the absence of regulation is associated with little or none of the behavior defined as appropriate by behavioral standards.

Operation of the Theory in Group Settings

Group settings are likely to influence each of the major components of self-attention theory. For example, consider the effect of a group on behavioral standards. Individuals enter a group with a collection of cultural, normative standards as well as personal, idiosyncratic standards. However, a group can be very powerful in establishing the salience and legitimacy of its own behavioral standards. For example, the persistence of group norms beyond the duration of membership of any individual has been repeatedly demonstrated (Jacobs & Campbell, 1961; MacNeil & Sherif, 1976; Montgomery, Hinkle, & Enzie, 1976). In addition, consider the effects of dissension on delegitimization of behavioral standards in social influence settings. For example, Milgram (1974) observed that a disobedient co-worker mitigated subjects' destructive obedience, presumably by delegitimizing the behavioral standards established by the authority's commands. Similarly, Allen and Levine (1971) demonstrated that the behavioral standard established by the behavior of a majority was delegitimized by a dissenting group member.

The group may also affect the outcome expectancies which the individual develops. Obviously, outcome expectancies might be influenced by one's own previous success or failure (Albert, 1977; Heider, 1958; Suls & Mullen, 1982). However, the performances of similar others might be used by the individual to formulate the subjective probability of their own successful performance (Festinger, 1954; Goethals & Darley, 1977, and Chapter 2, this volume). In addition, the encouragement and support offered by intimates and confidants might be reasonably inferred to enhance the individual's outcome expectancy (Bloom, Ross, & Burnell, 1978; Dean & Lin, 1977; Lang, 1980).

It is the influence of the group setting on the individual's awareness of the self that has received the most attention. Psychologists have long recognized the inherently social medium of self-awareness phenomena (e.g., Angell, 1904; Heider, 1958; James, 1890; Kohler, 1947; Krueger & Reckless, 1932; LeBon, 1895/1960; McDougall, 1908; Mead, 1934; Peirce, 1868; Ross, 1908; Royce, 1895). For example, consider Mead's observation that:

> Selves can only exist in definite relationships to other selves. No hard and fast line can be drawn between ourselves and the selves of others, since our own selves exist and enter as such into our experience only insofar as the selves of others exist and enter into our experience also. (Mead, 1934, pp. 227–228)

In a similar vein, Kohler noted that:

> Just like any other object, the self may become a member of perceptual groups. . . . At times, these facts confer upon the self a central position within the total field; but even this is by no means always the case. After all, in many situations experience includes other persons, and there are circumstances under which such people occupy a more conspicuous position in the field than the self does. (Kohler, 1947, p. 175)

Consistent with this earlier thinking, recent research efforts (e.g., Diener, 1980; Duval & Siegal, 1978; Gerard & Hoyt, 1974; Mullen, 1983; 1984, 1985a, b, in press a, b; Mullen, Johnson, & Drake, 1985; Wegner & Schafer, 1978; Wicklund, 1980, 1982; Ziller, 1964) reveal that members of a heterogeneous group become more self-attentive and more concerned with standards of behavior as the relative size of their subgroup decreases. This appears to be the result of a tendency for the smaller subgroup to become the figure of group members' attention (e.g., Coren, Porac, & Ward, 1979; Koffka, 1935; Riley, 1958). That is, individuals in the group will tend to focus upon the small subgroup as the figure of their attention. This leads members of the small subgroup, in turn, to focus their own attention more closely on themselves and thereby become more concerned with discrepancies between present states and salient standards. Conversely, this leads members of the larger subgroup to become less self-attentive (or de-individuated; cf. Diener, 1980; Festinger, Pepitone, & Newcomb, 1952; Simmel, 1950; Zimbardo, 1970) and thereby less concerned with matching their behavior to salient standards.

A numerical representation of this compositional effect of the group on the individual is the Other–Total Ratio. This Other–Total Ratio is the ratio of the number of people in the Other subgroup to the sum of the number of people in the Other subgroup and the number of people in the Self

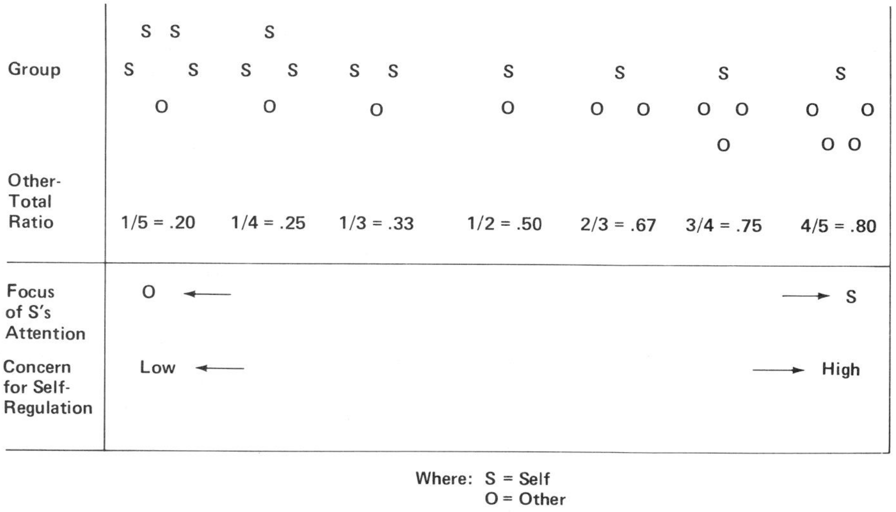

Group	S S	S							
	S	S	S	S	S	S	S	S	S	S
	O		O		O		O	O O	O O	O O
									O	O O

Other-Total Ratio	1/5 = .20	1/4 = .25	1/3 = .33	1/2 = .50	2/3 = .67	3/4 = .75	4/5 = .80

Focus of S's Attention	O ←———						———→ S
Concern for Self-Regulation	Low ←———						———→ High

Where: S = Self
O = Other

Figure 7.1. General Overview. Self-attention theory, Other–Total Ratio, and the effect of the group on the individual.

subgroup. In a sense, the Other–Total Ratio represents the proportion of the Total group that is comprised of people in the Other subgroup. For example, for one person speaking in front of an audience of eight other people [Other–Total Ratio = 8/(8 + 1)], the Other–Total Ratio = .888. Similarly, for six people speaking in front of an audience of one other person [Other–Total Ratio = 1/(1 + 6)], the Other–Total Ratio = .143. Figure 7.1 illustrates the general application of this approach.

This simple algorithm has been demonstrated to be an accurate predictor of the effect of the group on the individual's level of self-attention (cf. Mullen, 1983, Study 1 and Study 2, 1985a; Mullen & Peaugh, 1985). In addition, the Other–Total Ratio has been demonstrated to be an accurate predictor of the individual's attempts to match to standards of behavior (cf. Mullen, 1983, Studies 3, 4, 5, and 6, 1984, 1985a, b, in press a, b; Mullen & Peaugh, 1985; Mullen, Johnson, & Drake, 1985). We will now consider the application of this perspective to a number of group phenomena.

Applications

Participation in Classroom Settings

The typical classroom setting might be viewed in this light as a hetero-geneous group comprised of two subgroups: students and teachers. As the number of students in the classroom increases relative to the number of teachers, a given student is likely to become less self-attentive and thereby less likely to match to standards of "participating in class discussion." As the number of students in the class decreases relative to the number of teachers, a given student is likely to become more self-attentive and thereby more likely to match to standards of "participating in class discussion." This is consistent with Glass and Smith's (1979) meta-analytic review of the effects of class size on student achievement. Glass and Smith observed that classes of increasing size produced decreasing amounts of student achievement.

Mullen (1985a) reported an analysis of transcripts of class discussion in 27 highschool classes of various sizes. In this procedure (cf. Dillon, 1982), Other–Total Ratios can be calculated for students of each class as the number of teachers in the class divided by the sum of the number of teachers and the number of students in the class. First, these analyses revealed that the students' proportionate use of first person singular pronouns increased as a function of the Other–Total Ratio ($R = .515$, $R^2 = .265$, $F(1,25) = 9.011$, $p < .003$). In light of previous reliance upon first person singular pronouns as an index of self-focused attention (e.g., Wegner & Guiliano, 1980, 1983), this supports the fundamental premise that self-attention varies as a function of group composition. In addition, these analyses revealed that students' participation in classroom discussion increased as a function of the Other–Total Ratio, on a variety of measures of participation (number of student turns taken: $R = .697$, $R^2 = .486$, $F(1,25) = 23.642$, $p = .00005$; number of student seconds spent talking: $R = .754$, $R^2 = .568$, $F(1,25) = 32.874$, $p = .00005$; number of student words spoken: $R = .758$, $R^2 = .574$, $F(1,25) = 33.730$, $p = .00005$). Thus, participation in classroom discussion did in fact vary as a function of group composition.

Subsequent analyses (reported in Mullen, 1985a) indicated that these effects were independent of any influence of the inherent interest value of the topics under discussion, or of any influence of the number of times the teacher asked questions or the number of times the teacher offered encouragements. The increased participation which occurred in smaller classes represents what Carver and Scheier (1981) referred to as self-regulation, whereas the decreased participation which occurred in larger classes represents what Carver and Scheier referred to as the absence of regulation. Thus, the self-attention perspective appears to be a viable approach to participation in classroom settings.

Group Psychotherapy

Consider the application of this perspective to group psychotherapy settings. As the number of active participants increases relative to the number of passive participants, a given active participant is likely to become less self-attentive. As the number of active participants decreases relative to the number of passive participants, a given active participant is likely to become more self-attentive. The therapeutic application of self-attention principles has received a considerable amount of research attention in recent years (e.g., Brehm, 1976; Damsteegt & Christoffersen, 1982; Gibbons, Smith, Ingram, Pearce, Brehm, & Schroeder, 1985; Liese, 1983). There are two ways in which group psychotherapy manipulated self-attention could affect the client.

On the one hand, it may be desirable to enhance self-attention processes in some therapeutic settings, in order to facilitate client awareness of problem behaviors, and in order to facilitate matching to standards of appropriate behavior. Practically any psychotherapeutic approach can be viewed in this light, from Freudian concern for insight to Rogerian concern for increased accuracy of self-perceptions to Skinnerian concern for self-monitoring of target behaviors. Thus, it is not surprising that a number of group psychotherapy techniques involve setting the client off from the group as a lone performer in front of an audience. For example, the techniques of soliloquy, behind the back, the hot seat, and "change 'It' to 'I'" (Shaffer & Galinsky, 1979) can be viewed as attempts to enhance the self-attention of the client.

On the other hand, it may be desirable to reduce self-attention in other contexts, in order to mitigate the negative affect that can result from failure experiences (Carver & Scheier, 1981). Thus, it is not surprising that a number of group psychotherapy techniques are directed toward immersing the client in the group. First and foremost, when one client is in the hot seat, the others are by definition immersed in the large observing audience. In addition, reducing the client's self-attention could be facilitated through the use of a double and through efforts directed toward helping the client to see that he or she are not alone in having troubles.

Participation in Religious Groups

Religious groups provide another context within which to examine the application of the self-attention theory approach to group behavior. As the number of congregation members increases relative to the number of ministers, a given congregation member is likely to become less self-attentive and thereby less likely to match to standards of "participating in the religious group." As the number of congregation members decreases relative to the number of ministers, a given congregation member is likely to become more self-attentive and more concerned with matching to standards of "participating in the religious group." This inference is consistent with Wicker (1969), Latané (1981), and Pinto and Crow (1982), who observed that participation in religious groups was negatively related to group size.

This application of the self-attention perspective has been examined using 10 different archival records of participation in religious groups (Mullen, 1984). Participation was variously operationalized in these archival records as the proportion of the congregation attending worship service, becoming lay ministers, or "inquiring for Christ." Other–Total Ratios can be calculated for congregation members as the number of ministers in the congregation divided by the sum of the number of ministers and the number of congregation members. Meta-analytic summary[1] (cf. Mullen & Rosenthal, 1985; Rosenthal, 1980, 1984) of the 10 regression analyses revealed that the Other–Total Ratio was able to predict participation in the religious groups in a manner that was both statistically significant (weighted Z for combination of significance levels $Z = 14.048$, $p <$ .0000000000000000001) and of considerable magnitude (mean weighted coefficient of regression $\bar{R} = .602$, mean weighted coefficient of determination $\bar{R}^2 = .362$). The increased participation in the religious group associated with the increased Other–Total Ratio represents what Carver and Scheier (1981) referred to as self-regulation, whereas the decreased participation associated with the decreased Other–Total Ratio represents the absence of regulation. Thus, the self-attention perspective appears to be a viable approach to understanding the process of participation in religious groups.

Note that these analyses examined participation in the sense of intentional behaviors. Different results might emerge if one were to examine unintentional, expressive behaviors. Decreased self-attention may be necessary to facilitate expressive, uninhibited behavior (e.g., Diener, 1980). Further, certain individuals may be attracted to the religious group because it offers a means of reducing self-attention after personal failure [similar to Hull's (1981) consideration of the effects of alcohol consumption, and the possible self-attention reducing effects of some group psychotherapy techniques described above]. Hammersla (1983) and Hoffer (1951, 1954) have described religious groups that seem to thrive by offering a reduction in self-attention processes among congregation members. This work has recently been examined from the present self-attention theory perspective (Mullen & Hu, 1986).

The application of self-attention theory to participation in religious groups gives rise to an interesting paradox. On the one hand, it may be better to decrease the individual's self-attention in order to attract the individual to the group and in order to propagate the uninhibited, expressive experiences that the recruit may be seeking. On the other hand, it may be necessary to increase the individual's level of self-attention in order to elicit from congregation members the intentional behaviors that are necessary for the effective functioning of the religious group. As suggested by Mullen (1984), this paradox may be resolved by periodic vacilation between inductions of self-attention and reductions of self-attention, or by a

---

[1]The meta-analytic statistics employed in this chapter provide a numerical integration of the results of multiple hypothesis tests. The Z for significance (and the associated one-tailed probability level) indicate the likelihood that the observed significance levels could have been obtained as a result of chance alone. The mean correlation coefficient (and the associated mean coefficient of detrmination) provide a general unbiased estimate of the magnitude of the effects under consideration. The interested reader is directed to Mullen and Rosenthal (1985) and Rosenthal (1980, 1984) for more detailed discussion.

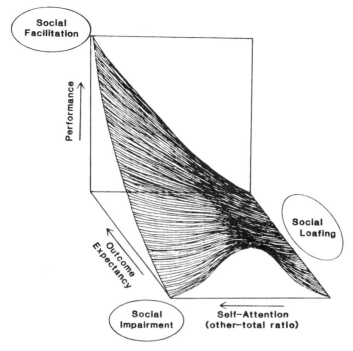

Figure 7.2. Three dimensional representation of the predicted effects of self-attention and outcome expectancy on performance.

two-step process of deindividuated assimilation into the group and self-attentive participation in the group.

Worker Productivity

Consider the application of this perspective to worker productivity. As the number of performers increases relative to the number of observers, a given performer is likely to become less self-attentive, and thereby less concerned with matching to salient standards of excellence in performance. As the number of performers decreases relative to the number of observers, a given performer is likely to become more self-attentive and thereby more concerned with matching to salient standards of excellence in performance. Figure 7.2 illustrates the requisite conditions for each of three general categories of group effects on the individual's performance.

Social facilitation occurs when the performers' Other–Total Ratio increases, as the performers become proportionately more rare in the group, and as the performers become more self-attentive, and when performers have developed a good outcome expectancy (and when attention to one's performance and task feedback does not interfere with task performance). This represents an example of what Carver and Scheier (1981) refer to as self-regulation.

Social impairment occurs when the performer's Other–Total Ratio increases, as the performers become proportionately more rare in the group and the performers become more self-attentive, and when performers have developed a poor outcome expectancy. This represents an example of what Carver and Scheier (1981) refer to as withdrawal.

Social loafing occurs when the performer's Other–Total Ratio decreases as the performers become proportionately less rare in the group, and as the performers become less self-attentive. This represents an example of what Carver and Scheier (1981) refer to as the absence of regulation.

A thorough examination of this perspective would require variation in both outcome expectancies and group-induced self-attention. Such an examination has been accomplished (Mullen & Story, 1985). However, the discussion of this research is postponed until a later section of this chapter because this procedure has relied upon a slightly different approach to the effects of the group on self-attention. Partial tests of this perspective can be accomplished by examining the Other–Total Ratio's prediction of performance in the absence of manipulations of outcome expectancy. Such partial examinations of this perspective are thus based on the assumption that the workers' outcome expectancies were sufficiently high to permit the workers to begin to match their performance to standards of excellence.

For example, Mullen (1983, Study 5) examined the Other–Total Ratio's prediction of social facilitation–social loafing in the results of 18 previously published studies. Standardized mean performance levels were accurately predicted by the Other–Total Ratio in a manner that was both significant ($Z = 8.14$, $p < .0000000001$) and of considerable magnitude ($\bar{R} = .97$), $\bar{R}^2 = .95$). Similarly, Mullen *et al.* (1985) examined organizational productivity in the context of 58 offices of a federal agency in a five-state region in the southwestern United States. The Other–Total Ratios for the subordinates in each office were calculated as the number of supervisors divided by the sum of the number of supervisors and the number of subordinates. Productivity was operationalized as the speed of processing applications for retirement pensions (the primary function of this agency). The Other–Total Ratio accurately predicted productivity in this real organizational setting ($R = -.314$, $R^2 = .099$, $F(1,56) = 6.122$, $p = .0164$; note that the negative relationship indicates that shorter processing times were associated with higher Other–Total Ratios). Subsequent analyses indicated that this effect was independent of any effects of subordinate workload. Thus, as performers' Other–Total Ratios decreased, performance decreased; as performers' Other–Total Ratios increased, performance increased.

Note that this self-attention integration provides a theoretical alternative to the Drive-Arousal Hypothesis (Bond, 1983; Geen, 1980; Geen & Bushman, Chapter 5, this volume; Zajonc, 1965). Several recent studies have examined performance in social contexts in terms of self-attention induced matching to standard processes; these processes can be demonstrated to lead to nondominant but correct responses, in contradiction to the Drive-

Arousal Hypothesis (cf. Baumeister, 1984; Baumeister & Steinhilber, 1983; Bond, 1982; Hormuth, 1982). In addition, the many demonstrations of social loafing are not easily reconciled with the Drive-Arousal Hypothesis. Demonstrations of social loafing tend to use simple tasks, such as shouting and clapping (Harkins, Latané, & Williams, 1980), rope pulling (Ingham, Levinger, Graves, & Peckham, 1974), and pumping sphygmographic bulbs (Kerr & Brunn, 1981). Individuals performing these tasks in a group context should, according to the Drive-Arousal Hypothesis, exhibit performance facilitation; in actuality, individuals performing these tasks in the context of a group tend to exhibit performance impairment, as predicted in terms of a non-self-attentive lack of concern for matching to standards of excellence.

Antisocial Behavior

The application of this perspective to antisocial behavior has received a considerable amount of currency. As the size of a crowd increases, the members of the crowd are likely to become less self-attentive and thereby less likely to match their behavior to normative standards of conduct. The effects of deindividuation on antisocial behavior have often been viewed in this light (e.g., Diener, 1980; Festinger et al., 1952; Simmel, 1950; Zimbardo, 1970). This is consistent with Mann's (1981) observation that "baiting crowds" were more likely to urge and taunt a suicidal individual to jump from a bridge or building as the size of the crowd increased.

In support of this perspective, Mullen (1983, Study 6) examined the Other–Total Ratio's predictions of antisocial behavior in the results of five previously published studies. Standardized mean antisocial behaviors were accurately predicted by the Other–Total Ratio in a manner that was both statistically significant ($Z = 4.78$, $p = .0000009$) and of considerable magnitude ($\bar{R} = .95$, $\bar{R}^2 = .90$).

A recent archival analysis (Mullen, in press b) has evaluated this perspective in a context with high ecological validity (Bjorkman, 1969) by examining the atrocities committed by lynch mobs upon their victims. Sixty newspaper reports of lynching events (derived from Ginzburg, 1962) were coded for information regarding group composition and atrocity of the lynching event. Other–Total Ratios could be calculated for members of each lynch mob as the number of victims divided by the sum of the number of victims and the number of lynchers. Atrocity was operationalized in terms of a composite index of the occurrence or nonoccurrence of hanging, shooting, burning, lacerating, or dismembering of the victim, as well as the duration of the lynching. The atrocity of the lynching events decreased as the Other-Total Ratio increased ($R = -.350$, $R^2 = .122$, $F(1,58) = 8.069$, $p = .0031$). Subsequent analyses (reported in Mullen, in press b) indicated that these results did not owe to variability in newspaper coverage of lynchings involving more people, newspaper coverage of lynchings involving a greater degree of atrocity, or the nature of the crime alleged to have been perpetrated by the victim of the lynching. Thus, as the lynch mob increased in size, the members of the mob grew less self-attentive (or more deindividuated) and thereby became more subject to the absence of regulation represented by the antisocial behavior of lynching.

It must be recognized that this non-self-attentive absence of regulation represents just one way in which undesirable, antisocial behavior might be engaged. As discussed by Mullen (1983), antisocial behavior could be observed in two different contexts. Antisocial behavior in the sense of the absence of regulation could be observed among non-self-attentive individuals (as in the lynching atrocity analysis). Alternatively, antisocial behavior in the sense of self-regulation of behavior could be observed among self-attentive individuals when behavioral standards are made salient which support the otherwise antisocial behavior. For example, Scheier, Fenigstein, and Buss (1974) observed more aggression among non-self-attentive subjects than among self-attentive subjects in a context where standards prohibiting aggression were salient. This represents antisocial behavior in the sense of the absence of regulation. Alternatively, Carver (1974) observed more aggression among self-attentive subjects than among non-self-attentive subjects in a context where standards supporting aggression were salient. This represents antisocial behavior in the sense of the self-regulation of behavior toward otherwise antisocial behavioral standards.

A preliminary examination of this line of reasoning was made in a secondary analysis of data originally reported by Diener, Westford, Diener, and Beaman (1973). This procedure entailed the unobtrusive observation of the stealing of candy by trick or treaters on Halloween in the presence of a lone homeowner. In the original analysis, it was reported that children were more likely to steal when in groups than when alone, and that this pattern was exaggerated when arousal was induced (via exercise or scary noises). It seemed reasonable to examine the precise effects of group composition among the control subjects of this study (i.e., the trick or treaters who were not subjected to an arousal manipulation). Other–Total Ratios can be calculated for these 173 trick or treaters as the number of homeowners divided by the sum of the number of homeowners and the number of trick or treaters. Unexpectedly, a regression analysis revealed that the Other–Total Ratios had essentially no predictive relationship with the number of candies stolen ($R = -.008$, $R^2 = .00007$, $F(1,171) = .011$, $p = .912$). This would seem to suggest that the group setting had no effect on transgressive behavior in this realistic setting.

However, some previous research suggests that self-attention processes, and the effects of social stimuli on self-attention processes, may not fully develop until late childhood or early adolescence (Buss, Iscoe, & Buss, 1979; Tice & Baumeister, 1984; Cooley, 1908; Kagan, 1981). Therefore, separate regression analyses were conducted for four separate age groups of trick or treaters, and an interesting pattern emerged. For the 1- to 4-year-olds, there was absolutely no correlation between Other–Total Ratio and stealing (there was no variability in the stealing behavior of this group, since not a single piece of candy was stolen). Similarly, for the 5- to 8-year-olds, practically no relationship emerged ($R = -.006$, $R^2 = .00004$, $F(1,77) = .003$, $p = .954$). For the 9- to 12-year-olds, a marginally significant negative relationship emerged ($R = -.209$, $R^2 = .044$, $F(1,63) = 2.875$, $p = .091$). Finally, for the 13- to 15-year-olds, a highly significant positive relationship emerged ($R = .663$, $R^2 = .439$, $F(1,12) = 13.311$, $p = .002$).

These results might be interpreted in the following manner. Up to and including 9 to 12 years of age, the prohibition made by the adult homeowner against stealing represents a legitimate behavioral standard, and stealing represents a real antisocial behavior. As children grow older, they become more responsive to group effects on self-attention processes, so that they become more likely to steal in the larger group than in the smaller group. Stealing represents antisocial behavior in the sense of the absence of regulation, brought about by an increase in group size. However, among the 13- to 15-year-olds, the prohibition made by the adult homeowner represents something other than a legitimate behavioral standard. In fact, one might argue that the legitimate behavioral standards for adolescents on Halloween encourage the making of mischief and engaging in acts of petty theft and vandalism. Thus, for these young adolescents (who are sufficiently responsive to the effects of group settings on self-attention processes), stealing represents antisocial behavior in the sense of the self-regulation to otherwise antinormative standards of behavior. These adolescent trick or treaters were more likely to steal in a smaller group, whereas the larger groups apparently interfered with self-attention processes and made stealing less likely to occur. Thus, antisocial behavior, typically conceived in terms of the absence of self-regulation, might occur in certain circumstances as a result of self-regulation toward otherwise antisocial standards of behavior.

Verbal Disfluencies among Stutterers

One phenomenon of special interest is the effect of group contexts on verbal disfluencies among stutterers. Stuttering has often been conceptualized as a consequent of self-focused attention (Brown, 1945; Dittman & Lewellyn, 1969; Schwartz, 1976; Wicklund, 1975). Therefore, a larger audience would be assumed to increase the stutterer's level of self-attention and thereby exacerbate the stutterer's verbal disfluencies.

This line of reasoning has recently been examined in the context of two procedures that measured verbal disfluency on the part of stutterers speaking in front of audiences of varying sizes (Mullen, in press a). In these procedures (cf., Hahn, 1940; Porter, 1939), Other–Total Ratios can be calculated for stutterers as the number of people in the audience divided by the sum of the number of people in the audience and the number of stutterers. The percentage of words stuttered by each subject under each audience condition was regressed upon the corresponding Other–Total

Ratios for each subject, yielding a regression analysis for each of Hahn's 52 subjects and for each of Porter's 13 subjects. These analyses revealed that the Other–Total Ratio accurately predicted the extent of stuttering in a manner that was both statistically significant and of considerable magnitude, both for Hahn's subjects ($Z = 5.522$, $p = .000000019$; $\bar{R} = .889$, $\bar{R}^2 = .790$) and for Porter's subjects ($Z = 5.504$, $p = .00000002$, $\bar{R} = .808$, $\bar{R}^2 = .652$). Thus, stutterers exhibited greater verbal disfluencies in front of larger audiences, as predicted by the Other–Total Ratio.

The Effects of Multiple Subgroups

The foregoing examination of verbal disfluencies among stutterers sets the context for a more substantive extension of the self-attention theory, Other–Total Ratio perspective. The applications described previously in this chapter were limited to relatively simple group contexts involving two subgroups (e.g., teachers and students). However, we can begin to consider more complex groups comprised of multiple subgroups. For example, in a class setting, a minority student is confronted with two distinct Other subgroups: the nonminority students, and the teacher. If a complex group is comprised of multiple subgroups that do in fact serve as distinct stimulus entities to the members of the group setting (Campbell, 1958), it is reasonable to expect the effects of each subgroup on the individual to combine in an additive manner. The individual might experience exaggerated self-attention when confronted with multiple, distinct Other subgroups. This is consistent with Stonequist's (1937) treatment of the "marginal man," Hartley's (1951) seminal consideration of the effects of multiple group memberships, and more recent examinations of the effects of multiple subgroups (cf., Brewer & Kramer, 1984; Wong-Rieger & Taylor, 1981).

In a sense, the complex group may be best characterized in terms of multiple Other–Total Ratios, derived for the Self subgroup with reference to each distinct subgroup of Others. For example, consider a group of 10 people comprised of two subgroups. The lone Self confronted with one Other subgroup of nine Others would be expected to experience relatively high self-attention [Other–Total Ratio $= 9/(9 + 1)$], the Other–Total Ratio $= .900$. However, consider the group of 10 people comprised of three distinct subgroups. If those nine Others belong to two distinct Other subgroups of four Others and five Others, then the lone Self would be expected to experience even higher self-attention [Additive Other–Total Ratio $= (4/(4 + 1)) + (5/(5 + 1)) = .800 + .833$], the Additive Other–Total Ratio $= 1.633$. This exaggerated effect of multiple distinct subgroups is precisely the type of result obtained by Wilder (1977), in studying the effects of multiple subgroups on conformity. Wilder's (1977) study takes on special significance in light of the applicability of this self-attention theory Other–Total Ratio approach to conformity behavior (Mullen, 1983, Study 3).

In order to determine whether these additive effects of multiple subgroups can be predicted in the manner specified above, an analysis was conducted on the effects of multiple subgroups on stuttering (Mullen, 1985b). Barber (1939) reported the results of a procedure similar to those of Hahn (1940) and Porter (1939) discussed above. The major difference was that three subgroups could be identified in Barber's procedure: the number of stutterers (Self), the number of Others actively listening to and tabulating the stutterers' verbal disfluencies (Active Other), and the number of Others passively sitting and waiting (Passive Other). The simple Other–Total Ratio can be calculated for stutterers as the total number of Others divided by the sum of the total number of Others and the number of stutterers. The Additive Other–Total Ratio can be calculated for the stutterers as the sum of the simple Other–Total Ratio derived with reference to the Active Others and the simple Other–Total Ratio derived with reference to the Passive Others.

Although the simple Other–Total Ratio was a relatively strong predictor ($Z = 5.86$, $p = .000000003$, $\bar{R} = .732$, $\bar{R}^2 = .535$), the Additive Other–Total Ratio was even stronger ($Z = 6.978$, $p = .000000001$, $\bar{R} = .814$, $\bar{R}^2 = .662$). For 17 of Barber's 18 subjects, the Additive Other–Total Ratio was superior to the simple Other–Total Ratio, with the Additive Other–Total Ratio accounting for an additional 13% of the variability in stuttering beyond that accounted for by the simple Other–Total Ratio.

Mullen and Story (1985) have recently replicated this Additive Other–Total Ratio approach. In this procedure (cf. Dabbs, Ruback, Purvis, & Hopper, 1983), college students participated in five-person discussion groups. Group composition varied in terms of race and gender, producing up to four subgroups in any given five-person group (male Caucasian, female Caucasian, male non-Caucasian, female non-Caucasian). The behavior of the non-Caucasian subjects was not examined (being invariably a minority in these groups, there were very few of these subjects, and their simple and Additive Other–Total Ratios were extremely high with little or no variability). For the Caucasian subjects, males were assumed to have a relatively good outcome expectancy, and females were assumed to have relatively poor outcome expectancy, regarding their group discussion participation (cf. Dweck, Goetz, & Strauss, 1980; Sutherland, 1978; Terborg, 1977). The simple Other–Total Ratio provided marginally significant predictions of discussion participation for males ($R = .269$, $R^2 = .072$, $F(1,43) = 3.349$, $p = .0742$), and insignificant predictions for females ($R = -.036$, $R^2 = .001$, $F(1,36) = .046$, $p = .831$). The Additive Other–Total Ratio did provide statistically significant predictions of discussion participation for males ($R = .403$, $R^2 = .162$, $F(1,43) = 8.328$, $p = .0061$), but not for females

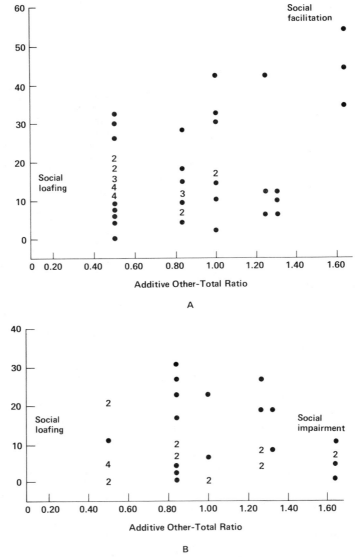

Figure 7.3. Discussion participation as a function of Additive Other–Total Ratios and gender/outcome expectancy. A. Male Caucasian subjects. B. Female Caucasian subjects.

$(R = -.070, R^2 = .005, F(1,36) = .176, p = .678)$. Visually, these results (presented in Figure 7.3) bear a striking resemblance to the predictions presented previously in Figure 7.2. This analysis both replicates the utility of the Additive Other–Total Ratio and lends support to the self-attention theory integration of social facilitation–impairment–loafing effects.

Conclusion

This chapter has described the application of self-attention theory to the effect of the group on the individual. This perspective is similar to alternative current theoretical approaches in its concern with the effects of group composition (e.g., Brewer & Kramer, 1985; Latané, 1981; Tanford & Penrod, 1984). However, some of the distinguishing attributes of the self-attention theory perspective should also be highlighted. First and foremost, this approach is based upon the measurable mediating mechanism of self-attention. Research continues to accumulate regarding the variations in self-attention that can be predicted as a result of variations in group composition. Second, variations in self-attention and associated intentional behaviors are predictable a priori, based upon knowledge of the group's composition, rather than a posteriori, postdicting the behavior of concern. Third, this approach to the effect of the group on the individual can be successfully extended to those group contexts comprised of multiple subgroups.

The inherently nonlinear and relativistic nature of the effect of the group on the individual should be emphasized. It is important to recognize that the Other–Total Ratio is not merely redundant to, or an inaccurate distortion of, the effects of the mere size of any given subgroup alone. Correlations between the Other–Total Ratio and the group behavior of concern are invariably higher than the corresponding correlations based on mere group size. In those analyses where both subgroups vary in size, the differences between mere size predictions and Other–Total Ratio predictions become quite dramatic. For example, recall the magnitude of the relationships between participation in religious groups and the Other–Total Ratio ($\bar{R} = .602$, $\bar{R}^2 = .362$). The results of similar analysis based upon the mere number of congregation members ($\bar{R} = -.376$, $\bar{R}^2 = .106$) or the mere number of ministers ($\bar{R} = .011$, $\bar{R}^2 = .0001$) highlight this point: the individual's focus of attention and resultant social behaviors appear to be affected by the size of the individual's own subgroup relative to the other subgroup, and not by the mere size of any given subgroup alone.

Acknowledgments. This chapter is based, in part, on a paper presented at the annual meeting of the Eastern Psychological Association in Baltimore, MD, April 12–15, 1983. The author would like to thank Marilynn Brewer, Charles Carver, Ed Diener, and Al Goethals for helpful comments on an earlier version of this manuscript, and Ed Diener and James Dabbs for providing original data to be used for reanalysis.

References

Albert, S. (1977). Temporal comparison theory. *Psychological Review, 84*, 485–503.
Allen, V.L., & Levine, J.M. (1971). Social support and conformity: The role of independent assessment of reality. *Journal of Experimental Social Psychology, 7*, 148–158.
Angell, J.R. (1904). *Psychology.* New York: Henry Holt.

Barber, V. (1939). Studies in the psychology of stuttering, XV. Chorus reading as a distraction in stuttering. *Journal of Speech Disorders, 4*, 371–383.

Baumeister, R.F. (1984). Choking under pressure: Self-consciousness and paradoxical effects of incentives on skillful performance. *Journal of Personality and Social Psychology, 46*, 610–620.

Baumeister, R.F., & Steinhilber, A. (1984). Paradoxical effects of supportive audiences on performance under pressure: The home killer choke effect in sports championships. *Journal of Personality and Social Psychology, 47*, 85–93.

Bjorkman, M. (1969). On the ecological relevance of psychological research. *Scandanavian Journal of Psychology, 10*, 145–157.

Bloom, J.R., Ross, R.D., & Burnell, G. (1978). The effect of social support on patient adjustment after breast surgery. *Patient Counseling and Health Education, 1*, 50–59.

Bond, C.F. (1982). Social facilitation: A self-presentational view. *Journal of Personality and Social Psychology, 42*, 1042–1050.

Bond, C.F. (1983). Social facilitation: A meta-analysis of 241 studies. *Psychological Bulletin, 94*, 265–292.

Brehm, S.S. (1976). *The application of social psychology to clinical practice.* New York: Wiley.

Brewer, M.B., & Kramer, R.M. (1984). Subgroup identity as a factor in the conservation of resources. Paper presented at the meeting of the American Psychological Association, Toronto, Canada. August 24–28.

Brewer, M.B., & Kramer, R.M. (1985). The psychology of intergroup attitudes and behavior. In *Annual Review of Psychology* (Vol. 36). Palo Alto, CA: Annual Reviews, Inc..

Brown, S.F. (1945). The loci of stutterings in the speech sequence. *Journal of Speech Disorders, 10*, 181–192.

Buss, A.H., Iscoe, I., & Buss, E.H. (1979). The development of embarrassment. *Journal of Social Psychology, 193*, 227–230.

Campbell, D.T. (1958). Common fate, similarity, and other indices of the status of aggregates of persons as social entities. *Behavioral Science, 3*, 14–25.

Carver, C.S. (1974). Facilitation of physical aggression through objective self-awareness. *Journal of Experimental Social Psychology, 10*, 365–370.

Carver, C.S. (1979). A cybernetic model of self-attention processes. *Journal of Personality and Social Psychology, 37*, 1251–1281.

Carver, C.S. (1984). Cybernetics: Meta-theoretical implications for social psychology. Paper presented at the annual meeting of the Society of Southeastern Social Psychologists.

Carver, C.S., & Blaney, P.H. (1977). Perceived arousal, focus of attention and avoidance behavior. *Journal of Abnormal Psychology, 86*, 154–162.

Carver, C.S., Blaney, P.H., & Scheier, M.F. (1979). Focus of attention, chronic expectancy and responses to a feared stimulus. *Journal of Personality and Social Psychology, 37*, 1186–1195.

Carver, C.S., Blaney, P.H., & Scheier, M.F. (1980). Reassertion and giving up: The interactive role of self-attention and outcome expectancy. *Journal of Personality and Social Psychology, 37*, 1859–1870.

Carver, C.S., & Scheier, M.F. (1981). *Attention and self-regulation: A control theory approach to human behavior.* New York: Springer-Verlag.

Cooley, C.H. (1908). A study of the use of self-words by a child. *Psychological Review, 15*, 334–357.

Coren, S., Porac, C., & Ward, L.M. (1979). *Sensation and perception.* New York: Academic Press.

Dabbs, J.M., Ruback, R.B., Purvis, J.A., & Hopper, C.H. (1983). Grouptalk: An investigation into group process. Paper presented at the meeting of the American Psychological Association, Anaheim, CA. August 23–27.

Damsteegt, D.C., & Christoffersen, J. (1982). Objective self-awareness as a variable in counseling process and outcome. *Journal of Counseling Psychology, 29*, 421–424.

Dean, A., & Lin, N. (1977). The stress-buffering role of social support. *Journal of Nervous and Mental Disease, 165*, 403–417.

Diener, E. (1980). Deindividuation: The absence of self-awareness and self-regulation in group members. In P.B. Paulus (Ed.), *Psychology of group influence*. Hillsdale, NJ: Erlbaum.

Diener, E., Westford, K.L., Diener, C., & Beaman, A.L. (1973). Deindividuating effects of group presence and arousal on stealing by Halloween trick-or-treaters. Paper presented at the meeting of the American Psychological Association, Washington, DC.

Dillon, J. (1982). Male-female similarities in class participation. *Journal of Educational Research, 75*, 350–353.

Dittman, A.T., & Lewellyn, L.G. (1969). Body movement and speech rhythm in social conversation. *Journal of Personality and Social Psychology, 11*, 98–106.

Duval, S., & Siegal, K. (1978). Some determinants of objective self-awareness: Quantitative novelty. Paper presented at the meeting of the American Psychological Association, Toronto, Canada.

Duval, S., & Wicklund, R.A. (Eds.). (1972). *A theory of objective self-awareness*. New York: Academic Press.

Duval, S., Wicklund, R.A., & Fine, R.L. (1972). Avoidance of objective self-awareness under conditions of high and low intra-self discrepancies. In S. Duval & R.A. Wicklund (Eds.), *A theory of objective self awareness*. New York: Academic Press.

Dweck, C.S., Goetz, T.E., & Strauss, N.L. (1980). Sex differences in learned helplessness: IV. An experimental and naturalistic study of failure generalization and its mediators. *Journal of Personality and Social Psychology, 38*, 441–452.

Exner, J.E. (1973). The self-focus sentence completion blanks: A study of egocentricity. *Journal of Personality Assessment, 37*, 437–455.

Feinberg, R.A., Miller, F.G., Mathews, G., & Denig, G. (1979). The social facilitation of learned helplessness. Paper presented at the meeting of the Midwestern Psychological Association, Chicago.

Fenigstein, A., Scheier, M.F., & Buss, A.H. (1975). Public and private self-consciousness: Assessment and theory. *Journal of Consulting and Clinical Psychology, 43*, 522–527.

Festinger, L. (1954). A theory of social comparison processes. *Human Relations, 7*, 117–140.

Festinger, L., Pepitone, A., & Newcomb, T. (1952). Some consequences of de-individuation in a group. *Journal of Abnormal and Social Psychology, 47*, 382–389.

Geen, R.G. (1980). The effects of being observed on performance. In P.B. Paulus (Ed.), *Psychology of group influence*. Hillsdale, NJ: Erlbaum.

Gerard, H.B., & Hoyt, M.F. (1974). Distinctiveness of social categorization and attitude toward ingroup members. *Journal of Personality and Social Psychology, 29*, 836–842.

Gibbons, F.X., Smith, T.W., Ingram, R.E., Pearce, K., Brehm, S.S., & Schroeder, D.J. (1985). Self-awareness and self-confrontation: Effects of self-focused attention on members of a clinical population. *Journal of Personality and Social Psychology, 48*, 622–675.

Ginzburg, R. (1962). *100 years of lynching*. New York: Lancer.

Glass, G., & Smith, M.L. (1979). Meta-analysis of research on the relationship of class size and achievement. *Educational Evaluation and Policy Analysis, 1*, 2–16.

Goethals, G.R., & Darley, J.M. (1977). Social comparison theory: An attribution approach. In J. Suls & R.L. Miller (Eds.), *Social comparison processes: Theoretical and empirical perspectives.* Washington, DC: Hemisphere.

Hahn, E.F. (1940). A study of the relationship between the social complexity of the oral reading situation and the severity of stuttering. *Journal of Speech Disorders, 5,* 5-14.

Hammersla, J.F., (1983). Cult conversions: The role of deindividuation in attitude change. Paper presented at the meeting of the American Psychological Association, Washington, DC. August 23-27.

Harkins, S., Latané, B., & Williams, K. (1980). Social loafing: Allocating effort or taking it easy? *Journal of Experimental Social Psychology, 16,* 457-465.

Hartley, E. (1951). Psychological problems of multiple group membership. In J.H. Roherer & M. Sherif (Eds.), *Social psychology at the crossroads.* New York: Harper & Brothers.

Heider, F. (1958). *The psychology of interpersonal relations.* New York: Wiley.

Hoffer, E. (1951). *The true believer.* New York: Harper.

Hoffer, E. (1954). *The passionate state of mind.* New York: Harper.

Hormuth, S.E. (1982). Self-awareness and drive theory: Comparing internal standards and dominant responses. *European Journal of Social Psychology, 12,* 31-45.

Hull, J.G. (1981). A self-awareness model of the causes and effects of alcohol consumption. *Journal of Abnormal Psychology, 90,* 586-600.

Ingham, A.G., Levinger, G., Graves, J. & Peckham, V. (1974). The Ringelmann effect: Studies of group size and group performance. *Journal of Experimental Social Psychology, 10,* 371-384.

Jacobs, R.C., & Campbell, D.T. (1961). Perpetuation of an arbitrary tradition through several generations of a laboratory microculture. *Journal of Abnormal and Social Psychology, 62,* 649-658.

James, W. (1890). *The principles of psychology.* New York: Holt.

Kagan, J. (1981). The emergence of consciousness in the second year. Paper presented at the meeting of the Eastern Psychological Association, New York, NY. April 22-25.

Kerr, N.L., & Bruun, S.E. (1981). Ringelmann revisited: Alternative explanations for the social loafing effect. *Personality and Social Psychology Bulletin, 7,* 224-231.

Koffka, K. (1935). *Principles of gestalt psychology.* New York: Harcourt, Brace.

Kohler, W. (1947). *Gestalt psychology.* New York: Mentor.

Krueger, E.T., & Reckless, W.C. (1932). *Social psychology.* New York: Longmans Green & Company.

Lang, L.H. (1980). A new prescription: The family. *America's Health, 2,* 6-7.

Latané, B. (1981). The psychology of social impact. *American Psychologist, 36,* 343-356.

LeBon, G. (1895/1960). *The Crowd.* New York: Viking Press.

Liese, B. (1983). Self-awareness in the therapeutic context. Unpublished doctoral dissertation, State University of New York at Albany.

MacDougall, R. (1916). The self and mental phenomena. *Psychological Review, 23,* 1-29.

MacNeil, M.K., & Sherif, M. (1976). Norm change over subject generations as a function of arbitrariness of prescribed norm. *Journal of Personality and Social Psychology, 34,* 762-773.

Mann, L. (1981). The baiting crowd in episodes of threatened suicide. *Journal of Personality and Social Psychology, 41,* 703-709.

McDougall, W. (1908). *An introduction to social psychology.* London: Methuen.

Mead, G.H. (1934). *Mind, self and society.* Chicago: University of Chicago Press.

Milgram, S. (1974). *Obedience to authority.* New York: Harper & Row.

Montgomery, R.L., Hinkle, S.W., & Enzie, R.F. (1976). Arbitrary norms and social change in high- and low-authoritarian societies. *Journal of Personality and Social Psychology, 33*, 698–708.

Mullen, B. (1983). Operationalizing the effect of the group on the individual: A self-attention perspective. *Journal of Experimental Social Psychology, 19*, 295–322.

Mullen, B. (1984). Participation in religious groups as a function of group composition: A self-attention perspective. *Journal of Applied Social Psychology, 14*, 509–518.

Mullen, B. (1985a). Participation in classroom discussion as a function of class composition: A self-attention perspective. Paper presented at the meeting of the American Educational Research Association, Chicago, IL. March 31–April 4.

Mullen, B. (1985b). The effect of multiple subgroups on the individual: A self-attention perspective. Paper presented at the meeting of the Eastern Psychological Association, Boston, MA. March 21–24.

Mullen, B. (in press a) Stuttering, audience size and the Other–Total Ratio: A self-attention perspective. *Journal of Applied Social Psychology.*

Mullen, B. (in press b) Atrocity as a function of lynch mob composition: A self-attention perspective. *Personality and Social Psychology Bulletin.*

Mullen, B., & Hu, L. (1986). Group composition, the self, and religious experience: East and west. Paper presented at the International Conference on Eastern Approaches to Self and Mind. Cardiff, Wales, July 11–14.

Mullen, B., Johnson, D.A., & Drake, S.D. (1985). Organizational productivity as a function of group composition: A self-attention perspective. Unpublished manuscript. Syracuse University, Syracuse, NY.

Mullen, B., & Peaugh, S. (1985). Focus of Attention in the Executive Office Building: A self-attention perspective. Unpublished manuscript, Syracuse University, Syracuse, NY.

Mullen, B., & Rosenthal, R. (1985). *BASIC meta-analysis: Procedures and programs.* Hillsdale, NJ: Erlbaum.

Mullen, B., & Story, J.E. (1985). Effects of multiple subgroups and outcome expectancy on participation in discussion. Unpublished manuscript. Syracuse University, Syracuse, NY.

Peirce, C.S. (1868). Questions concerning certain functions claimed for man. *Journal of Speculative Philosophy, 2*, 103–114.

Pinto, L.J., & Crow, K.E. (1982). The effect of size on other structural attributes of congregations within the same denomination. *Journal of the Scientific Study of Religion, 21*, 304–316.

Porter, H.V.K. (1939). Studies in the psychology of stuttering: XIV. Stuttering phenomena in relation to the size and personnel of audience. *Journal of Speech Disorders, 4*, 323–333.

Riley, D.A. (1958). The nature of the effective stimulus in animal discrimination learning. *Psychological Review, 65*, 1–7.

Rosenthal, R. (1980). *New directions for methodology of social and behavioral science: Quantitative assessment of research domains.* San Francisco, CA: Jossey-Bass.

Rosenthal, R. (1984). *Meta-analytic procedures for social research.* Beverly Hills, CA: Sage.

Ross, E.A. (1908). *Social psychology.* New York: Macmillan.

Royce, J. (1895). Self-consciousness, social consciousness and nature. *The Philosophical Review, 4*, 465–485; 577–602.

Scheier, M.F., Fenigstein, A., & Buss, A.H. (1974). Self-awareness and physical aggression. *Journal of Experimental Social Psychology, 10*, 264–273.

Schwartz, M.F. (1976). *Stuttering solved.* New York: McGraw-Hill.

Shaffer, J.B.P., & Galinsky, M.D. (1979). *Models of group therapy and sensitivity training.* Englewood Cliffs, NJ: Prentice-Hall.

Simmel, G. (1950). *The sociology of Georg Simmel* (K. Wolff, transl.). New York: Free Press.

Steenbarger, B.N., & Aderman, D. (1979). Objective self-awareness as a nonaversive state: Effect of anticipatory discrepancy reduction. *Journal of Personality, 47,* 330–339.

Stonequist, E.V. (1937). *The marginal man.* Chicago: Charles Scribner's Sons.

Suls, J., & Mullen, B. (1982). From the cradle to the grave: Comparison and self-evaluation across the life-span. In J. Suls (Ed.), *Psychological perspectives on the self* (Vol. 1). Hillsdale, NJ: Erlbaum.

Sutherland, S.L. (1978). The unambitious female: Women's low professional aspirations. *Signs, 3,* 774–794.

Tanford, S., & Penrod, S. (1984). Social influence model: A formal integration of research on majority and minority influence processes. *Psychological Bulletin, 95,* 189–225.

Terborg, J.R. (1977). Women in management: A research review. *Journal of Applied Psychology, 62,* 647–664.

Tice, D.M., & Baumeister, R.F. (1984). Development of self-consciousness: When does audience pressure disrupt performance? Paper presented at the annual meeting of the American Psychological Association, Toronto, Ontario. August 24–28.

Wegner, D.M., & Guiliano, T. (1980). Arousal-induced attention to self. *Journal of Personality and Social Psychology, 38,* 719–726.

Wegner, D.M. & Guiliano, T. (1983). On sending artifact in search of artifact: Reply to McDonald, Harris and Maher. *Journal of Personality and Social Psychology, 44,* 290–293.

Wegner, D.M., & Schaefer, D. (1978). The concentration of responsibility: An objective self-awareness analysis of group size effects in helping situations. *Journal of Personality and Social Psychology, 36,* 147–155.

Wicker, A.W. (1969). Size of church membership and members' support of church behavior settings. *Journal of Personality and Social Psychology, 13,* 278–288.

Wicklund, R.A. (1975). Objective self-awareness. In L. Berkowitz (Ed.), *Advances in experimental social psychology* (Vol. 8). New York: Academic Press.

Wicklund, R.A. (1980). Group contact and self-focused attention. In P.B. Paulus (Ed.), *Psychology of group influence.* Hillsdale, NJ: Erlbaum.

Wicklund, R.A. (1982). How society uses self-awareness. In J. Suls (Ed.), *Psychological perspectives on the self* (Vol. 1). Hillsdale, NJ: Erlbaum.

Wilder, D.A. (1977). Perceptions of groups, size of opposition and social influence. *Journal of Experimental Social Psychology, 13,* 253–268.

Wong-Rieger, D., & Taylor, D.M. (1981). Multiple group membership and self-identity. *Journal of Cross-Cultural Psychology, 12,* 61–79.

Zajonc, R.B. (1965). Social facilitation. *Science, 149,* 269–274.

Ziller, R.C. (1964). Individuation and socialization: A theory of assimilation in large organizations. *Human Relations, 17,* 341–360.

Zimbardo, P. (1970). The human choice: Individuation, reason and order versus deindividuation, impulse, and chaos. In W. J. Arnold & D. Levine (Eds.), *Nebraska symposium on motivation* (Vol. 18). Lincoln, NE: University of Nebraska Press.

Chapter 8

Social Cognition Theory of Group Processes

John B. Pryor and Thomas M. Ostrom

The perspective of social cognition researchers on group processes is unabashedly *intrapsychic*. All social organizations, be they face to face groups or loosely knit aggregates, have a corresponding existance in the perceiver's cognitive organization of social information. This perspective maintains that virtually all group processes are understandable through an analysis of how individual group members process group-relevant information.

We begin this chapter with an overview of some of the basic information processing principles that are employed in social cognition research. The reader will note that most of these principles are drawn from cognitive psychology. The social cognition perspective is part of a larger inter-disciplinary effort kown as *cognitive science*. Cognitive science draws from philosophy, neuropsychology, linguistics, social psychology, and cognitive psychology to understand better how people come to comprehend their physical and social environments. This perspective provides a coherent theoretical basis for understanding interpersonal behavior (Fiske & Taylor, 1984; Markus & Zajonc, 1985) and intergroup relations (Stephan, 1984).

Basic Concepts and Processes

It is convenient to divide information processing into three basic sub-processes: *encoding, representation,* and *retrieval* (Crowder, 1976; Hastie & Carlston, 1980; Pryor & Ostrom, 1981). In a simplistic sense one may think of these subprocesses as representing a linear chain of cognitive events. It is certainly true that an item cannot be retrieved unless it is cognitively represented and an item cannot be represented unless it has been first been encoded. It is more accurate, however, to view the three subprocesses as highly interrelated.

Common to all three subprocesses is the concept that humans are *active* information processors. An item of information is not passively shuttled from one phase to another. Rather, it is transformed by each subprocess in systematic ways. Further, each subprocess can affect the workings of the other two. Nevertheless, for expository purposes we shall retain this division. Below we examine each subprocess in turn.

Encoding

Our sense organs are receptive to a wide variety of physical stimulation. It is, of course, impossible for the brain to retain every detail of this stimulation. The encoding phase involves selecting what from the environment is to be retained. There are at least at least three important components involved in encoding processes: processing objectives, schematic expectations, and information structure.

Processing objectives. Processing objectives refer to the immediate goals of the social perceiver in using social information. Some examples of processing objectives that have been examined in previous research include the following: forming an impression of a person or a group, memorizing information about a person or a group, empathizing with a person, predicting a person's future behavior, and judging the relevance of information for the self (Greenwald & Pratkanis, 1984, Hamilton, Katz, & Leier, 1980; Hoffman, Mischel, & Mazze, 1981; Srull, 1981). Some studies have combined one or more of these objectives in the instructions given subjects (e.g., Hastie & Kumar, 1979; Pryor, Simpson, Mitchel, Ostrom, & Lydon, 1982).

Processing objectives may serve any of the following functions: First, they may influence the "depth" with which information is processed (Craik & Tulving, 1975). Some processing objectives seem to promote more extensive processing of social information than others. For example, the objective of forming an impression of a person or a group may encourage more consideration of apparent inconsistencies in social information (Srull, 1981) and more active attempts to impose an organization upon the information than the goal of simply memorizing social information (Hamilton *et al.*, 1980).

Second, processing objectives may influence the extent to which prior expectancies influence encoding. Those objectives that encourage deeper processing seem to promote an active comparison of incoming information to prior expectancies (Srull, 1981). Also, specific processing objectives may evoke certain schematic structures. For example, Ostrom, Lingle, Pryor, and Geva (1980) asked subjects to judge the suitability of a stimulus person for an occupation. This evoked subjects' expectatons of the characteristics stereotypically associated with the occupation (e.g., the characteristics associated with being a good pilot) which in turn affected what information subjects retained in memory. As another example, Hoffman *et al.* (1981) found that asking subjects to recall information about or to empathize with another person resulted in subjects' organizing information in terms of the actor's goals, whereas asking subjects to form an impression of the person or try to predict his future behaviors resulted in their organizing information in terms of underlying traits.

Third, processing objectives may guide attention during information acquisition, sensitizing the social perceiver to information and structures that are relevant to the goals at hand. For example, Pryor *et al.* (1982) have found that requiring subjects to make individual evaluations of the members of a group can result in subjects paying closer attention to which individuals were associated with specific facts.

Schemata and encoding. Below we shall elaborate on some conceptions of schematic knowledge, but for now let us consider a schema to be conveniently defined as any expectation a perceiver has about how information may go together (Hastie, 1981, employs a similar definition). During encoding schematic expectations are thought to guide information processing. They lend structure to what may be otherwise ambiguous social experience, help a perceiver to fill in missing information in an information configuration, and help the perceiver to quickly identify appropriate units or "chunks" (Taylor & Crocker, 1981). Some schematic structures, such as scripts, also help a perceiver anticipate the temporal flow of social events (Abelson, 1981). In sum, schemata determine what a perceiver will attend to and deem important in social experience and what he/she will ignore and deem irrelevant.

Structure. While a perceiver's expectations may impose organization upon a social experience, organization may also be inherent in the sequence and correlational structure of experiences (Garner, 1974; McArthur & Baron, 1985). For example, Pryor, Kott, and Bovee (1984) have found that the relative redundancy of different potential organizational structures influences their discriminability during encoding. In this study, subjects were asked to memorize 18 behaviors performed by a group of six persons (each person did three things). Three of the behaviors were also related to each of six personality traits. Pryor *et al.* found that the more the persons overlapped or were correlated with the traits (the more that behaviors from a common trait category were attributed to a specific individual) the more discriminable the persons were as organizing categories during encoding. Ostrom and Pryor (in press) have found conceptually similar effects in variations in the relationship between person categories and the temporal sequence of information. The more information about individuals in a group was arranged according to person units the more the individuals were discriminable as organizing categories during encoding (see also Pusateri, Devine, Ostrom, & McCann, 1984). All of these studies suggest that the naturally occuring structure of social experience may importantly influence encoding by making some ways of organizing information more salient than others.

Other variations of how information is structured may have important implications for encoding. Many of these variations influence attention. For, example the relative infrequency of the members of a specific social group in a social situation will draw attention to the members of the group. This may make their behaviors more memorable because of extensive encoding (Hamilton, Dugan, & Troiler, 1985). Other findings suggest that being the solo or "token" member of a minority group in a small group makes an individual appear to have a more prominent role in group discussions (Taylor, Fiske, Close, Anderson, & Ruderman, 1977). Several studies have documented that "figure–ground" configurations can encourage more extensive processing of a social entity and thereby enhance its memorability and the polarization of judgments made about it (Pryor & Kriss, 1977; Taylor & Fiske, 1978).

Representation

In this section we review two approaches to conceptualizing the cognitive representations of encoded information: the associative network approach and the schematic memory approach. Although other possible approaches could also be discussed (e.g., Fiske, Kenney, & Taylor, 1982; Lord, 1980; Wyer & Srull, 1980), these two basic approaches are those most commonly used in modern social cognition research.

The two approaches share the assumption that information, beliefs, inferences, and other cognitive products can be represented as descrete elements in memory. These elements are linked to one another to form meaningful structures, such that when one element in a structure is activated, the others become highly accessible.

The two approaches differ in their level of analysis. The associative network approach focuses on the detailed assumptions involved in representing information in terms of elements and links. These issues are of fundamental concern to researchers in cognitive psychology. The schematic representation approach employs a broader perspective, focusing more on the nature of the overall cognitive structures. It is less concerned with specific network assumptions, dealing more with properties of the structures that are invariant over different sets of assumptions. Although most work in social cognition has been at this latter level of analysis, the two levels must ultimately be combined.

Associative networks. The concept of human memory as an associative network is certainly not new to psychology. The interested reader should consult Anderson and Bower (1973) for an excellent review of the history of this idea. Part of the rejuvenated interest in the last dozen years is perhaps related to the use of this concept as a basic building block in computer simulations of human memory. The most notable of these simluations appears in the work of Anderson and his colleagues. The basic concept of an associative network describes human memory as a series of idea nodes linked by associative pathways of varying strength. The strength of any associative link is generally believed to be related to the frequency and recency of its activation (Hayes-Roth, 1977). Node–link arrangements may either be undifferentiated or hierarchically organized (Hastie, Park, & Weber, 1984).

Although nodes and pathways can describe the structure of information in memory they provide no clue about the dynamics of this structure. One concept that describes how associative networks function dynamically is "spreading activation" (Collins & Loftus, 1975). The probability of an idea being accessed is related to its level of activation. When an idea is activated, activation also spreads along the associative paths surrounding the node to connected neighboring nodes. This increases the probability of these additional nodes being accessed. Activation spreads most strongly between idea nodes that are most closely associated. Evidence for this process comes from "priming" studies, which have shown that inducing activation of a node through a task such as lexical decision making can facilitate subsequent judgments involving related nodes. For example, if a subject judges in a reaction time task whether "bacon" is a word, subsequent immediate judgments of whether "eggs" is a word are made more quickly (Warren, 1973). Thus, activation of the first concept "primes" the activation of the related second concept. Recent work in social cognition has shown that idea nodes may be primed unobtrusively (Higgins, Rholes, & Jones, 1977; Rholes & Pryor, 1982) and that idea nodes that are primed may importantly influence interpretative processes during encoding. Other work by Bargh (1984) has shown that priming may be accomplished without the subject's conscious awareness.

Crucial to social cognition is the distinction between *declarative* and *procedural* knowledge (Anderson, 1983). Earlier conceptions of associative network representations dealt primarily with declarative knowledge. This refers to knowledge about facts and things. Procedural knowledge is fundamentally different. It is "how to" knowledge that enables us to perform cognitive and behavioral tasks efficiently and automatically. It is knowledge that is goal oriented and allows us to use the cognitive system in social judgments and behavior.

Smith (1984) has suggested some interesting ways in which this distinction may apply to social inferences. For example, deciding one's attitude on a previously unconsidered issue may entail a deliberate review of related declarative knowledge. This could involve a review of one's past behavior as described by self-perception theory (Bem, 1972). Theoretically, this could be a relatively time-consuming process. However, if one has previously formed an attitude on this topic then the decision is retrieved as a previously formed procedural inference rule. Fazio, Chen, McDonel, and Sherman (1982) have found some evidence consistent with this analysis. They found that attitudes may be accessed automatically for attitude objects with which one has had direct past experience. Other research in social cognition based directly upon Smith's analysis has just begun to appear in the literature (Smith & Branscomb, 1985).

There are many unanswered questions about the specific workings of associative networks. As one example, does the system work in serial (only one node can be accessed at a time) or in parallel (can different parts of the system be accessed simultaneously) (McClelland & Rumelhart, 1981)? As a second example, are spatial images (such as visual scenes) represented as an array of descrete nodes or as a continuous information field (Klatzky, 1984; Shoben, 1984)? As a third example, what leads a person to terminate a search of memory when attempting to retrieve a specific information item (Anderson, 1983)? Although these questions are of special interest to cognitive psychology, their impact on social cognition research has yet to be felt.

Schematic representations. A schema is essentially a *generic* knowledge structure. It is a very general expectancy about how information goes together. It represents a summary of the components, attributes, and relationships that typically occur in specific exemplars. Some theorists view a schema as having *variables* that are filled by specific inputs as the schema guides comprehension (Graesser & Nakamura, 1982; Minsky, 1975; Rumelhart, 1984). Some variables may also be filled by *default values* or guesses about variables that are unobserved. Notions about the typical values and relationships of the variables in a schema are called *variable constraints*.

The concept of schema is silent regarding both the content and the configuration of the cognitive structures (Hastie & Carlston, 1980). Many traditional social psychology content domains can be represented via the schema concept. For example, *stereotypes* refer to the pattern of inferences linked to a group label, *impressions* consist of the inferences that derive from one or more personality trait labels, *attitudinal beliefs* are those evoked by the attitude object, *norms* are the set of acceptable behaviors associated with a particular setting, and *roles* are the functional obligations linked to various interpersonal orientations.

Different schematic configurations can exist. Many have the simple form of linking attributes to a common node, as when a person associates the characteristics of lazy, aggressive, and rhythm to Blacks. However, more complicated structures also exist. For example, we can have *linear orderings* (e.g., ranking group members in terms of intelligence or physical strength; Potts, 1975), *temporal structures* (e.g., scripts that guide behavior in settings such as restaurants; Abelson, 1981), and *hierarchies* (e.g., kinship patterns relating children, parents, and grandparents).

Two prominent theories concerning the role of schemata in representation are the Schema Copy plus Tag (SC + T) model developed by Graesser and his associates (Graesser & Nakamura, 1982) and the Encoding Elaboration model proposed by Hastie (Hastie, 1980, 1981; Hastie *et al.*, 1984, Srull, 1981). An analysis of schema–item relationships plays an integral role in both theories. The representation of any given information is determined by its relationship to a schema. For the SC + T model, the essential relationship of consequence to representation is typicality, the probability of the information given the schema. For example, "paying one's check" might be a highly typical event in a person's schema or script of a restaurant.

According to the SC + T model, a specific memory trace is constructed when a schema-based experience is comprehended. This memory consists of a partial copy of the generic schema that best fits the input experience and a set of *tags* for information that is atypical of the schema (marginally typical information may also receive tags). Tags are associative links that signify contrasts. The resulting memory representation consists of one organizational unit for the actually experienced or schematically inferred typical information and seperate units for each tagged item.

One consequence of this sort of representation is that subjects find it difficult to discriminate typical information actually experienced in some situation from typical information not actually experienced. On the other hand, atypical information is highly distinct and easily discriminated from other similar information. After long retention intervals memory for the specific trace decays, including the various tags. Thus, all that remains after a lengthy delay is likely to be the generic schema.

The encoding elaboration model also relies heavily upon an analysis of schema–item relationships in its account of how shemata influence representation. Here three relationships are distinguished: consistent, irrelevant, and inconsistent relationships. Hastie (1981) summarizes these relationships in terms of the probablity of the item given the schema. Items that are highly probable are considered schema consistent. Items that are of moderate probability (.50) are considered irrelevant. Finally, items that are improbable are considered inconsistent. In examples of these relationships, consider the schematic expectation that someone is friendly and outgoing. A consistent event might be, "He smiled at the delivery boy." An irrelevant event might be, "He ate a hamburger." An inconsistent event might be, "He yelled at his neighbor."

The focus of the encoding elaboration model is upon how a schema molds the episodic representation of the memory trace. According to this account, attention is drawn to inconsistent items during encoding owing to the fact that they are unexpected. The perceiver actively holds inconsistent items in memory during encoding for a longer time than consistent (expected) or irrelevant items, for the purpose of trying to explain them. During this time the perceiver may compare and contrast the inconsistent information with other information experienced in an attempt to under-stand it. In the process a rich associative network is developed connecting

the inconsistent information items to other items. This model concep-
tualizes retrieval as entering the associative network and traversing the
associative links between information items in a random fashion. Because
there are more links connecting the inconsistent items, they have a greater
probability of being retrieved. This model makes many of the same
predictions as the SC + T model. For a further comparison and contrast of
these two models, the reader may consult Hastie *et al.* (1984).

Retrieval

Retrieval is a particularly important part of information processing for
social cognition theorists because all social behaviors are at least in part
memory driven. Consider the following example of an everyday social
interaction:

> The first author of this chapter gets off the elevator on the fourth floor
> and passes by the new receptionist's desk on his way to his office. "Good
> morning, Dr. Pryor. How are you today? Is your cold better?" asks the
> receptionist.
> "Yes, thank you, Patty. Did you have a good weekend?" replies Pryor.
> "Yes, I did," says the receptionist. "My husband and I visited some
> relatives in Peoria. We had a picnic by the river on Sunday afternoon. It was
> relaxing. What did you do?"
> "It sounds like you had more fun than I did," laments Pryor. "I was up
> here most of the weekend working on a chapter that is overdue. By the way,
> did a student drop by on Friday afternoon to pick up the book I left with
> you?"
> "No," says the receptionist.
> "I guess she forgot. See you later," says Pryor as he wanders on to his
> office.

This brief encounter is ripe with examples of how memory influences
social behaviors. The two individuals immediately recognize each other and
recall specific information about each other (e.g., Pryor's cold) as well as
general information (e.g., she remembers that he is a professor and he that
she is the receptionist). A large portion of their conversation involves
recollecting past events (what happened over the weekend or what
happened Friday afternoon). Much of what we do and say in everyday
social encounters is thus driven by our memories for people and situations.
   Two basic types of retrieval processes are illustrated by the example: recall
and recognition. Recall is often considered to involve two stages. First, the
subject must retrieve a item of information from memory and then perform
some sort of recognition check to determine whether the item is the one
desired. Recognition, on the other hand, is commonly thought to bypass the
retrieval stage and involve only the second recognition check. Recognition
memory is often more accurate than recall. One explanation for this is that
it simply involves fewer processes and fewer things can go wrong (Srull,
1984). Other theorists (e.g., Mandler, 1980), however, suggest that recognition

also involves a two-stage process. The first stage involves the detection of familiarity and the second a retrieval check. The receptionist in the example above might first note to herself, "I know that guy who just got off the elevator" and then after retrieving information from memory decide, "He looks like Pryor."

The organization of the representation from which information is retrieved can affect both recognition and recall processes. The influence of organizational factors from an associative network perspective is illustrated by a pair of studies reported by Pryor and Ostrom (1981). Both of these studies involved having subjects memorize several facts about each of several persons. The facts were presented in a random order. In some conditions the persons were familiar and in other conditions the persons were unfamiliar.

Pryor and Ostrom postulated that subjects would form cohesive person by person cognitive representations of the information when the persons were familiar, but not when they were unfamiliar. In one study (Pryor & Ostrom; 1981, Study 2), this hypothesis was tested using a recognition reaction time paradigm. Subjects were presented pairs of facts from the list they memorized on a tachistoscopic device. Interspersed were also items previously unseen. They were asked to judge as quickly as possible whether both of the items in each given pair had been from the list. When the two facts were from a single familiar person this judgment was accomplished more quickly than when the two were from two different familiar people. No such difference was observed for similar comparisons involving information about unfamiliar people. Pryor and Ostrom interpret this as evidence that the information items about a particular person were stored in a proximate location when the persons were familiar, but not when the persons were unfamiliar.

A second study by Pryor and Ostrom (1981, Study 3) serves to illustrate the influence of an associative network organization upon recall. The initial exposure to the information list was roughly the same as in the previous experiment. Only here subjects were asked to freely recall the information. Person clustering patterns were examined in the free-recall protocols. *Person clustering* refers to the tendency to recall items about the same person in sequential order, even though they appeared in a random sequence during learning. These suggested a strong tendency to organize recall by persons when the persons were familiar, but not when they were unfamiliar. In terms of an associative network representation, the activation of a node in the network spreads most strongly to those nodes that are closely associated. Pryor and Ostrom (1981) conceptualize the representation of a familiar person as node link network in which individual feature nodes (facts about the person) are linked to a central person node and also possibly to each other directly. This forms a cohesive unit of information that has implications for access during retrieval. Put into simple terms terms, remembering one fact about a familiar person serves to bring other facts to mind.

Schematic organizations are also thought to have effects upon recognition and recall. Effects regarding the amount of information accurately retrieved have already been discussed in the section above on representation. The presence of a schema enhances the recognition and recall of both schema-consistent and schema-inconsistent information over schema-irrelevant information.[1] Consistent with the encoding elaboration perspective, these enhancements seem more probable when the schema is instantiated (brought to mind) during encoding (Hastie, 1981; Ostrom et al., 1980). However, research has also shown that retrieval of schema-relevant information is facilitated by instantiation during retrieval only (Dooling & Christiaansen, 1977; Hasher & Griffin, 1978; Spiro, 1977).

One of the most widely observed retrieval effects involves schema-consistent errors (Graesser & Nakamura, 1982; Spiro, 1977). In recognition studies these are usually called *false alarms*, while in recall studies they are often called *schema-consistent intrusions*. They represent an inability of subjects to discriminate schema-relevant information that actually has occurred from schema-relevant information that has not actually occurred. This tendency has been found to increase with longer time intervals between exposure and retrieval. These sorts of findings have often been used to support the argument that much of retrieval is a *reconstructive* process (Bartlett, 1932); that is, it involves schematic inferences about what probably happened instead of remembering what actually happened in a given situation. For example, if asked to recall the events that transpired when you last visited a restaurant, you would probably rely on your general knowledge of what ususlly transpires in a restaurant in formulating an answer rather than your actual memory of a specific experience.

Social Cognition in Group Settings

What is a social group? Across the seemingly endless mass of group research there seems to be no real consensus as to the definition of a social group (DeLamater, 1974; Cartwright & Zander, 1968; Mullen, Chapter 1, this volume). In this chapter we will employ a definition that emphasizes the phenomenology of the individual. A social group is any collection of persons that the individual perceives as related. Thus, in a sense, a social group is like a category.

In associative network terms, a social group is a central idea node to which is connected a collection of information pertaining to two or more

---

[1]It is important to take note that these enhancements in the recognition of consistent information are related to hit rate (i.e., correctly recognizing information that was experienced). At the same time schematic processing also frequently produces more errors in the form of schema-consistent false alarms (Graesser & Nakamura, 1982).

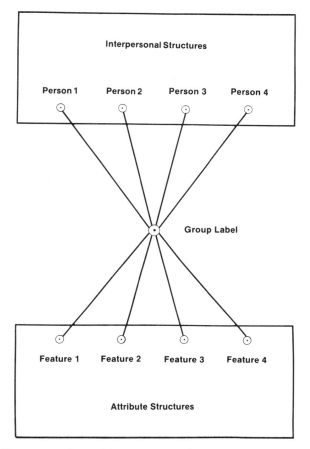

Figure 8.1. Two types of cognitive structures that can be related to a group label.

persons (Rothbart, Fulero, Jensen, Howard, & Birrell, 1978). As we discussed in the previous section on basic processes, an associative network model of cognitive representation is largely concerned with the indexing and accessing functions of memory. In this conceptual model, a group label indexes and provides an access route to knowledge about a collection of individuals. For example, "people in the weight room at the gym" could index information about a group of people one might encounter in a particular social context. When you think about this group label, specific individuals may come to mind (e.g., the guy who checks your ID at the door) or assorted facts about various people (e.g., the sound of heavy breathing). All of this information is organized by the social group label. Figure 8.1 illustrates two group label structures.

In schematic memory terms, a group is a collection of features or attributes that are expected of persons who are attributed a group label

(Cohen, 1977). Thus, the identification of the group label may help the social perceiver to understand ambigious behaviors of an individual or to infer information that is unseen. For example, imagine that you are standing in line at a ticket counter in an airport. A stranger walks up, gives you a flower and then starts to make a conversation with you. This seemingly ambiguous encounter is given meaning if you identify the person as a member of a religious cult known to acost strangers in airports in search of handouts. Given this social group label you can render an interpretation of ongoing behavior and come to expect what the mysterious stranger is leading up to in his act of generosity.

Both of these frameworks provide some interesting insights into social cognition processes that are relevant to understanding groups. It is convenient to think of these frameworks as describing two different types of cognitive structures evoked by a group label: *interpersonal structures* and *attribute structures*. Interpersonal structures involve the linkages between the nodes representing individual group members and the group node. They are invoked when the perceiver is considering the relationships between and among group members. Attribute structures involve linkages between the group label and general features that characterize the group as a whole. These two types of relationships are depicted in Figure 8.1. They emphasize two different functions that the identification of group membership may have for the individual: an organizational function and an inferential function. Below we describe two areas of social cognition research that have grown out of these frameworks.

Interpersonal structures

Basic to all interpersonal structures is the existance of nodes representing individual group members. For such structures to emerge for one specific group (e.g., a neighboring fraternity), the social perceiver must acquire knowledge about individual members of that group. The process through which such nodes are developed and subsequently used by the perceiver have been studied under the label of *person organization*.

We have conceptualized person organization as a continuum. At one end are social groups whose members are represented by distinct propositional networks. At the other end information about each individual is undifferentiatedly connected to a single group node. These extremes are represented in Figure 8.2.

Much of the original work on person organization began with the study of how people cognitively represent groups of familiar and unfamiliar people (Pryor & Ostrom, 1981). In these initial studies, high person organization was found to be characteristic of the cognitive representations of groups of familiar persons, whereas, low person organization was found to be characteristic of the cognitive representations of groups of unfamiliar persons. Although this might not seem a surprising finding on the surface,

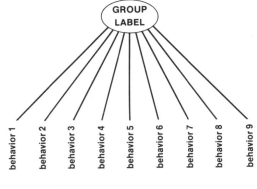

LOW PERSON ORGANIZATION

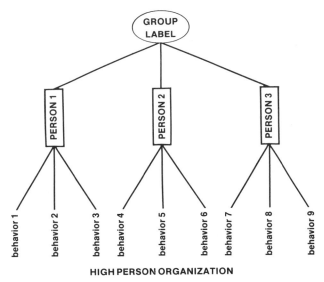

HIGH PERSON ORGANIZATION

Figure 8.2. Conceptual representation of high and low person organization in the cognitive representation of a social group.

much of the previous work on person perception processes had assumed that persons automatically emerged as organizational foci from the stream of social experience (Asch, 1951). This assumption had led person perception researchers to devote much of their effort to studying subjects' reactions to isolated individuals (Anderson, 1978). This work demonstrated that person organization does not occur automatically when subjects encounter several pieces of information about several strangers in a random order. Thus, issues of how person organizations develop must be considered when trying to understand person perception processes involving groups of unfamiliar people.

An associative network model proved a useful tool conceptualizing the factors that contribute to a strong person organization. Across several studies the following factors emerged as related to strong person organizations: (1) strong nodal associations (i.e., features pertaining to individuals are closely associated to seperate person nodes—for example, the feature "greasy hair" might be strongly associated with a Ronald Reagan node in the minds of many people); (2) strong interfeature associations (i.e., features pertaining to individuals are strongly associated to one another independently of their relationship to a specific person—for example, the behavior: "He frequently listens to Mozart" and the behavior: "He plays the piano" might describe a person under high person organization conditions); and (3) high discriminability (i.e., unique information is associated with each person) (Ostrom & Pryor, in press; Ostrom, Pryor, & Simpson, 1981; Pryor & Ostrom, 1981; 1982).

In previous sections of this chapter, we alluded to studies that showed that processing objectives and information structure can influence the degree of person organization (see the preceding section on encoding). Another factor (related to our preceding discussion of structure) that influences the degree of person organization is the presence of competing organizational alternatives. Pryor et al. (1982) found that the presence of salient organizational alternatives (e.g., knowing the hometown, occupation, and hobbies of each person in a group) can diminish person organization. Pryor et al. (1984) found that it is not the mere presence of organizational alternatives that diminishes person organization, but their relationship to persons as organizing categories. Under circumstances where organizational alternatives are orthogonal to person categories (i.e., they are uncorrelated), person organization may be diminished. However, under circumstances where organizational alternatives are redundant with person categories, person organization may be enhanced.

This summarizes our efforts to date of trying to understand some of the antecedants of person organization. Below we describe how this concept is important in understanding some specific group processes.

Judgments of individual group members. One of our initial speculations concerning person organization was that it might be related to judgments that are made about the members of a group. When person organization is high then a social perceiver may be more capable of judging each group member individually according to his/her faults and merits. When person organization is low then the judgments of group members may be less differentiated and regress toward some sort of group mean (Ostrom et al., 1981).

In the first study to test this hypothesis, Ostrom, Pryor, Pusateri, & Mitchell (1985, Study 2) induced high or low person organization in subjects' representation of a group of four unfamiliar stimulus persons using a procedure which strengthened nodal associations and accentuated interfeature associations and discriminability. The descriptions of the four stimulus persons were: highly positive, moderately positive, moderately negative, and highly negative. The evaluative judgments made of these four persons are depicted in Figure 8.3. Under conditions of high person organization subjects showed more evaluative differentation in their judgments of the four persons. A confirmatory causal analysis indicated that the manipulation used to handle person organization affected the latent variable, *person organization* (indexed by measures of clustering in free recall), which, in turn, affected the evaluative differentiation in judgments depicted in Figure P.3. This finding suggests that performance appraisals in industry (Feldman, 1981) may more accurately reflect individual variability under conditions that facilitate high person organization.

Group judgments. The degree of person organization may also be an influential factor in judgments concerning the group as a whole. Rothbart *et al.* (1978) presented subjects with evaluative information concerning the

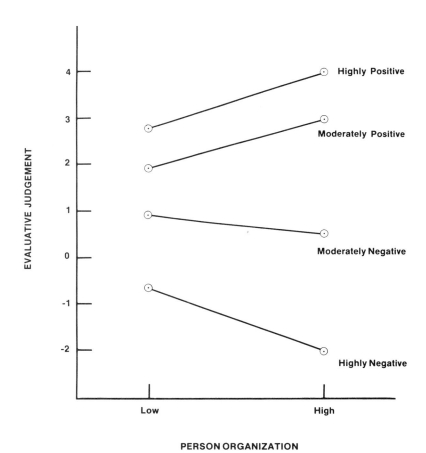

Figure 8.3. Evaluative differentiation as a function of high and low person organization.

members of a group under low and high information load conditions. Rothbart *et al.* suggest that under low information load conditions subjects are more likely to develop a seperate propositional network representation for each person in the group, whereas under high information load conditions their representations are more likely to be undifferentiated links to a single group node. These descriptions closely parallel our descriptions of high and low person organization depicted in Figure 8.2. Also varied in this experiment was the degree to which information was ascribed to specific group members. Under some conditions, each evaluative information item was ascribed to a seperate individual. Under other conditions several items were ascribed to each of several individuals.

Rothbart *et al.* found that in the low information load condition judgments made concerning the likability of the group as a whole increased as a function of the number of positively described individuals. In the high information load condition, the group evaluations increased as a function of the total number of positive items presented irrespective of the number of individuals to which they had been ascribed. Thus, under conditions that promote low person organization, the evaluation of a group may be strongly influenced by the presence of a few individuals who perform many good or bad deeds.

Social influence. One of the most consistent findings in the area of social influence is that the impact of a group upon an individual increases with group size or the number of sources of social influence (e.g., Harkins & Petty, 1981). The most commonly observed relationship between group size and social influence is a negatively accelerating power function (Jackson, Chapter 6, this volume; Latané, 1981; Mullen, 1983). Most of this research has involved manipulations of the actual number of group members and has not been concerned with manipulations designed to influence the cognitive representation of group members. An exception is the work of Wilder (1981).

Wilder (1977, 1978) asked subjects to listen to the opinions of six other people before stating their own opinions on a legal case involving personal injury. The opinions of the six other people were presented in a videotape. All six unanimously agreed in their opinions. Wilder varied the organization of the six persons in the following manner: By segmenting the videotape, the six persons were made to appear as one group of six people, two groups of three, three groups of two or six seperate individuals. Wilder found that the social influence of the six increased linearly as a function of the number of distinct social units. In explaining these results, Wilder suggests that when people are categorized into social units their opinions are no longer perceived as independent, that is, the social perceiver guesses that they may have influenced each other. Thus, the opinions of individuals who are part of the same social unit are viewed as essentially one opinion.

Wilder's (1977, 1978) manipulations of social unitization may be viewed as having induced different degrees of person organization in subjects' cognitive representations of the group. Under conditions of higher person organization (where the group members were more individuated), the opinions expressed may have been perceived as having come from more distinct sources (Harkins & Petty, 1981). This view of Wilder's studies does not necessarily conflict with his account, but it puts the findings into a more explicit cognitive representational framework. One implication of this view not derivable from Wilder's analysis is that other factors which also diminish person organization in a group should diminish the group's social influence. One such factor is the presence of salient alternative organizations (Pryor *et al.*, 1982).

In a direct test of these ideas, Ostrom *et al.* (1985) presented subjects with three recreational preferences ascribed to each of three individuals. The preferences (e.g., "On Tuesday, Frank enjoyed racing through the woods on a snowmobile") involved the stimulus persons' behaviors in one of two difference vacation resorts (the beach or the mountains). All preferences were unanimously positive for a specific type of resort activity. Through a manipulation involving processing objectives and information structure, subjects were induced to remember the information organized by persons or organized by a categorical structure orthogonal to persons (days of the week on which the activities occurred). Both free-recall and social influence measures were subsequently assessed. Person clustering in free recall indicated a high degree of person organization in the condition where it was induced and a low degree in the other condition. A key social influence measure involved the subjects' own vacation preferencs were they to vacation with this group. Subjects were more influenced by the preferences of the group under high person organization conditions than under low person organization conditions.

The results of this initial investigation are promising. It is interesting to note that this study found these social influence differences where neither the number of persons nor the number of social entities were manipulated. It is also interesting to note that analyses of the subjects' recall protocols revealed no differences across conditions in subjects' ability to recall at least one behavior about each person. So, subjects did not recall more sources of social influence in one condition as compared to the other. These results support our contention that the *distinctness* of the sources of social influence is the key variable underlying the relationship between cognitive representation and social influence.

In future investigations it might be interesting to examine other social influence findings that could be related to person organization. For example, the diminishing impact of adding more and more members to a group (Latané, 1981) could be partially a function of the decreasing distinctness of the individual group members. This follows from Rothbart's finding that information overload creates difficulties in associating specific facts with individual group members (Rothbart et al., 1978).

In-groups and out-groups. One application of the person organization concept concerns the perception of in-groups and out-groups (Brewer, 1979; Wilder, 1981). The cognitive representation of in-group members may be higher in person organization than the representation of out-group members. Several findings are consistent with this hypothesis. First, many of our own studies found that person organization was higher for familiar than for unfamiliar persons. In many of the studies of in-groups/out-groups (e.g., Linville, 1982, 1983; Linville & Jones, 1980) it may be surmised that subjects are more familiar with in-groups than out-groups. (There are some exceptions to this generality, e.g., Tajfel, 1970). Second, out-group members are often assumed by in-group members to be homogeneous in their beliefs (Allen & Wilder, 1979), attitudes (Quattrone & Jones, 1980), and behaviors (Park & Rothbart, 1982). This finding is consistent with the idea that a single group node is used to organize information about the out-group, whereas an individual node are used to organize information about each of the in-group members.

Other theorists have previously suggested that the representation of out-groups is less cognitively complex than the representation of in-groups. For example, Linville (1982) has found evidence that people consider fewer dimensions when evaluating the members of an out-group than when evaluating the members of an in-group. Linville relates this to a tendency to make polarized judgments of outgroup members (rate them as extremely positive or extremely negative) and make more moderate judgments of in-group members. Whereas Linville's theoretical perspective is similar the one we are suggesting in that it assumes a more cognitively complex representation of in-groups, a different kind of complexity is assumed. Linville's theory assumes that more dimensions are used to represent in-groups and we assume that more individual propositional networks are used.

Research by Carpenter and Ostrom (1985) has examined the prediction that in-groups are more person organized than out-groups. Male and female subjects learned facts about eight unfamiliar stimulus persons, four of whom were male and four, female. The facts pertained to different stereotyped characteristics of the persons, such as college major, favorite sport, and personality trait. Subjects were later asked to recall the in-group (same sex) facts on one page and the out-group (other sex) facts on another page. The recall protocols were scored for two kinds of clustering, one on the basis of person and the other on the basis of stereotype category.

In support of the prediction, it was found that person clustering was greatest for in-group information and that stereotype clustering was greatest for out-group information. These findings suggest that the reason out-group members are perceived as similar to one another is that people tend to link them into the group attribute structures rather than develop individuating interpersonal structures.

Attribute Structures

Knowing that a person is a group member can automatically evoke response-relevant attribute structures (see Figure 8.1). Ths structure most widely studied to date by researchers in social cognition is the group stereotype. The cognitive view of stereotypes (Hamilton, 1981) does not make any assumptions about their veridicality as traditional views often do (e.g., Lippman, 1922). The cognitive view simply assumes that stereotypes involve expectations about social groups.

Acquisition of group schemata. One of the most important processes in the formation of expectations about a group is the simple act of categorizing people. Allport (1954) first noted that the leap from categorizing to stereotyping is a small one. Simple categorization leads to a minimization of within-group differences and a maximization of between-group differences (Taylor, 1981). Wilder (1981) and Tajfel (1981) have shown that even with arbitrary categorizations, people expect the members of a group to respond similarly in social situations.

One question that arises in considering the nature of social categorization is: at what level does categorization typically take place? After all, there is a myriad of different ways with which one can divide up the social world. Taylor (1981) has suggested that while people probably use the most salient social and physical distinctions to categorize other people (e.g., race, sex ethnicity), they may also employ more basic-level social categories (Cantor & Mischel, 1979) that are perhaps more informative. For example, nested under the category "Jews" might be Jewish American princesses, rabbis, Jewish mothers, and nice jewish boys. Taylor (1981) speculates that such stereotypes as these (which are not as abstract or all inclusive as more superordinate stereotypes) may be more frequently used in everyday thinking about social groups. While some evidence exists which suggests that people employ such middle-level stereotypes (Brewer, Dull, & Lui, 1981), we suspect that the level at which people categorize social groups probably varies greatly across situations depending on such factors as processing objectives and knowledge domains (see Pryor, McDaniel, & Kott-Russo, in press, for a related discussion).

A useful way of thinking about social group stereotypes is that they are like correlational concepts (Hamilton, 1981). For example, we may think that such characteristics as laziness, stinginess, and volatility are correlated with Blacks, Jews, and Italians, respectively. If our ideas of what characteristics or behaviors are correlated with specific groups grew only out of our veridical experience with these groups, then stereotypes would in essence be accurate representations of reality. Unfortunately, our correlational concepts about social groups may often reflect the influence of information-processing biases. Hamilton (1981) has identified at least two biases that result in *illusory correlations* (Chapman & Chapman, 1967) about the relationship between social groups and social features: *distinctiveness* and *prior associations*. The first bias provides a cognitive basis for the formation of some social group stereotypes and the second, a basis for how they may grow stronger over time.

The first study to explore how information distinctiveness might contribute to the formation of group stereotypes was done by Hamilton and Gifford (1976, Study 1). Subjects in this study read 26 statements describing the behaviors of individuals belonging to a hypothetical group, A, and 13 statements describing the behaviors of individuals belonging to another hypothetical group, B. In each case 31% were negative and 69% were positive. Subsequently, the subjects were asked to evaluate the two groups, to recognize which behaviors were attributed to each group and to estimate the number of positive and negative behaviors attributed to each group. Hamilton and Gifford found that subjects evaluated the smaller group (B) more negatively than the larger group (A), attributed more negative behaviors to B in the recognition task and estimated that B had performed more negative behaviors.

Hamilton and Gifford suggest that members of group B and negative behaviors were more distinctive in this context than members of group A and positive behaviors, respectively. This distinctiveness is the result of the relative infrequency of B members and negative behaviors. This distinctiveness draws attention to the cooccurence of group B membership and negative behaviors during information acquisition and makes such co-occurences particularly available during retrieval when subjects are asked to make various social judgments (Tversky & Kahneman, 1973). A consequence of this information-processing bias is that people see group B membership and negativity as correlated, when in reality they are not. Thus, subjects perceive an illusory correlation. Later research substantiated the role of distinctiveness as a mediating mechanism over alternative explanations (Hamilton *et al.*, 1985).

Hamilton (1981) views this study as a possible analog for how negative stereotypes may be formed for minority groups in naturalistic settings. If we assume that socially undesirable behaviors and minority group membership are both relatively infrequent in the experiences of majority group members, then we can see a mechanism through which an illusory correlation between minority groups and negative behaviors may be perceived by majority group members. Recent research by Pryor (1986) has suggested that illusory correlations such as those reported in Hamilton and Gifford (1976) are more likely to be formed when subjects are in a nonintegrative processing set, that is, when subjects are not making on-line judgments of group members during information acquisition. Pryor found that subjects who were asked to form impressions of the two groups in a Hamilton and Gifford procedure were not affected by illusory correlations in their judgments of these groups. This suggests some possible limitations in applying this concept to naturalistic information processing. The actual role of illusory correlations in the development of minority stereotypes would presumably be, in part, a function of the relative frequency of nonintegrative processing in everyday experience.

In another series of experiments, Hamilton and Rose (1980) investigated the role of prior associations in the perception of correlations between social groups and various behaviors. For example, in Hamilton and Rose (1980, Study 1) subjects received two traits about each of eight members of three occupational groups (doctors, accountants, and salesmen). Traits stereotypically associated with each group (e.g., salesmen–talkative) were presented with equal frequency across the descriptions of each group. Afterwards, subjects were asked to estimate the frequency with which the various traits had cooccurred with each occupational label. Subjects tended to overestimate the frequency with which stereotypic traits had described the members of each group. Thus, subjects' expectations about a group resulted in their perceiving an illusory correlation.

The theoretical explanation for this result again involves availability (Tversky & Kahneman, 1973). Stereotypically expected cooccurrences can either be remembered well because one term provides a strong retrieval cue for the other or else be easily constructed later when actual memory fades. In either case, the availability of such cooccurrences at retrieval results in the overestimation of their actual experience. This basic bias provides a basis for the maintenance and possibly strengthening of stereotypic expectancies over time. How many times have we heard an assertion such as: "I wouldn't believe that blacks are lazy if I had not seen evidence for this myself time and time again"? Such statements are possibly related to illusory correlations.

Hamilton's work on illusory correlations is an important contribution to our understanding of the development of stereotypes because it provides a nonmotivation account for how negative stereotypes may develop. According to this view stereotypic expectations of groups can emerge from biases inherent in how we process information about other people. Thus, this view is particularly cogent for the theme of this chapter. For other views of stereotype acquisition, the reader should consult Ashmore and Del Boca (1981).

Unit of analysis. One function of a group label is in creating expectations. Group-based expectations may function at either an individual or a group level. You may have expectations about an individual because he is a member of a group ("Fred is a black—he is probably lazy") or you may have expectations about the group as a whole ("Blacks as a group are more lazy than whites"). In this sense a group label may function like any other schematic expectation.

There are, however, differences between the way a group label may affect our perceptions of a specific individual as compared to our perceptions of a group as a whole. For example, suppose you have an expectation that Texans will be loud and obnoxious. Upon meeting a person at a party who is a Texan, you may find his quiet and courteous behavior unexpected. This might evoke some sort of extensive processing of the individual's behavior in a manner similar to that described by Hastie's (1984) encoding elaboration model. However, if your unit of analysis was the group, "Texans," instead of just an individual, then inconsistencies might be more expected. Thus, if you moved to Dallas and encountered several Texans who were quiet and courteous, this probably would not as strongly violate your expectations of the group as a whole and would probably not evoke extensive processing. The reason is that expectations that we hold about a group as a whole are usually not as strong as the expectations we hold about individuals. Group expectations usually allow for more variability. Individuals, on the other hand, are expected to be consistent.

Several studies support the idea that the schematic expectancies we hold for groups are often not as strong as the schematic expectations we hold for individuals. For example, Srull (1981) gave subjects schematic expectations about an individual, a meaningful group (one that frequently interacted and had a common goal—a political caucus) or a nonmeaningful group (described as simply a "group") and then presented specific behaviors enacted by the social entity that were either consistent, inconsistent, or irrelevant to the schematic expectation. Subjects who were asked to form an impression of the social entity later recalled more inconsistent than consistent or irrelevant information about an individual or a meaningful group. This fits the encoding elaboration model's predictions (Hastie, 1980). There was no superior recall for inconsistent information, however, when the social entity was a nonmeaningful group. Many social groups may be similar to what Srull (1981) terms a "nonmeaningful" group, that is, they may neither necessarily interact nor have common goals. Consider the following examples: Blacks, Jews, Texans, or women. These are nevertheless social groups using our definition of a group as simply a collection of people who are perceived as related.

Additional evidence concerning the idea that schemata may function differently at the group as compared to the individual level comes from Tessor and Leone (1977). These researchers described either an individual or a group with a set of either moderately positive or moderately negative adjectives. Subjects rated the favorability of the social entity and then, after a delay, rerated it. Some were distracted during the delay while others were asked to think about their impressions. Both the individual and the group subjects showed polarization in their reratings after thought; however, the degree of polarization was much greater for the individual than the group.

Tessor and Leone (1977) suggest that people have more well-developed schemata about individuals than groups. Across a variety of other studies Tessor (1978) found that when people have a well-developed schema about something, thought produces schema-consistent cognitions and attitude polarization as demonstrated above.

A final study demonstrating a difference between group and individual expectations comes from Coovert and Reeder (1985, described in Reeder, 1985). Subjects were presented with one moral and one immoral behavior. In some conditions these were both ascribed to an individual, while in others these were ascribed to two individuals. Subjects were asked to form an impression either of the individual or of the two people as a group and rate the social entity's morality. In the individual condition, subjects demonstrated a distinct negativity effect; that is, they assigned more weight to the immoral than the moral behavior. In the group condition, they equally weighted the two behaviors. In accounting for these results, Reeder suggests that people typically hold strong expectations that moral people do not do immoral acts. Therefore, even just one immoral behavior is enough to tip judgments to the immoral side of the scale. No such strong expectations seem to necessarily mediate the judgments of a group.

Interpretive functions. One of the most important functions of group schemata is that they provide us with interpretations of ambiguous behaviors. Since the interpretations they provide are often schema consistent, schemata may be described as generating evidence necessary for their own perpetuation. An example of this tendency is found in the work of Duncan (1976). Subjects viewed a film in which an actor gently shoved another actor. When the actor was white, this ambiguous act was interpreted as playfulness. When the actor was black, the act was interpreted as reflecting hostility.

Another study by Darley and Gross (1983) shows a similar effect. Subjects were given a stereotypic label about a child. The child was said to come from either a high or a low socioeconomic background. Subsequently, subjects viewed a film in which the child answered questions from an acheivement test. Her performance was arranged to provide an ambiguous picture of her abilities. She answered both easy and difficult questions correctly as well as incorrectly. Both groups subsequently made a series of ratings concerning the child's academic abilities. The group given the high stereotypic expectancy rated the child higher that the group given the low stereotypic expectancy. Both groups cited evidence from the film to support their conflicting conclusions.

A final example comes from a recent study by Bodenhausen and Wyer (1985). In this study, subjects were found to use an ethnic stereotype to infer reasons for a crime. Subsequently, subjects reviewed available information in an attempt to find further confirmation of the stereotype. Later subjects were found to recall information consistent with the stereotypical judgment.

These studies all indicate that a schema can bias the interpretations that people make concerning ambiguous information, but what about interpretations of information that is *inconsistent* with a schematic expectation? Results from several studies show that attributional processes are evoked when people encounter information inconsistent with their expectations (e.g., Hastie, 1984). The result of this attributional processing may be to preserve the original expectation.

For example, Bell, Wicklund, Manko, and Larkin (1976) found that behaviors that violate expectations we hold about a person are often attributed to environmental forces. In a recent study, Kulik (1983) found that prior schematic expectations concerning an actor evoked equally strong dispositional attributions for an actor's behavior whether or not the behavior was enacted in the presence of strong situational pressure. In contrast, behaviors that were inconsistent with prior expectations were attributed to situational forces even in situations normally believed to inhibit such behaviors. Kulik's results suggest a "confirmatory attributional analysis" may often be evoked when expectations are threatened by disconfirming information. The attribution of inconsistent behaviors to situational factors may also have important implications for the memory of these behaviors. For example, Crocker, Hannah, and Weber (1983) found that the often noted superiority of memory for behaviors that violate a schematic expectation (e.g., Hastie & Kumar, 1979) is eliminated when subjects are given feasible situational explanations for inconsistent behaviors.

Other attributions may also be evoked in the service of maintaining expectations in the face of disconfirming evidence. For example, violations of stereotypic expectations concerning ability have often been found to be attributed to *unstable* causes (Weiner, 1979). White males are stereotypically expected to be more skillfull on a variety of intellectual tasks than women or blacks. When women or blacks are observed to succeed on these tasks, the attribution of the performance to effort (e.g., "She probably succeeded because she tried very hard") allows the social perceiver to maintain the original stereotypic expectation (Yarkin, Towne, & Wallston, 1982).

Pettigrew (1981) has expanded these and similar ideas into a generalized system of hypotheses he calls the "ultimate attributional error." He suggests that our stereotype of outgroups are generally negative. When we observe negative acts performed by out-group members, we tend to attribute them to enduring dispositions. However, when we observe positive acts performed by out-group members we tend to attribute them to situational or transitory causes. In support for this idea Pettigrew, Jenmont, and Johnson (cited in Pettigrew, 1981) found that the good performances of black contestants in a staged quiz show were often attributed to "luck" by whites, whereas the blacks' bad performances were often attributed to less general knowledge and poor college preparation.

Schematic expectations and behaviors. Perhaps one of the reasons that schematic expectations are so obdurate to change is that they are often instrumental in bringing about the behaviors they anticipate. They often function as *self-fulfilling prophecies* in social interactions (Merton, 1948). More recently, Darley and Fazio (1980) have examined the typical social interaction sequence through which expectations are transformed into reality. This begins with the social perceiver's formulation of an expectancy about a target. This expectation may be derived from a social stereotype or other sources. This expectancy guides the perceiver's behaviors directed toward the target. The target, in turn, interprets the perceiver's behaviors and responds accordingly. This interaction continues with behavior followed by interpretation followed by behavior. Darley and Fazio's main point is that biasing factors leading to self-fulfilling prophecies may occur at any point in the interaction sequence, both in the interpretations and in the actual behaviors.

Early studies of expectancy confirmation effects examined how teachers' expectations influence student achievement (Rosenthal & Jacobson, 1968; Zanna, Sheras, Cooper, & Shaw, 1975). Expectancy confirmation processes have also been documented in studies of social interaction. For example, Snyder, Tanke, and Berscheid (1977) found that males' stereotypic expectations of females based upon physical attractiveness serve as self-fulfilling prophecies in dyadic interaction. Men who believed they were interacting with an attractive woman over the telephone behaved in such a way as to bring out those qualities they expected of attractive women (e.g., warmth, sociability) (see also Andersen & Bem, 1981).

Another study by Word, Zanna, and Cooper (1974) illustrates how nonverbal behavior can also communicate expectations and bring about self-fulfilling prophecies. In an initial experiment white and black confederates posed as job applicants and were interviewed by white job interviewers. Relative to the white applicants, the black applicants received shorter interviews, greater physical distancing, and more speech disfluencies (stuttering and repetitions) from the white interviewers.

In a companion experiment, Word *et al.* trained white confederates to simulate the typical behaviors of the interviewers to white and black applicants in the previous experiment. These trained confederates then interviewed white subjects. Subjects exposed to these two types of interviewers tended to reciprocate their behaviors. That is, they tended to sit close or far and make speech disfluencies in a manner that paralleled the behavior of their interviewer. Subjects also tended to rate their interviewer as more hostile when he behaved in a distant manner as compared to when he behaved in a more intimate manner. Finally, blind raters judged the subjects interviewed by the distant interviewer as less calm and less qualified for the job than the subjects interviewed by the more intimate interviewer.

Snyder (1981) has proposed that interpersonal expectations often serve as hypotheses when people gather information about others. However, instead of gathering evidence in a more or less objective fashion as scientists presumably do, the social perceiver engages in what Snyder calls a *confirmatory hypothesis-testing strategy*. In one experiment, Snyder and Swan (1978) asked subjects to determine whether another person's behavior and life experiences matched those of a prototypical *extrovert*. Other subjects were asked to determine whether the target's behavior and life experiences matched those of a prototypical *introvert*. Participants in both conditions chose to ask the target questions that solicited hypothesis-confirming evidence. For example, they chose to ask such questions as: "What kinds of situaitons do you seek out if you want to meet new people?" to test an extrovert hypothesis. It is not surprising that when these questions were posed to randomly selected subjects, they tended to elicit evidence confirming the hypothesis being tested.

In summary, schematic expectations seem to frequently guide the behaviors of those who hold them in such a way so as to create evidence consistent with these expectations. The studies we have reviewed in this section demonstrate an important link between cognition and behavior.

On changing schematic expectations. As stated above a great deal of interest has been generated in studying how schematic expectations guide the processing and representation of social information and how they also guide behaviors. However, until recently little has been done to examine how schemata can change in response to varying information over time. The powerful effects of schemata over behavior and incoming information provide a basis for understanding how schemata resist change, but how can they be changed?

Crocker, Fiske, and Taylor (1984) describe two general ways in which schemata may change. The first is a gradual maturing process in which the schema becomes more and more differentiated in order to account for the varying input encountered by the perceiver. This sort of change has been described in terms of a general associative learning process (Anderson, Kline, & Beasley, 1979). The second form of change is through exposure to inconsistent information.

There are at least three conceptual models that describe the changes schemata could make in response to inconsistent information. Two of these models were discussed by Rothbart (1981) in an analysis of stereotypes. The first is a *Bookkeeping model*. In this model, schema revision is a gradual incremental process where each new piece of information results in some minor adjustment or "fine tuning" of the schema. The second model is a *Conversion model*. In this model, a single salient disconfirming instance may produce a sudden and perhaps drastic revision of the schema. Moderately or slightly inconsistent information has little effect on the schema.

Taylor (1981) has proposed a third possible model, called *Subtyping*. This involves the development of subcategories to accommodate inconsistent instances. For example, when a college professor who has the stereotype of college athletes as unintelligent encounters a couple of football players who are outstanding students, he may have to develop a subtype of "smart athletes." This allows the social perceiver to retain the general stereotype and still deal with the inconsistent information.

Weber and Crocker (1983) have recently put these different models to empirical test. In studying group stereotypes they found evidence for the bookkeeping and the subtyping models under different circumstances. When a social perceiver encounters schema-inconsistent information dispersed across a group, this seems to result in some incremental change in the schema. This supports the Bookkeeping model. However, when the inconsistent information is concentrated in a few individuals, these individuals are seen as nonrepresentative of the group and no overall changes are made in the expectations for the other group members. This apparently reflects a Subtyping process. While Weber and Crocker (1983) have found no evidence for a Conversion model, Crocker *et al.* (1984) suggest that this model is more likely to apply when a new schema is available to take the place of the old one.

Some Possible Applications

In this section we turn to a selective sample of applications of the social cognition approach to some specific group phenomena. Our goal is not to be comprehensive. Indeed, the social cognition perspective is relevant to all interpersonal settings. Our intent, rather, is to simply demonstrate the usefulness of social cognition theories in understanding some applied domains.

Person organization and jury decision making. One important social situation in which a social perceiver is faced with integrating multiple pieces of information from multiple sources is in a criminal trial. Judges and jurors may hear testimony from several witnesses bearing on several important issues. Testimony from a specific witness may be required on more than one occasion. The ability of jurors to form interpersonal structures for witness information in this setting can directly affect decisions of guilt or innocence. Devine and Ostrom (1985) examined how different degrees of person organization in the cognitive representation of witnesses' testimonies might influence mock jurors' perceptions of inconsistency in the witnesses' testimonies. In conditions designed to produce high person organization, lawyers questioned each of four witnesses individually about each of four evidence issues (e.g., motive, opportunity). In conditions designed to promote low person organization, lawyers' questioning was organized by evidence categories. Thus, they asked all four witnesses about motive issues, then about opportunity issues, and so forth. An examination of the person-clustering patterns in subsequent free recall of the testimony revealed that this manipulation did indeed result in different degrees of person organization.

Under high person organization subjects were more likely to identify and discount low-credibility witnesses. Consequently, the testimony of these witnesses had less impact on judgments of guilt and innocence under high conditions of high person organization.

While most of the previous research in this area has focused upon how person organization influences the ability of subjects to retrieve information on a person by person basis (e.g., Ostrom & Pryor, in press), this study found evidence for a another way in which person organization may influence social information processing. Subjects' judgments regarding guilt or innocence were apparently not so much influenced by a person-organized *retrieval* of information about the individual witnesses at the time of the decision as they were influenced by spontaneous cognitive reactions to the witness information during *encoding*. Subjects were making their judgments *on line* while learning what each witness had to say. Higher degrees of person organization apparently resulted in subjects' noticing and dis-counting the testimony of specific low-credibility witnesses. This was established by examining subjects' cognitive responses to the testimony during acquisition. This study demonstrates the reciprocal benefits of examining theoretical issues in applied contexts. Our understanding of some of the possible effects of person organization is enriched as well as our appreciation of the complexity of information processing in a jury setting.

Perceptions of leaders. What is leadership? At different times, organizational psychologists have taken the view that leadership is (1) a function of personality factors (Constantini & Craik, 1980; Fodor & Smith, 1982), (2) a function of situational factors (Hollander & Jullian, 1978), or (3) a interactive function of both personality and situational factors (Stein, Hoffman, Cooley, & Pearse, 1980). Another more cognitive perspective is that leadership is a concept people use to explain organizational outcomes (Calder, 1977; Pfeffer, 1977). Research by Meindl, Ehrlich, and Dukerich (1983) suggests that the notion most people have of leadership may be a romanticized one. They found that extremely positive organizational outcomes are more likely to be attributed to a leader's influence than less positive or negative outcomes.

If people have general expectations about leaders, then such expectations should have some schematic effects upon the processing of information in organizational settings. Several studies have indicated that this is indeed the case. Dukerich, Nichols, and Meindl (1984) asked subjects to freely recall randomly ordered information about the members of a small group. In an examination of clustering patterns, they found that subjects tended to chunk information about a leader into an organized unit apart from information about the other group members. Recall about the other group members was much less organized. This suggests that leaders play an important role in the organization of information in small group settings.

Research by Lord and his associates have investigated the idea that people have implicit theories of leadership and that these act as cognitive schemata in processing information in organizational settings. Phillips and Lord (1982) presented subjects with videotapes in which a small group worked on a cooperative task. The leader in the group displayed five behaviors that are prototypically associated with an effective leader, five behaviors that are prototypically associated with an ineffective leader and five behaviors neutral with respect to leadership. Subsequently, subjects were given bogus feedback concerning how the group did relative to other groups working on the same task. Finally, they were given a recognition task concerning the behaviors of the leader. Results showed that subjects tended to recognize effective behaviors better in the positive feedback condition than in the negative feedback condition. Also, they recognized ineffective behaviors better in the negative feedback than the positive feedback condition. There was also some tendency for subjects to make false alarms, particularly with regard to ineffective behaviors. This indicates that people may have a generalized schema for leadership. In other studies, Lord and his colleagues (Foti, Fraser, & Lord, 1982; Lord, Foti, & DeVader, 1984) make a case for the existence of more specific or middle-level leader schemata (Cantor & Mischel, 1979; Rosch, 1978) that vary according to the specific tasks facing a leader. For example, people may have prototypes concerning "political leaders" that are distinct from their more general "leader" schema. This idea is similar to Taylor's (1981) discussion of the hierarchical structure of stereotypes.

Self-fulfilling prophecies. Some of the research presented in the previous discussion on how expectancies influence behaviors immediately suggests applications by virtue of its methodology. For example, Word et al. (1973) used an interview situation to study how nonverbal mediators are important in self-fulfilling prohecies. The selection–recruitment interview is a particularly important social setting in which to study social cognition processes because this remains one of the most important means by which employers make hiring decisions. Dipboye (1982) has recently proposed a model of how expectancy-confirmation processes may operate in interviews. His model is very similar to the more general model proposed by Darley and Fazio (1980). An important input in Dipboye's model is preinterview information on the interviewee. This is usually provided by application materials. These materials provide the basis for forming expectations concerning the interviewee which guide information processing during the interview. Relevant to the present chapter's theme, social group information (e.g., the applicant's sex) is often an important determinent of the expectations formed from these application materials (Dipboye, Arvey, & Terpstra, 1977). Consistent with Dipboye's theoretical analysis, Binning, Lemke, & Goldstein (1985) have found that hypotheses formed from applications can importantly influence the selection of questions chosen for an interviewee. Subjects who reviewed positive applications tended to select questions that would confirm a positive impression of a job candidate and subjects who reviewed negative applications tended to select questions that would confirm their negative impressions.

All three of the application areas in this section suggest that social cognition ideas may be applied successfully outside the laboratory to further understanding of group-related social phenomena. The diversity of these examples illustrates the potential breadth of this application.

Conclusions

We stated in the beginning of this chapter that the social cognition perspective is unabashedly intrapsychic. We hope that this chapter achieves the goal of convincing the reader that at least *many,* if not all, group processes may be understood by examining the cognitive processes that underlie them. While the social cognition approach focuses on mental processes, it does not neglect the task of relating these to overt behaviors. We wish to make clear that we are not advocating some sort of modern day mentalism as was popular around the turn of the century among introspectionists. At the same time, we believe that all social processes have roots in the ways people characteristically process social information.

Another common misconception concerning social cognition theories is that they necessarily presuppose some sort of conscious awareness of the cognitive processes which they dscribe. In fact, social cognition theory is essentially silent for the most part concerning the role of consciousness. Some social cognition processes that are important in group dynamics could very well operate beyond the realm of normal conscious awareness (see Bargh, 1984, for example), while others might be typically open to conscious inspection. We take no stand on this issue but see it as an interesting empirical question.

Prior to 1980, most conceptual models of psychological structures popular in social psychology were "point on a continuum" models. For example, the characterization of an individual's attitude involved a point on an attitude continuum. Thus, attitudes were described in a *quantitative*, more or less fashion. One of the major thrusts of the social cognition approach is a reformulation of this basic approach to theorizing. Social cognition theories emphasize "categorical" models of psychological structures. Thus, an attitude, for example, might be described as a cognitive structure that an individual might or might not possess and the individual substructures associated with the attitude could vary across individuals. In a sense, this is a more *qualitative* view of psychological structures.

Cognitive theories have a long and venerable history in social psychology (Ostrom, 1984). We hope that this chapter will help to further stimulate the pursuit of cognitive theories in the study of group processes.

References

Abelson, R. P. (1981). The psychological status of the script concept. *American Psychologist, 36*, 715–729.

Allen, V., & Wilder, D. (1979). Group categorization and attribution of belief similarity. *Small Group Behavior, 10*, 73–80.

Allport, G. (1954). *The nature of prejudice.* Cambridge, MA: Addison-Wesley.

Andersen, S., & Bem, S. (1981). Sex stereotyping and androgeny in dyadic interactions: Individual differences in responsiveness to physical attractiveness. *Journal of Personality and Social Psychology, 11*, 279–287.

Anderson, J. R. (1983). *The architecture of cognition.* Cambridge, MA: Harvard University Press.

Anderson, J. R., & Bower, G. H. (1973). *Human associative memory.* Washington, DC: V. H. Winston.

Anderson, J. R., Kline, P. J., & Beasley, C. (1979). A general learning theory and its application to schema abstraction. In G. H. Bower (Ed.), *The psychology of learning and motivation.* New York: Academic press.

Anderson, N. (1978). Cognitive algebra: Integration theory applied to social attribution. In L. Berkowitz (Ed.), *Cognitive theories in social psychology* (pp. 1–102). New York: Academic Press.

Asch, S. (1952). *Social psychology.* New York: Prentice-Hall.

Ashmore, R., & Del Boca (1981). Conceptual approaches to stereotypes and stereotyping. In D. L. Hamilton (Ed.), *Cognitive processes in stereotyping and intergroups behavior* (pp. 1–36). Hillsdale, NJ: Erlbaum.

Bargh, J. A. (1984). Automatic and conscious processing of social information. In R. S. Wyer & T. K. Srull (Eds.), *Handbook of social cognition.* Hillsdale, NJ: Erlbaum.

Bartlett, F. C. (1932). *Remembering.* London: Cambridge University Press.

Bell, L., Wicklund, R., Manko, G., & Larkin, C. (1976). When unexpected behavior is attributed to the environment. *Journal of Research in Personality, 10*, 316–327.

Bem, D. J. (1972). Self-perception theory. In L. Berkowitz (Ed.), *Advances in experimental social psychology* (Vol. 6 pp. 2–62). New York: Academic Press.

Binning, J., Lemke, R., & Goldstein, M. (1985 May). Sex effects on hypothesis testing in the employment interview. Paper presented at the Midwestern Psychological Association Meeting, Chicago.

Bodenhausen, G., & Wyer, R. S., Jr. (1985). Effects of stereotypes on decision making and information processing strategies. *Journal of Personality and Social Psychology, 48*, 267–282.

Brewer, M. (1979). In-group bias in the minimal intergroup situation: A cognitive-motivational analysis. *Psychological Bulletin, 86*, 307–324.

Brewer, M., Dull, V., & Lui, L. (1981). Perceptions of the elderly: Stereotypes as prototypes. *Journal of Personality and Social Psychology, 41*, 656–670.

Calder, B. J. (1977). An attribution theory of leadership. In B. Staw & G. Salancik (Eds.), *New directions in organizational behavior* (pp. 179–204). Chicago: St. Clair Press.

Cantor, N., & Mischel, W. (1979). Prototypes in person perception. In L. Berkowitz

(Ed.), *Advances in Experimental Social Psychology* (Vol. 12 pp. 4–52). New York: Academic Press.

Carpenter, S., & Ostrom, T. M. (1985, May). Person organization in the perception of outgroups. Paper presented at the Midwestern Psychological Association Convention, Chicago IL,

Cartwright, D., & Zander, A. (1968). *Group dynamics* (3rd ed.). New York: Harper & Row.

Chapman, L. J., & Chapman, J. P. (1967). The genesis of popular but erroneous psychodiagnostic observations. *Journal of Abnormal Psychology, 72*, 193–204.

Cohen, C. (1977). Cognitive basis of stereotyping. Paper presented at the American Psychological Association Meeting, San Francisco, August.

Collins, A., & Loftus, E. (1975). A spreading activation theory of semantic processing. *Psychological Review, 82*, 407–428.

Coovert, M., & Reeder, G. L. (1985). Impressions of morality: Differences when a target is an individual vs. a pair of persons. Unpublished manuscript, Illinois State University, Normal, Illinois.

Costantini, E., & Craik, K. (1980). Personality and politicians: California party leaders, 1960–1976. *Journal of Personality and Social Psychology, 38*, 641–661.

Craik, F. M., & Tulving, E. (1975). Depth of processing and the retention of words in episodic memory. *Journal of Experimental Psychology: General, 104*, 268–294.

Crocker, J., Fiske, S. T., & Taylor, S. E. (1984). Schematic bases of belief change. In R. Eisen (Ed.), *Attitude judgment*. New York: Springer.

Crocker, J., Hannah, D., & Weber, R. (1983). Person memory and causal attributions. *Journal of Personality and Social Psychology, 44*, 55–66.

Crowder, R. B. (1976). *Principles of learning and memory*. Hillsdale, NJ: Erlbaum.

Darley, J. M., & Fazio, R. H. (1980). Expectancy confirmation processes arising in the social interaction sequence. *American Psychologist, 35*, 867–881.

Darley, J. M., & Gross, P. (1983). A hypothesis-confirming bias in labeling effects. *Journal of Personality and Social Psychology, 44*, 20–33.

DeLamater, J. (1974). A definition of "group." *Small Group Behavior, 5*, 30–44.

Devine, P., & Ostrom, T. M. (1985). Cognitive mediation of inconsistency discounting. *Journal of Personality and Social Psychology, 49*, 5–21.

Dipboye, R. (1982). Self-fulfilling prophecies in the selection-recruitment interview. *Academy of Management Review, 7*, 579–586.

Dipboye, R., Arvey, R., & Terpstra, D. (1977). Sex and physical attractiveness of raters and applicants as determinants of resume evaluation. *Journal of Applied Psychology, 62*, 288–294.

Dooling, D., & Christiaansen, R. (1977). Episodic and semantic aspects in memory for prose. *Journal of Experimental Psychology: Human learning and memory, 3*, 428–436.

Dukerich, J., Nichols, M., & Meindl, J. (1984). An investigation of leader schemas as a basis of leadership attributions. Paper presented at the National Academy of Management Meeting, August.

Duncan, B. (1976). Differential social perception and attribution of intergroup violence: Testing the lower limits of stereotyping blacks. *Journal of Personality and Social Psychology, 34*, 590–598.

Fazio, R. H., Chen, J., McDonel, E. C., & Sherman, S. J. (1982). Attitude accessibility attitude-behavior consistency and the strength of the object-evaluation association. *Journal of Personality and Social Psychology, 18*, 339–357.

Feldman, J. M. (1981). Beyond attribution theory: Cognitive processes in performance appraisal. *Journal of Applied Psychology, 66*, 127–148.

Fiske, S. T., Kenney, D., & Taylor, S. E. (1982). Structural models for the mediation of salience effects on attribution. *Journal of Personality and Social Psychology, 18*, 105–127.

Fiske, S. T., & Taylor, S. E. (1984). *Social cognition.* Reading, MA: Addison-Wesley.

Fodor, E., & Smith, T. (1982). The power motive as an influence on group decision making. *Journal of Personality and Social Psychology, 42*, 178–185.

Foti, R., Fraser, S., & Lord, R. (1982). Effects of leadership labels and prototypes on perceptions of political leaders. *Journal of Applied Psychology, 67*, 326–333.

Garner, W. (1974). *The processing of information and structure.* Hillsdale, NJ: Erlbaum.

Graesser, A. C., & Nakamura, G. V. (1982). The impact of a schema on comprehension and memory. In G. H. Bower (Ed.), *The psychology of learning and motivation: Advances in research and theory* (Vol. 16). New York: Academic Press.

Greenwald, A. G., & Pratkanis, A. R. (1984). The self. In R. S. Wyer & T. K. Srull (Eds.), *Handbook of social cognition* (Vol. 3 pp. 129–178). Hillsdale, NJ: Erlbaum.

Hamilton, D. L. (1979). A cognitive-attributional analysis of stereotyping. In L. Berkowitz (Ed.), *Advances in experimental social psychology* (Vol. 12 pp. 53–85). New York: Academic Press.

Hamilton, D. L. (1981). Illusory correlation as a basis for stereotyping. In D. L. Hamilton (Ed.), *Cognitive processes in stereotyping and intergroup behavior* (pp. 115–144). Hillsdale, NJ: Erlbaum.

Hamilton, D. L., Dugan, P., & Troiler, T. (1985). The formation of stereotypic beliefs: Further evidence for distinctiveness-based illusory correlations. *Journal of Personality and Social Psychology, 48*, 5–17.

Hamilton, D. L., & Gifford, R. K. (1976). Illusory correlations in interpersonal perception: A cognitive basis of stereotype judgments. *Journal of Experimental Social Psychology, 12*, 392–407.

Hamilton, D. L., Katz, L. B., & Leier, V. O. (1980). Cognitive representation of personality impressions: Organizational processes in first impression formation. *Journal of Personlity and Social Psychology, 39*, 1050–1063.

Hamilton, D. L., & Rose, T. (1980). Illusory correlation and the maintenance of stereotypic beliefs. *Journal of Personality and Social Psychology, 39*, 832–845.

Harkins, S., & Petty, R. (1981). Effects of source magnification of cognitive effort on attitudes: An information processing analysis. *Journal of Personality and Social Psychology, 40*, 401–413.

Hasher, L., & Griffin, M. (1978). Reconstructive and reproductive processes in memory. *Journal of Experimental Psychology: Human Learning and Memory, 4*, 318–330.

Hastie, R. (1980). Memory for information that confirms and contradicts a personality impression. In R. Hastie, T. Ostrom, E. Ebbesen, R. Wyer, D. Hamilton, & D. Carlston (Eds.), *Person memory: The cognitive basis of social Perception* (pp. 155–178). Hillsdale, NJ: Erlbaum.

Hastie, R. (1981). Schematic principles in human memory. In E. T. Higgins, C. D. Herman, & M. P. Zanna (Eds.), *Social cognition: The Ontario symposium* (Vol. 1 pp. 39–88). Hillsdale, NJ: Erlbaum.

Hastie, R. (1984). Causes and effects of attribution. *Journal of Personality and Social Psychology, 41*, 656–670.

Hastie, R., & Carlston, D. (1980). Theoretical issues in person memory. In R. Hastie, T. M. Ostrom, E. Ebbesen, R. S. Wyer, D. L. Hamilton, & D. Carlston (Eds.), *Person memory: The cognitive basis for social perception* (pp. 1–54). Hillsdale, NJ: Erlbaum.

Hastie, R., & Kumar, A. P. (1979). Person memory: Personality traits as organizing principles in memory for behaviors. *Journal of Personality and Social Psychology, 37*, 25–38.

Hastie, R., Ostrom, T. M. Ebbesen, E., Wyer, R. ., Hamilton, D. L., & Carlston, D. E. (Eds.) (1980) *Person Memory: The cognitive basis of social perception*. Hillsdale, NJ: Erlbaum.

Hayes-Roth, B. (1977). Evolution of cognitive structures and processes. *Psychological Review, 84*, 260–278.

Higgins, E. T., Rholes, W. S., & Jones, C. R. (1977). Category accessibility and impression formation. *Journal of Experimental Social Psychology, 13*, 141–154.

Hoffman, C., Mischel, W., & Mazze, K. (1981). The role of purpose in the organization of information about behavior. *Journal of Personality and Social Psychology, 40*, 211–225.

Hollander, E., & Jullian, J. (1978). A further look at leader legitimacy, influence and innovation. In L. Berkowitz (Eds.), *Crosscurrents in leadership*. Carbondale: Southern Illinois Univ. Press.

Jackson, J. (1986). Social impact theory. In B. Muller & G. R. Goethals (Eds.), *Theories of group behavior*. New York: Springer-Verlag.

Klatzky, R. L. (1984). Visual memory: Definitions and functions. In R. S. Wyer & T. K. Srull (Eds.), *Handbook of social cognition* (Vol. 2 pp. 233–270). Hillsdale, NJ: Erlbaum.

Kott-Russo, T. L., & Pryor, J. B. (1985). Person memory: Schematic processes in storage and retrieval. Unpublished manuscript, University of Notre Dame.

Kulik, J. (1983). Confirmatory attribution and the perpetuation of social beliefs. *Journal of Personality and Social Psychology, 44*, 1171–1181.

Latané, B. (1981). Social impact theory. *American Psychologist, 36*, 343–356.

Linville, P. (1982). The complexity-extremity effect and age-based stereotypes. *Journal of Personality and Social Psychology, 42*, 193–211.

Linville, P. (1983). Affective consequences of complexity regarding the self and others. In M. S. Clark & S. T. Fiske (Eds.), *Affect and cognition: 17th annual Carnegie symposium on cognition*. Hillsdale, NJ: Erlbaum.

Linville, P., & Jones, E. E. (1980). Polarized appraisals of outgroup members. *Journal of Personality and Social Psychology, 38*, 689–703.

Lippman, W. (1922). *Public opinion*. New York: Harcourt, Brace, Jovanovitch.

Lord, C. G. (1980). Schemas and images as memory aids. Two modes of processing social information. *Journal of Personality and Social Psychology, 38*, 257–269.

Lord, R., Foti, R., & DeVader, C. (1984). A test of leadership categorization theory: Internal structure, information processing and leadership perceptions. *Organizational Behavior and Human Performance, 34*, 343–378.

Mandler, G. (1980). Recognizing: The judgment of previous occurrence. *Psychological Review, 87*, 252–271.

Markus, H., & Zajonc, S. (1985). Cognitive theories in social psychology. In G. Lindzey & E. Aronson (Eds.), *Handbook of social psychology* (Vol. 1 pp. 137–230). Reading, MA: Addison-Wesley.

McArthur, L. Z., & Baron, R. M. (1985). Toward an ecological theory of social perception. *Psychological Review, 90*, 215–238.

McClelland, J. L., & Rummelhart, D. E. (1981). An interactive model of context effects in letter perception: I. An account of basic findings. *Psychological Review, 88*, 375–407.

Meindl, J., Ehrlich, S., & Dukerich, J. (1983). Understanding organizational outcomes: An initial study in the romance of leadership. Paper presented at the National Academy of Management Meeting, August.

Merton, R. K. (1948). The self-fulfilling prophecy. *Antioch Review, 8*, 193–210.

Minsky, M. (1975). A framework for representing knowledge. In P. H. Winston (Ed.), *The psychology of computer vision*. New York: McGraw-Hill.

Mitchell, M. L., Ostrom, T. M., & McCann, C. D. (1982). The effect of exposure pattern on the cognitive differentiation of persons. Eastern Psychological Association Convention, Baltimore, MD.

Ostrom, T. M. (1984). The sovereignty of social cognition. In R. Wyer & T. Srull (Eds.), *Handbook of social cognition* (Vol. 1 pp. 1–38). Hillsdale, NJ: Erlbaum.

Ostrom, T. M., Lingle, J. H., Pryor, J. B., & Geva, N. (1980). Cognitive organization of person impressions. In R. Hastie, T. Ostrom, E. Ebbesen, R. Wyer, D. Hamilton, & D. Carlston (Eds.), *Person memory: The cognitive basis of person perception* (pp. 55–88). Hillsdale, NJ: Erlbaum.

Ostrom, T. M., & Pryor, J. B. (in press) Person organization in small groups. *Representative Research in Social Psychology.*

Ostrom, T. M., Pryor, J. B., Pusateri, T. P., & Mitchell, M. L. (1985). Judgmental consequences of person organization. Unpublished manuscript, Ohio State University.

Ostrom, T. M., Pryor, J. B., & Simpson, D. D. (1981). The organization of social information. In E. T. Higgins, C. P. Herman, & M. P. Zanna (Eds.), *Social cognition: The Ontario symposium* (Vol. 1 pp 3–38). Hillsdale, NJ: Erlbaum.

Park, B., & Rothbart, M. (1982). Perception of outgroup homogeneity and levels of social categorization: Memory for the subordinate attributes of ingroup and outgroup members. *Journal of Personality and Social Psychology, 42,* 1050–1068.

Pettigrew, T. (1981). Extending the stereotype concept. In D. L. Hamilton (Ed.), *Cognitive processes in stereotyping and intergroup behavior.* Hillsdale, NJ: Erlbaum.

Pfeffer, J. (1977). The ambiguity of leadership. *Academy of Management Review, 3,* 104–112.

Phillips, J., & Lord, R. (1982). Schematic information processing and the perception of leadership in problem-solving groups. *Journal of Applied Psychology, 67,* 486–492.

Potts, G. R. (1975). Bringing order to cognitive structures. In F. Restle, R. Shiffrin, N. Castellan, H. Lindman, & D. Pisoni (Eds.), *Cognitive theory* (Vol. 1). Hillsdale NJ: Erlbaum.

Pryor, J. B. (1986). The influence of different encoding sets upon the formation of illusory correlations and group impressions. *Personality and Social Psychology Bulletin, 12,* 216–226.

Pryor, J. B., Kott, T. L., & Bovee, G. R. (1984). The influence of information redundancy upon the use of persons and traits as organizing categories. *Journal of Experimental Social Psychology, 20,* 246–262.

Pryor, J. B., & Kriss, M. (1977). The cognitive dynamics of salience in the attribution process. *Journal of Personality and Social Psychology, 35,* 49–55.

Pryor, J. B., McDaniel, M., & Kott-Russo, T. L. (in press). The influence of the level of schema abstractness upon the processing of social information. *Journal of Experimental Social Psychology.*

Pryor, J. B., & Ostrom, T. M. (1981). The cognitive organization of social information: A converging operations approach. *Journal of Personality and Social Psychology, 41,* 628–641.

Pryor, J. B., & Ostrom, T. M. (1982). Perception of persons in groups. In H. Hiebsch, H. Brandstrafter, & H. H. Kelley (Eds.), *Social psychology* (pp. 124–133). Amsterdam: North-Holland.

Pryor, J. B., & Ostrom, T. M., Dukerich, J., Mitchell, M. L., & Herstein, J. A. (1983). Pre-integrative categorization of social information: The role of persons as organizing categories. *Journal of Personality and Social Psychology, 44,* 923–932.

Pryor, J. B., Simpson, D. D., Mitchell, M. L., Ostrom, T. M., & Lydon, J. E. (1982). Structured selectivity in the retrieval of social information. *Social Cognition, 1,* 336–357.

Pusateri, T. P., Devine, P. G., Ostrom, T. M., & McCann, C. D. (1984). Blocking and

schema activation independently facilitate the categorization of social information. Midwestern Psychological Association Convention, Chicago, May.

Quattrone, G., & Jones, E. E. (1980). The perception of variability within ingroups
and outgroups: Implications for the law of small numbers. *Journal of Personality
and Social Psychology, 38*, 141–152.

Reeder, G. L. (1985). Implicit relations between dispositions and behaviors: Effects
on dispositional attributions. In J. Harvey & G. Weary (Eds.), *Attribution: Basic
Issues and applications* (pp. 87–116). Orlando, FL: Academic Press.

Rholes, W. S., & Pryor, J. B. (1982). Cognitive accessibility and attributions.
Personality and Social Psychology Bulletin, 8, 719–727.

Rosch, E. (1978). Principles of categorization (pp. 87–116). In E. Rosch & B. B. Loyd
(Eds.), *Cognition and categorization*. Hillsdale, NJ: Erlbaum.

Rosenthal, R., & Jacobson, L. (1968). *Pygmalion in the classroom*. New York: Holt,
Rinehart & Winston.

Rothbart, M. (1981). Memory processes and social beliefs. In D. Hamilton (Ed.),
Cognitive processes in stereotyping and intergroup behavior (pp. 145–182). Hillsdale,
NJ: Erlbaum.

Rothbart, M., Fulero, S., Jensen, C., Howard, J., & Birrell, P. (1978). From individual
to group impressions: Availability heuristics in stereotype formation. *Journal of
Experimental Social Psychology, 14*, 237–255.

Rumelhart, D. E. (1984). Schemata and the cognitive system. In R. S. Wyer & T. K.
Srull (Eds.), *Handbook of social cognition* (Vol. 1 pp. 161–188). Hillsdale, NJ:
Erlbaum.

Shoben, E. J. (1984). Semantic and episodic memory. In R. S. Wyer & T. K. Srull
(Eds.), *Handbook of social cognition* (Vol. 2 pp. 213–232). Hillsdale, NJ: Erlbaum.

Smith, E. (1984). Model of social inference processes. *Psychological Review, 91*, 392–
413.

Smith, E., & Branscomb, N. (1985). Procedurally mediated social inferences: The
case of category accessibility effects. Unpublished manuscript, Purdue University.

Snyder, M. (1981). Seek, and ye shall find: Testing hypotheses about other people. In
E. T. Higgins, C. P. Herman, & M. P. Zanna (Eds.), *Social cognition: The Ontario
synposium* (Vol. 1 pp. 277–304). Hillsdale, NJ: Erlbaum.

Snyder, M., & Swann, W. B. (1978). Hypothesis-testing in social interaction. *Journal
of Personality and Social Psychology, 36*, 1202–1212.

Snyder, M., Tanke, E. D., & Berscheid, E. (1977). Social perception and interpersonal
behavior: On the self-fulling nature of social stereotypes. *Journal of Personality and
Social Psychology, 35*, 656–666.

Spiro, R. J. (1977). Inferential reconstruction in memory for connected discourse. In
R. C. Anderson, R. J. Spiro, & W. E. Montague (Eds.), *Schooling and the acquisition
of knowledge*. Hillsdale, NJ: Erlbaum.

Srull, T. K. (1981) Person memory: Some tests of associative storage and retrieval
models. *Journal of Experimental Psychology: Human Learning and Memory, 7*, 440–
463.

Srull, T. K. (1984) Methodological techniques for the studyof person memory and
social cognition. In R. S. Wyer & T. K. Srull (Eds.), *Handbook of social cognition*
(Vol. 2 pp. 2–72). Hillsdale, NJ: Erlbaum.

Stein, R., Hoffman, L., Cooley, S., & Pearse, R. (1980). Leadership valence: Modeling
and measuring the process of emergent leadership. In J. Hunt & L. Larson (Eds.),
Crosscurrents in leadership. Carbondale: Southern Illinois Univ.

Stephan, W. (1984). Intergroup relations. In E. Aronson & G. Lindzey (Eds.),
Handbook of social psychology (Vol. 2, pp. 599–658). Reading, MA: Addison-
Wesley.

Tajfel, H. (1970). Experiments in intergroup discrimination. *Scientific American, 223*,
96–102.

Tajfel, H. (1981). *Human groups and social categories: Studies in social psychology.* Cambridge: Cambridge University Press.

Taylor, S. E. (1981). A categorization approach to stereotyping. In D. L. Hamilton (Ed.), *Cognitive processes in stereotyping and intergroup behavior.* Hillsdale, NJ: Erlbaum.

Taylor, S. E., & Crocker, J. (1981). Schematic bases of social information processing. In E. T. Higgins, C. P. Herman, & M. P. Zanna (Eds.), *Social cognition: The Ontario symposium* (pp. 89–134). Hillsdale, NJ: Erlbaum.

Taylor, S. E., & Fiske, S. T. (1978). Salience, attention & attribution. In L. Berkowitz (Ed.), *Advances in experimental social psychology* (Vol. 11 pp. 250–289). New York: Academic Press.

Taylor, S. E., Fiske, S. T., Close, M., Anderson, C., & Ruderman, A. (1977). Solo status as a psychological variable: The power of being distinctive. Unpublished manuscript, Harvard University.

Taylor, S. E., Fiske, S. T., Etcoff, N. L., & Ruderman, H. J. (1978). Categorical and contextual bases of person memory and stereotyping. *Journal of Personality and Social Psychology, 36,* 778–795.

Tessor, A. C. (1978). Self-generated attitude change. In L. Berkowitz (Ed.), *Advances in experimental social psychology* (Vol. 11 pp. 290–338). New York: Academic Press.

Tessor, A. C., & Leone, C. (1977). Cognitive schemas and thought as determinants of attitude change. *Journal of Experimental and Social Psychology, 13,* 340–356.

Tversky, A., & Kahneman, D. (1973). Availability: A heuristic for judging frequency and probability. *Cognitive Psychology, 5,* 207–232.

Warren, R. E. (1973). Stimulus encoding and memory. *Journal of Experimental Psychology, 94,* 90–100.

Weber, R., & Crocker, J. (1983). Cognitive processing in the revision of stereotypic beliefs. *Journal of Personality and Social Psychology, 45,* 961–977.

Weiner, B. (1979). A theory of motivation for some classroom experiences. *Journal of Educational Psychology, 71,* 3–25.

Wilder, D. (1977). Perception of groups, size of oppositiion and social influence. *Journal of Experimental Social Psychology, 13,* 253–268.

Wilder, D. (1978). Homogeneity of jurors: The majority's influence depends on their perceived independence. *Law and Human Behavior, 2,* 363–376.

Wilder, D. (1981). Perceiving persons as a group: categorization and intergroup relations. In D. L. Hamilton (Ed.), *Cognitive processes in stereotyping and intergroup behavior* (pp. 213–258). Hillsdale, NJ: Erlbaum.

Word, C., Zanna, M. P., & Cooper, J. (1974). The nonverbal mediation of self-fulfilling prophecies in interracial interaction. *Journal of Experimental and Social Psychology, 10,* 109–120.

Wyer, R. S., Jr., & Gordon, S. E. (1984). The cognitive representation of social information. In R. S. Wyer & T. K. Srull (Eds.), *Handbook of social cognition* (Vol. 2 pp. 13–150). Hillsdale, NJ: Erlbaum.

Wyer, R. S., Jr., & Srull, T. K. (1980). The processing of social stimulus information: A conceptual integration. In R. Hastie, T. Ostrom, E. Ebbesen, R. Wyer, D. Hamilton, & D. Carlston (Eds.), *Person memory: Cognitive bases of social perception* (pp. 227–300). Hillsdale, NJ: Erlbaum.

Wyer, R. S., Jr., & Srull, T. K. (1984). *Handbook of social cognition.* Hillsdale, NJ: Erlbaum.

Yarkin, K., Towne, J., & Wallston, B. (1982). Blacks and women must try harder: Stimulus person's race and sex attributions of causality. *Personality and Social Psychology Bulletin, 8,* 21–24.

Zanna, M., Sheras, P., Cooper, J., & Shaw, C. (1975). Pygmalion and Galatea: The interactive effect of teacher and student expectancies. *Journal of Experimental Social Psychology, 11,* 279–287.

Chapter 9

Transactive Memory: A Contemporary Analysis of the Group Mind

Daniel M. Wegner

The most influential theory of group behavior that has ever been developed is currently in disfavor. This is the theory of the *group mind*. Social commentators once found it very useful to analyze the behavior of groups by the same expedient used in analyzing the behavior of individuals. The group, like the person, was assumed to be sentient, to have a form of mental activity that guides action. Rousseau (1767) and Hegel (1807) were the early architects of this form of analysis, and it became so widely used in the 19th and early 20th centuries that almost every early social theorist we now recognize as a contributor to modern social psychology held a similar view. McDougall, Ross, Durkheim, Wundt, and LeBon, to name just a few, were willing to assume that the group has a mental life that plays a part in the patterning of group behavior.

Theories of the group mind fell victim to the behavioral revolution in psychology and have not yet returned. Even as research in cognition, memory, artificial intelligence, and information processing reaches feverish intensity in the field, group mind ideas seem generally ignored, perhaps because the group mind concept still reminds many of the worst excesses of mentalistic theorizing—from genetic theories of thought content (e.g., Pareto, 1935) to explanations based on telepathy and the supernatural (e.g., Jung, 1922). Obviously, these ideas do not represent the only direction in which group mind theories may develop (cf. Bartlett, 1932), and this chapter presents a fresh start toward a more useful formulation. The study of transactive memory is concerned with the prediction of group (and individual) behavior through an understanding of the manner in which groups process and structure information. Like early theories of the group mind, transactive memory draws deeply on the analogy between the mental operations of the individual and the processes of the group. Unlike early theories of group mind, the new notion of transactive memory benefits from recent advances in the study of the thinking processes of the individual.

General Principles

A transactive memory system is a set of individual memory systems in combination with the communication that takes place between individuals (Wegner, Giuliano, & Hertel, 1985). To understand how such a system operates, it is useful to consider its components. We begin, then, by looking at the individual's memory system and turn subsequently to see how this system becomes connected with those of other individuals.

Individual Memory

The processes of a person's memory are commonly understood to occur at three different stages. Information is entered into memory at the *encoding* stage, it resides in memory during a *storage* stage, and it is brought back during the *retrieval* stage. This breakdown of stages is useful for analysis because the successful operation of memory at one stage may have little consequence for the operation of memory at another. We have all had the experience of feeling we had encoded something, for instance, but found it impossible to retrieve. When this happens, it is not obvious where the memory failure has occurred. Did the item get into memory but somehow fall out? Did it get in and stay in, but we could not find it? Or did it really never get in at all? These questions highlight the possibility that separate processes may operate on information at each of these junctures. We may witness a robbery and, in the excitement, fail to encode the robber's face or clothing; we may fail in storing this information because someone asks us confusing questions about the robbery and suggests things to us we did not even see; we may fail to retrieve the information because later the prosecutor does not jog our memory by asking us the proper questions.

A further set of issues in individual memory centers on how the stored information is organized. Obviously, it takes a marvelous filing system to retrieve the color of a tomato in under a second—when one considers the millions of other questions that can be answered successfully by most people in the same short interval. Memory theorists have proposed a variety of organizational processes whereby items of information are not merely stored one by one but are stored as connected sets. This means that whole sentences may be stored as connected sets of items or, in the case at hand, that *tomatoes* may be stored with the color *red*. Processes that make or break such connections can occur during encoding to create organization, and complementary processes that operate at retrieval can locate the item by taking advantage of the organized storage that has been produced. By this logic, at some point early in one's experience with vegetables, the words *tomato* and *red* were encoded and the connection between them was encoded as well. Subsequent retrieval of either one then is often accompanied by retrieval of the other. At the same time, retrieval of one of these items very seldom yields the memory of a *waterfowl*, allowing us to recognize that disconnections can also be stored (perhaps as absent connections) for later retrieval.

The description of individual memory entertained to this point is not very far from what one might find in an introductory psychology text. To advance a bit more, we can incorporate the idea of *metamemory* in our discussion. In the last few years, memory theorists have noted that people have beliefs about their own memory facilities (Flavell & Wellman, 1977). One person who reads a book chapter may say she "knows" it, for instance, whereas another person who reads it may say he does not "know" it. The two may have precisely the same pattern of retrieval when they are tested, however, and so it becomes clear that they have differed primarily in what they meant by saying they "knew" it. This is thus a matter of memory about memory, or metamemory. As it turns out, metamemory is important in determining how well we use our memory skills. If we know how much we have to study before something is fully encoded, for example, we are in a better position for retrieval than someone who has little inkling of how much or what kind of studying to do. In essence, a person with a strong metamemory is able to take full advantage of whatever memory capacities he or she has. Someone with a weak metamemory, on the other hand, is like a person who has lost the instructions for operating a computer. No matter how much memory capacity is available in the computer, without good instructions the capacity may never be used. Metamemory can include knowledge about encoding, storage, and retrieval processes, and so may be useful at each of these stages.

External Memory

Now, introductory text views of memory begin receding into the distance at a faster rate—as we discuss an aspect of individual memory that has seldom received formal recognition in the scientific literature. It is surprising, actually, that the psychological study of memory has dwelt so little upon the extraordinary human tendency to record items in external storage media. Our walls are filled with books, our file cabinets with papers, our notebooks with jottings, our homes with artifacts and souvenirs, our floppy disks with data records, and at times, our palms with the scribbled answers to a test. Quite simply, we seem to record as much outside our minds as within them.

People use external storage for many everyday memory tasks (Harris, 1978). Remembering an upcoming engagement, for example, is not something people have to do forever, so they commonly rely on placing reminders in conspicuous places or on following their calendars (Meacham & Leiman, 1982). External storage is not only used as an "aid" in this way, however; often it is the central storage area for large bodies of information that cannot be retrieved elsewhere. The scrawlings one may make in a diary or daily log, for example, typically become the only record of many of the day's mundane activities. Internal storage of many details is rather sketchy, and although we may be able to reconstruct our day in general without recourse to a diary (e.g., "I went to work"), the external source provides some startling reminders. In a larger sense, realms of information we have never even encoded may become available for our retrieval because we are able to access external storage in the form of books, files, microfilm, and other media.

Externally stored items of information are retrievable, however, only when we know something about what they are and where they are. Although external memory aids such as notes may stare at us from the desktop and so present no identity or location mystery, the more frequent case is that we need some item of information and only know generally what and where it is. In search of a phone number, for instance, we may know we're looking for "Rudy's number" but not know the number itself. To retrieve the number we may need to look it up in the telephone directory, check the notepad by the phone, or call Rudy's ex-girlfriend to find out. The successful retrieval of a memory item (such as this number) thus requires the prior encoding of at least two additional pieces of information—a retrieval cue or *label* for the item (e.g., "Rudy's number"), and a notion of the *location* of the item (e.g., in the book). This seems to be a general requirement for the use of external storage.

The notions of a memory item, its label, and its location have their parallels in internal storage. As a rule, we can retrieve items from internal storage merely by knowing their labels, but these labels often can be broadly defined. If we are searching for "Rudy's number" internally, of course, it usually just pops to mind when we think of that label. We may sit down by the phone and be reminded of the number, however, without having a very clear prior thought of that particular label for it. We may be thinking instead of some other idea that happens to be organized with the number in memory (e.g., Rudy's toothless grin), and so have the number come to mind. The memory item is thus reached through any of a number of cues that perform the function of a label only implicitly (Graf & Schacter, 1985).

Location information, on the other hand, is something we never have to specify to ourselves in searching for internally stored items. Rather than wondering "Where did I put that?" we simply retrieve the item or not. We do, however, hold a certain kind of location information about our own memory items—in the form of our metamemories. We have opinions about what we know and do not know, and these allow us to judge whether an item or set of them is to be found in our own memories. Using this facility we can report, for instance, that we know Rudy's number without even reviewing it; or, without trying to reproduce the number, we can assert that we do not have it. Such judgments of location allow us to make both general and specific assessments of our internal information stores.

The processes of encoding, storage, and retrieval can now be understood to have both internal and external manifestations. When an item of information is encountered, it may be encoded internally or externally.

Successful encoding of either type requires that a label of some kind be attached to the information, that the label be encoded internally, and that at least one other piece of information be encoded internally as well. What we normally think of as internal encoding requires that the *item* be encoded internally along with the label. External encoding, however, requires that that *location* be encoded internally with the label—and for this reason, the item itself need not even be known. As an example of this, suppose that one encodes this book in memory. To encode it internally requires learning some sort of label (e.g., the book's title), and then memorizing the rest of it from cover to cover. To encode it externally also requires learning the label, but then only calls for learning where the book can be found. In either encoding process, the minimum requirement is that two categories of information are placed in internal storage.

In the course of a day, much of what we encounter is encoded internally, but probably much more is encoded externally. This is because the labels we encode for externally stored information can be very general, referring to hundreds or even millions of items. We surely cannot encode this much information internally in a short time, and it is for this reason that a large part of our internal storage capacity is devoted to location information that allows us to retrieve external items. For example, the average college professor may have an impressive internal store even when caught off guard in the classroom by an inquisitive student. However, this professor will have access to more information, enough to stupefy even the most challenging questioner, as the result of a brief sortee to the office, the microcomputer, or the library. Knowing where things are to be found can be a more important consequence of education than merely knowing things.

Transactive Memory

Other people can be locations of external storage for the individual. The professor may be the prime location for certain arcane bits of knowledge occasionally desired by the student, for example. For that matter, the student may also be an external storage facility for the professor; the professor may fail to learn the student's name, for instance, knowing that this is retrievable because the student is available in the classroom on a regular basis for consultation. In either case, one person has access to information in another's memory by virtue of knowing that the other person is a location for an item with a certain label. This allows both people to depend on communication with each other for the enhancement of their personal memory stores. At the same time, however, this interdependence produces a knowledge-holding system that is larger and more complex than either of the individuals' own memory systems. Each individual may know the system from one perspective—having in internal storage many items, labels, and locations, and knowing that the locations are in the other's memory. However, this individual usually will not be aware of the complementary location information held internally by the other, information that the other uses to keep track of what the individual knows. The transactive memory system, in short, is more than its individual component systems.

If we ask a question of a person who is a well-integrated part of a transactive memory network, this person often is able to answer (after consultation with other network members, of course) with information well beyond his or her own internal storage. Asking any member of a family a question about the family's summer vacation, for example, can prompt the retrieval of several members' accounts of the experience. The success we have in retrieving certain items depends on the degree to which the person we begin with has location information about the items we label. Even if we ask the person to retrieve an item with an obscure label, however, the person may be able to help us enter the storage system. Asking Bud how much the family paid for gasoline in Orlando, for instance, may lead him to quiz Dad—who generally knows about car-related items. Or perhaps Bud suspects that Father knows nothing and so instead asks Mom about the gas prices. There are a variety of potential paths to the information, and it may even be the case that no one knows, or everyone knows. Gaining entry to the group's stored knowledge is likely to be an efficient enterprise, however, even when we begin with a fairly inexpert member. This person may not have internal access to many items but is likely to have stored the main locations of information in the group.

The transactive quality of memory in a group is evident also in the transactions that take place during encoding and retrieval. In transactive encoding, people discuss incoming information, determining where and in what form it is to be stored in the group. Transactive encoding sometimes takes the simple form of direct instruction for one group member to encode information internally (e.g., "Lulu, remember this phone number"), but more often involves complex negotiations regarding the common labels that should be assigned to items (e.g., "What *was* that?"), the matter of responsibilities for internal storage (e.g., "Isn't this your bailiwick?"), the preferred locations of items (e.g., "I'll take care of that"), and the like. In this process, the very nature of incoming information can be changed, translated into a form that the group can store.

Transactive retrieval, in turn, requires determining the location of information and sometimes entails the combination or interplay of items coming from multiple locations. Transactive retrieval begins when the person who holds an item internally is not the one who is asked to retrieve it. A client asks the boss for information, for instance, that the boss has no idea about—but thinks the secretary may know. If the secretary can produce the item and pass it along, transactive retrieval comes to a successful conclusion. However, it may be that the secretary fails to find the item internally, perhaps finding instead some other information related to the label. As it turns out, perhaps the secretary recalls that the boss asked for this information at another time and reports this to the boss: "I gave that to you last Tuesday." The boss may now be able to use the new lead to retrieve some item internally or externally. He might now recall that the information he asked for Tuesday was in the top desk drawer in a file labeled "THIS IS IT." The item is found, then, thanks to neither the boss nor the secretary—but to the combined transaction of the boss and the secretary. The transactive process may thus operate at retrieval to search for a label that can prompt access to the desired item in the internal or external storage of at least one group member.

The Transactive Memory System

The transactive memory system in a group involves the operation of the memory systems of the individuals and the processes of communication that occur within the group. Transactive memory is therefore not traceable to any of the individuals alone, nor can it be found somewhere "between" individuals. Rather, it is a property of a group. This unique quality of transactive memory brings with it the realization that we are speaking of a constructed system, a mode of group operation that is built up over time by its individual constituents. Once in place, then, the transactive memory system can have an impact on what the group as a whole can remember, and as a result, on what individuals in the group remember and regard as correct even outside the group. In short, transactive memory derives from individuals to form a group information-processing system that eventually may return to have a profound influence upon its individual participants. In what follows our discussion centers on these developments in sequence.

Constructing the Transactive System

A transactive system begins when individuals learn something about each others' domains of expertise. Usually, such information is not at all difficult to obtain. When we walk along a crowded sidewalk, we can make inferences on the basis of dress, race, sex, possessions, and the like about the domains of expertise that may be afforded us by every person we see. In impromptu groups, these superficial bases of inference may be all we have and lead us, therefore, to make only some fairly broad distinctions. The other members of a jury decide that the retired Air Force General is likely to be smart, for instance, and so elect him foreman. Expertise judgments based on stereotypes are prone to exaggeration and error, however, and it is thus not surprising that impromptu groups may be poor memory systems. In longer standing groups, however, the history of conversation about who has done what and heard what and been where and studied what and with whom and under what circumstance could be exceedingly rich, and so allows members to discern with much greater precision just who is expert in each of a variety of information domains.

Known experts in a domain are usually held responsible for the encoding, storage, and retrieval of any new information encountered in that domain. The family member who is the known expert on the fleet of rusting cars and machinery out behind the barn, for example, is likely to be faulted if any harm comes to the fleet without his or her knowledge. The expert is responsible for continuing to encode incoming information. Questions about the domain (e.g., "How long has that hornets' nest been in the Chevy?") are typically directed to this person by default, and it is sometimes difficult for the person to escape continuing responsibility for storage in the domain once expertise is generally acknowledged. Other group members usually contribute to this centralization of information by delivering new information to the appropriate expert. The phone call from the Sheriff regarding the fleet will soon be conveyed to the family rusting machinery expert, allowing other family members to relax knowing that the information is properly stored in the group.

It is when a clear candidate of this kind is not available that difficulties arise in the allocation of information within the group. Very commonly, formal groups will make the assignment of responsibility for information domains to individuals on other bases. The classroom teacher will ask Ricky to become an expert on teeth by the weekend, the restaurant owner will ask a waiter to begin looking into wine, or the church choir will vote to appoint someone to keep track of the robes. In the absence of such explicit assignments, more subtle rules are used to direct continuing responsibility. For example, the person who initially reports a domain to the group may be held responsible; when the wife learns first of an upcoming party she and her husband may attend, for instance, she is subsequently held responsible for finding out additional information about the party. The person who most recently encounters a domain of information may also incur responsibility for it; when the husband intercepts a telephone update on the party plans, he may become accountable for the successful conduct of the whole enterprise. Overall, then, there are two sources of information people use to decide who is to be the acknowledged location of a set of labeled knowledge in the group. Individuals are seen as linked to knowledge on the basis of their *personal expertise*, or through the *circumstantial knowledge responsibility* that accrues as a result of how the knowledge has been encountered by the group.

An effective transactive memory in a group should not leave the responsibility for information to chance. If a clear expert does not exist in a domain, a channel for the processing of that information should nevertheless be established, either explicitly or implicitly. A study by Giuliano and Wegner (1985) supports this general hypothesis by showing that in intimate couples, transactive memory operates to keep one or the other partner responsible for information at all times. Couples selected for the study had been seeing each other exclusively for at least 3 months and were given the

Table 9.1. Percentage Recall as a Function of Perceived
Expertise and Circumstantial Responsibility
for Knowledge[a]

	Self-expertise	
Partner expertise	Self not expert	Self expert
Self is circumstantially responsible for knowledge		
Partner not expert	29.8	34.3
Partner expert	24.2	27.3
Partner is circumstantially responsible for knowledge		
Partner not expert	17.3	24.9
Partner expert	19.8	23.6

[a]Cell means are based on a within-subjects analysis for 20 dating couples (40 subjects). When the self is circumstantially responsible, there is a reliable main effect for partner expertise, $F(1,39) = 5.85$, $p < .01$. When the partner is circumstantially responsible, there is a reliable main effect for self expertise, $F(1,39) = 5.79$, $p < .03$. Data from Giuliano and Wegner (1985).

laboratory task of *together* remembering 64 items of information. Each of these items was drawn from an area of expertise; the item "Kaypro II," for example, was drawn from the area of computer expertise. The items were embedded in context sentences (e.g., "The Kaypro II is a personal computer") that made it clear even to the nonexpert what area of expertise they represented. Each partner was asked (either before the memory experiment or afterwards) to review the 64 domains of expertise and to indicate in each case whether a particular area was one in which the male was more expert, the female was more expert, both were expert, or neither was expert. For the memory portion of the study, eight trials were conducted in which each subject was given a set of four items to study for 1 minute, and then was instructed to pass these to the partner, who was asked to review them for 30 seconds. In this way, both partners became aware of their relative advantage (or disadvantage) in encoding time for each item.

These manipulations placed couples in the position of trying to remember information that varied in both personal expertise and circumstantial responsibility. Items had been sorted by each participant into four categories of personal expertise (self, partner, both, or neither), and then were encountered under circumstances that led either self or partner to be more responsible for them—in that either self viewed the items longer than partner or vice versa. The results, presented in Table 9.1, show the proportion of items recalled by each partner in these conditions. The most general effect was for the personal expertise of self. Across the board, subjects remembered items from categories they had judged to be their own areas of expertise. This is not particularly surprising and can be expected solely on the basis of a theory of individual metamemory; people know which areas of their own experience are most richly elaborated and well developed and simply predict their own memory performance on this basis.

The other effect of interest here reveals a clearly transactive phenomenon. Subjects who were circumstantially responsible for a topic more often recalled items from that topic when they believed their partner was not personally expert in that topic. In other words, members of these couples accepted the responsibility for information placed upon them by their circumstance, even when they were not expert, but did so only when they knew their partner had no history of personal expertise in the area. This, then, is a case in which an individual's internal memory retrieval is affected by transactive constraints—knowledge of what someone else's memory can or cannot do.

These transactive memory strategies combine to ensure that information the couple needs will always be captured by at least one of the partners. When either partner encounters a piece of information useful to the pair, that partner is placed in the position of having circumstantial responsibility for the knowledge. Normally the person lets the item "pass by"—to be remembered by the partner—only when the partner is known to be expert in the domain of that item. Because individuals regularly remember items in their own domains of expertise, moreover, the partner comes forward to "catch" the item before it escapes the group. It should be noted, however, that this efficient group encoding and storage system is critically dependent on each partner's knowledge of the other's domains of expertise. Faulty location knowledge on either member's part dooms the system, allowing items to pass through the group without being stored. Early in the development of the relationship, this is to be expected; later on, it signals the improper construction of the transactive system and can result in chronic memory failure for the dyad. Such a couple can lose the laundry, forget to pick up the children, and arrive at the theater just in time to watch the carpenters renovate the mezzanine.

The construction of a working transactive memory in a group is a fairly automatic consequence of social perception. We each attend to what others are like and in this enterprise learn as well what we can expect them to know. Then, when the group is called upon to remember something, information is channeled to the known experts. When no expert is known to exist, the individual who is entrusted with the information by circumstance holds on to it, allowing the group subsequent access. In sum, transactive memory can be built because individuals in a group accept responsibility for knowledge.

Transactive Processes in the Group

There is no guarantee that an item of information presented to an individual can subsequently be retrieved in the same form. Likewise, the group has an effect on the information it encounters, sometimes retrieving it unscathed, but sometimes losing it and sometimes changing it. These changes can take place because of individual memory effects but are perhaps just as likely to accrue as a result of transactive phenomena. When people talk about items of information, the information can change dramatically.

Individuals may talk about some items of information as they are encoding them. When such transactive encoding occurs, labels are linked to the item by the conversants as a group. Although this has the benefit of allowing each group member subsequent access to details of this item unknown to self but known to others, it also tends to color what is perceived by the group. Whatever label is applied first, perhaps arbitrarily, becomes the catchword for the item. This label may even be incorrect, but it serves as the common denominator for discussion and so becomes part of the item for everyone. This is particularly likely because individuals tend to encode items well when there is elaborative rehearsal—reviewing of the item's organization ties to other items (Anderson & Reder, 1979). Group commentary on incoming memory items provides just such rehearsal, and for this reason, individuals are more inclined to remember items as discussed than items as perceived. The group-acknowledged label thus can become more than a tag, growing to provide the major portion of what is remembered of the item by all group members. The term "UFO," for instance, might serve as a rallying point for a wide array of specific memories held by individuals who witnessed an event one evening. The label suggests a common experience and provides a common foundation for explanation and elaboration. Without this label, individuals might variously speak of seeing, say, "funny lights" or a "bright object," but with the label, a core memory is formed that provides an interpretive scheme for many different items of information—and so provides the group a night to remember.

Discussion that occurs well after the intake of information can have similar consequences. Modification of information may take place during storage, as has been shown to occur in individuals (Loftus, Miller, & Burns, 1978). This modification can occur much more quickly and with greater impact than in the case of individual memory, however, because the storage of information in the group may be more scattered and, hence, easily replaced by misinformation. In the UFO case, for instance, one family member may come home to tell the story of the unusual experience; other family members hear the story and get it wrong in places; members who have not even seen the event talk about it and resolve inconsistencies in their stories; finally, the group as a whole may end up with a majority opinion of the event that differs in many details from what the original witness saw. When they are asked what this person experienced, they will introduce their version as fact, and eventually may even convince the witness that certain things were encoded that truly were not present at all.

When the group attempts to retrieve information, transactive effects could occur that render individual memories more or less available for retrieval. The label that is used at the beginning of the transactive retrieval attempt can be translated into another label, as noted earlier, because one person finds internally stored information related to the initial label that serves as a useful cue for the internal search being conducted by another person. It is quite possible for groups to forget what they were looking for in this process, however, or to find useful items that they did not actually set out to find. The interesting aspect of transactive retrieval, then, is its "traveling" character, its tendency to wander.

Consider, by way of illustration, your visit to the computer store to ask why your new machine keeps saying "Invalid command." In short order, you find yourself in a conversation among all the salespeople. Each one seems to mention something different. Cryptic references to the software arise in certain quarters, are replaced by "loose chip" talk at one point, and amidst further murmurs, the person you first asked nods knowingly. An anticipatory shiver runs through you, and then you are apprised of several factors about your computer that you already knew. You eventually leave, perhaps with the solution, maybe suspecting only vaguely what must be done, but certainly with some new facts about the machine that you did not intend to find. In most cases, the person who you ask for group-stored information acts as your guide, checking to ascertain that your question has been answered. In the process, however, much other information is retrieved as well.

The transactive processes that occur at each stage of memory processing do not only produce errors. Although the examples we have entertained to this point suggest that transactive memory is often the source of departures from reality, it must be emphasized that useful creative products are just as likely to be produced by transaction. This occurs when different items of information that are held separately by individuals or subgroups are brought together. In essence, a group is capable of achieving integrative processes in memory that parallel the integration that can occur at the individual level. Hayes-Roth & Thorndyke (1979) describe integrative memory in the individual, noting that when memory items can be integrated or combined, the individual is more likely to remember those items. In transactive memory, this can occur when individuals respond to a particular information label, and one group member retrieves one item whereas a second member retrieves something quite different. In their subsequent discussion, it is determined that the two items add up to yet a third idea, one that is a qualitative departure from either of its constituents. Aircraft mechanics who are asked about a plane's safety, for example, might each volunteer different facts; Betty might note an unexplained bit of oil on the runway, while Veronica remembers that a hydraulic indicator light was not functioning. Taken one at a time, these observations may not be noteworthy. Taken together, however, they point to an oil leak, and this integration could turn out to be significant indeed. Both mechanics thus are likely to remember both facts, as well as their integrated meaning.

Integrative processes are among the most important transactive events in groups because they manufacture new knowledge for the group—and so for all the group members. Information coming from different locations in the transactive system is tied together by a common label, and during this juxtaposition is discovered to mean something new. And in well-developed transactive systems, there seems to be a strong press for just such integration. Intimate couples, for instance, strive for integrative agreement in their group solutions to problems, often abandoning solutions suggested by each partner alone in favor of a solution that emerges at the group level (Wegner *et al.*, 1985). The group exerts a strong directive pressure on what is to be encoded, stored, and retrieved and places a special premium on integrative transactions. Integration affirms the need to have a group in the first place, showing all members the utility of coming together to remember.

Impact on Individuals

The usefulness of a transactive memory for the individual is beyond question. The individual's expertise is expanded dramatically on the construction of a transactive system with others, and the specialization of knowledge that individuals can develop within such a system becomes beneficial to all. The individual gains others' domains of expertise, of course, but also gains access to the knowledge that is created through integrations occurring within the transactive memory. There is another benefit of company in that information relevant to the individual often is encoded and stored when the individual alone would miss it. Others can process knowledge and make decisions even as the individual sleeps. Moreover, a group with a smoothly functioning transactive memory is likely to be effective in reaching its goals and will thereby satisfy its members. Individuals thus benefit both directly and indirectly from transactive systems. These various advantages of transactive memory systems no doubt promote the formation of transactive memories within groups and, to be sure, provide the impetus for the formation of many groups that would not even be formed otherwise.

Transactive memory is not without its drawbacks, however. The complexity that is added to an individual's memory system by the existence of connections to other memory systems creates the potential for new sources of confusion and error. The most obvious source of difficulty is the incomplete specification of paths of knowledge responsibility within the group. As mentioned earlier, a partially constructed transactive system may leave certain individuals not knowing who is expert in important domains of knowledge or may leave everyone wondering how to decide when circumstance confers responsibility for knowledge. When an organizational system is built that channels information away from experts, for instance, things may be forgotten. When expertise is in dispute, information may fall in the cracks as well. Likewise, when clear group expectations regarding circumstantial knowledge responsibility are not developed, trouble may arise. These problems can exact a serious toll on the individual's information-processing capacities.

Typically, for instance, the person one reaches by phone in a household is responsible for bringing the desired family member to the phone. If the desired member is not home, a message is taken. This "first contact" person is crucial for connecting the family to outside information sources, and this person's job is typically to maintain contact with the outside source until some connection with the proper location of information in the family has been made. In many businesses, however, the first contact person knows little if anything of the expertise structure in the organization; the person is an "operator" who is hired to "work the phone equipment," and this person is never heard from after setting up the initial connection. The caller is sent to some contact and, if that does not work out, may have to start all over with redialing the phone. Such faulty connections in business mean that members of the company lose contact with each other and with outside information. What is really needed in the first contact position is a transactive memory expert, a person with quite extensive knowledge of who knows what in the company. This person must understand the requirement to maintain the responsibility for incoming information and continue to do so until a clear connection with someone who is the proper expert is established.

Individuals can suffer from transactive memory, though, even when it is well established and running smoothly. This happens when they overestimate its capabilities. Just as a person's metamemory offers information about what the person knows, a transactive memory system provides individuals information about what knowledge they may access in the group. This may result in a brand of the "feeling of knowing" (Hart, 1967) that yields an overconfidence in one's own ability to access knowledge. In the presence of one's Scout troop, for instance, one might fairly bristle with the lore of the woods and so set forth to conquer nature without doing much information seeking for oneself. If there are any shortcomings in the information provided by the troop, they are not likely to be met by one's own keen analysis. Thus, if the camporee factsheet has no mention of insect repellent, one may fail to think this a worthwhile accessory and so spend an uncomfortable weekend courtesy of one's confidence in the troop's preparedness. Such trust in the group for information makes one's own contribution less useful, of course, and also paves the way for the group to make poor decisions (cf. Janis, 1983).

The impact of transactive memory on the individual may be most clearly seen in its absence. When a group dissolves, formerly interdependent individuals are left with the individual remnants of what was once a transactive system. These remnants can be not only useless but troublesome in themselves. Much location information held by the individual is now unimportant; indeed, the knowledge that a departed spouse knew all about, say, balancing the checkbook, serves only as a bitter reminder that one does not now know these things for oneself. Labels for information that the individual shared with fellow group members may be unintelligible to others; the terms for bodily sensations or symptoms used in one's family may be confusing or just plain silly to one's physician. Items of information themselves, if the individual has been holding them for the group, become quite valueless; one may have been the only manager who could name every company employee—as the company drifted into bankruptcy proceedings. Major elements of the information that is shared in transactive memory thus become, at best, irrelevant and, at worst, misleading in the person's quest to form an independent individual memory.

Applications

Despite its roots in a tradition of group mind theorizing that stretches back many years, transactive memory is relatively new and unexamined. For this reason, it is important to chart the domains in which the idea may find useful application and empirical investigation. Transactive memory was first introduced to account for certain phenomena of intimate relationships, and that topic begins the discussion. Then the utility of transactive memory analysis is examined in the study of health behavior, instructional psychology, and organization management.

Intimate Relations

The most intricate and accurate transactive memories can be formed by people when they spend their whole lives together. The bonds of intimacy bring with them a large degree of cognitive interdependence, a tendency for individuals' thought processes and structures to be mutually determined (Wegner et al., 1985). This means that the labels intimates use for knowledge domains are often idiosyncratic to the pair (Hopper, Knapp, & Scott, 1981), that there exists a mutually understood organization of expertise and responsibility for information (Atkinson & Huston, 1984), and that information is processed by the pair in certain typical ways that are partly negotiated and partly implicit (Reiss, 1981). Transactive memory in intimates, then, represents much more than the observation that intimates can fill in stories for one another, alternating in their retrieval of shared information. Although this is part of the idea, the transactive memory developed in close relationships is yet more central, both a sign and a foundation of the successful relationship itself.

Relationship development is often understood as a process of mutual self-disclosure (e.g., Archer, 1980). Although it is probably more romantic to cast this process as one of interpersonal revelation and acceptance, it can also be appreciated as a necessary precursor to transactive memory. After all, partners must learn about each other's areas of expertise, and one function of early self-disclosure is the development of such location information in each partner. It is interesting that couples who come to agree on who knows what in the relationship are generally more satisfied with their pairing than couples who disagree. This is particularly true when the couples are asked to indicate whether one partner knows more than the other on each topic. In responses of 60 heterosexual couples who completed a questionnaire (also used by Giuliano & Wegner, 1985) that called for each partner to judge whether self, other, both, or neither were expert in each of 64 knowledge domains, a couple's agreement on self versus other expertise judgments was significantly correlated with each member's assessment of satisfaction with the relationship. This was not the case for agreement on "both" or "neither" judgments, indicating that the differentiation of knowledge domains in the heterosexual dyad may be an important key to success.

Perhaps some proportion of the sex role differentiation that occurs in couples may be traced to the utility of differential expertise in transactive memory. Although the development of "experts" in families has been acknowledged before (Davis, 1976), it has not been emphasized that this development may produce more efficient functioning in the group. When each person has group-acknowledged responsibility for particular tasks and facts, though, greater efficiency is inevitable. Each domain is handled by the fewest people capable of doing so, and responsibility for the domains is continuous over time rather than intermittently assigned by circumstance. The allocation of tasks may be determined initially by minor variations in circumstantial responsibility; the female, for instance, may more often be present when memory items relevant to the baby become known to the group. This gathering of knowledge serves as a kernel of expertise that draws additional items from other group members. The female quickly becomes the "baby expert," and even in the pressure toward egalitarian relationships that comes in a dual-career family, the female's informational duties in mothering may progress more rapidly than the male's duties in fathering.

Ideally, the differentiation of transactive memory is not one sided. The most efficient couple would likely develop equally large and equally taxing domains of individual expertise. This means that breaking up is likely to reduce the memory capabilities of both dyad members. Indeed, much of the grief and disorientation that accompanies the dissolution of a close relationship can be traced to the loss of transactive memory capacities.

Divorced people who suffer depression and complain of cognitive dysfunctions may be expressing the loss of their external memory systems. They once were able to discuss their experiences to reach a shared understanding, but such transactive encoding is gone. They once could count on access to a wide range of storage in their partner, and this, too, is gone. Their former capacity to retrieve information in their own memories by bantering with their partner until a helpful label can be found, also, is gone. In short, much of the joy and much of the utility of close relationships can be found in their transactive memory systems. The loss of transactive memory feels like losing a part of one's own mind.

Health Behavior

Transactive memory phenomena are relevant to health behavior at several levels. The success of self-diagnosis, the success of physician diagnosis, and the success of medical compliance, at minimum, are all affected by transactive memory processes. This is because some form of group decision making is often involved at each stage—when the patient decides to seek medical care, when the patient and physician discuss the nature of the problem, and when the patient is sent away with a prescribed medical regimen.

People seldom reach self-diagnoses alone. They commonly contact family or friends to make initial expressions of their symptoms (Pennebaker, 1982), and the process of deciding that the symptoms need treatment is thus a social one. It has been argued that individuals judge symptoms and decide whether to seek treatment on the basis of their cognitive prototypes of illnesses (Bishop, Sikes, Schroeder, McGregor, & Holub, 1985). Having a stuffy nose and sore throat, for example, is usually sufficient to convince people only that their symptoms match the prototypic "head cold," and this self-diagnosis then leads them to whatever action they associate with that prototype. Illness prototypes can be supplied by friends and relatives, however, and so can multiply the complexity of the decision to seek treatment. A circle of friends who have relatively impoverished cognitive prototypes of illness may lead the individual to make infrequent or mistaken illness self-diagnoses, whereas friends who are all in medical school may lead the individual to make relatively more frequent (but perhaps equally mistaken) self-diagnoses. The illnesses that friends and acquaintances have had themselves, of course, provide a point of comparison for the individual's symptom constellation, and this suggests that people in groups will often all appear to come down with the same thing. They may in fact have a common illness, or they may have a transactive memory that has encoded each person's idiosyncratic symptoms in terms of the group-provided illness label (cf. Colligan, Pennebaker, & Murphy, 1982).

The physician–patient dialog can also be understood as a transactive memory process, one of a slightly different kind. Here, the physician is an expert on illness generally, while the patient is an expert on the symptoms and manifestations of his or her particular malady. Both interactants usually know this, and the effect they seek by coming together is the completion of a successful transactive retrieval procedure—a meeting of the minds. The process can be led by either physician or patient, but it is clearly a sequential search in which early interaction phases determine the path of later phases. The patient's illness prototype will probably constrain the patient's symptom reports at first to those most relevant to the suspected illness. The physician may learn this illness label from the patient at the outset and may subsequently be influenced by it. This can be problematic because the early, albeit tentative acceptance of the label can constrain the physician's line of inquiry, ultimately moving the investigation along a narrow path determined in large part by the patient, the lesser expert in the pair. At the same time, it is possible for the physician to give the patient's hypotheses too little credence, and in this way to fail in fulfilling the patient's desires to be reoriented and reassured.

The transactive memory system developed between the patient and physician may eventually be expanded to include the patient's relatives and friends. This is necessary when the patient is given a prescribed regime by the physician—medication, perhaps, or a special diet, exercise, or activity plan. The patient may fail to adhere to this prescription, as is often the case (Sackett & Snow, 1979), and such failure can undermine the entire health care delivery process that has occurred to this point. Noncompliance can happen because the transactive memory system surrounding the patient is not sufficiently developed to support the patient's compliance. The patient forgets to take a pill, for example, and because the patient is usually considered the expert on his or her own self-medication this is ignored by family. The patient forgets again and again, and the prescription is finally abandoned. The physician finds out several weeks later when the patient is back with further problems, or the physician may not find out at all. Perhaps physicians or health-care professionals in this position should convey information about the patient's prescription to the entire family. Emphasizing such knowledge to them may increase their acceptance of circumstantial responsibility for the patient's remembering, and so provide a "safety net" should the patient fail to self-medicate. This advice seems simple enough but it is often forgotten when the patient's memory is understood only as an individual system and not as part of a transactive system.

Instructional Psychology

A teacher and student form a transactive memory system that has some special properties. Their roles are defined, of course, in terms of a lopsided distribution of knowledge in the system, and the transmission of internal memory storage from the teacher to the student is typically the overarching goal of the group. The usual instructional setting, however, is only a temporary transactive memory system, the purpose of which is the formation of a permanent individual memory system on the part of the student. This means that instructional success occurs if the transactive memory system can replace itself. This would occur if the teacher could be replaced with some more portable or generally available external memory source (e.g., a library), or if the student could encompass in internal memory all that once was part of the transactive system.

This movement of memory from one location to another occurs most efficiently when frequent transaction is possible. Wood (1980) summarizes studies indicating that instruction through dialog is more effective than a number of seemingly comparable instruction techniques—including didactic communication and encouraged exploration. Mothers instructing their children, for instance, engage them in a conversation that creates a "scaffolding" of control around the child's activity, one which provides just that level of intervention necessary to get the child over his or her current difficulties. The mother steps in to offer control, suggestion, and information when the child fails at some attempted action, and steps back, in turn, offering progressive relaxation of such direction when the planning and execution of the action are going well. Wood finds that this technique is particularly likely to impart task mastery to children and that parents who use it are the best teachers.

This technique tends to insure optimal transmission of information from one locale in transactive memory (the teacher) to another (the student). Independent, internally guided action is allowed and encouraged in the student at every step, but the watchful instructor intervenes with externally stored information when this is necessary to keep the student progressing. The activities elicited in the student are likely to be remembered well because this ongoing transaction takes full advantage of the "generation effect" in memory—the tendency to remember better the information one has generated than the information one has merely encountered (Johnson & Raye, 1981; Slamecka & Graf, 1978). A limited context is imposed by the instructor, and in it the student generates new language and action. Because these self-generated responses have been guided and arranged through the "scaffolding" procedure, very few lengthy but wholly inappropriate lines of action are produced. Checks and interventions occur throughout the information transmission period, for transactions retrieve information from the teacher just to match points at which the student requires the encoding of the particular item. In the end, the new structures of expertise are transferred to the student with minimal amounts of communication and maximal resultant internal memory.

As an example, we might consider the interaction of a chemistry teacher and student when the student asks how to operate a balance. One teacher might take this as the opportunity for a lecture and launch into 20 minutes of balance theory, whereas another might encourage the student to experiment with the balance on his own. The first technique might be effective in the long run, but it would be inefficient indeed; the second might be easy for the teacher but has the potential of being completely fruitless. In contrast, a teacher using a transactive approach would encourage the experimentation but then would watch to find the student's first error, correct this, and then encourage more experimentation. Each subsequent mistake, as it is corrected, provides the opportunity for transmission of precisely the information the student needs to complete the operation. The instruction passes information easily and certainly, and the reorganization of the group's memory that results takes place with the minimum of confusion. It is interesting that people drift naturally toward such transactive instruction, and that it works so very well.

Organization Management

The managers of organizations are sometimes put in the unusual position of having to design a transactive memory from scratch. Although they may not know they are doing this, they go ahead and assemble a group of people, give them positions in the organization, tell them who to report to, write their job descriptions, and so on. More often, of course, managers do not have the luxury of starting fresh in this way and must manage instead by making revisions in the organizational structure when these become possible. In either case, however, the structuring of an organization is clearly an exercise in structuring transactive memory as well. Classic studies of organizational communication patterns (e.g., Leavitt, 1951; see Mullen, Chapter 1, this volume), have alerted many managers to the "connections" that are being made when an organization is put together.

The task of structuring organizations for the most effective transactive memory systems is a formidable one. It is helpful, however, to consider the dimensions along which such structures could vary. This at least allows the manager some sense of the appropriateness of the organization's memory to the organization's purpose. Wegner *et al.* (1985) have suggested that transactive memories can vary in the same structural dimensions often used to analyze individual memories—differentiation and integration. A differentiated transactive memory occurs when *different* items of information are stored in different individual memory stores, but the individuals know the general labels and locations of items they do not hold personally. An integrated transactive memory occurs when the *same* items of information are held in different individual memory stores, and the individuals are aware of the overlap because they share label and location information as well. Integrated transactive memory in an organization represents, then, an extreme of one kind; all organization members have duplicate knowledge. Differentiated transactive memory in an organization represents the opposing extreme; organization members share a limited core of labels and locations but otherwise diverge dramatically in their domains of storage.

These structural extremes vary in their effectiveness depending on the organization's task.

An organization with an integrated transactive memory is desirable when every member of the organization must personally carry out every function of the organization. A sales organization in which all employees are selling the same product, for instance, will give customers the most immediate information if every salesperson knows all about the product. The individual doing the selling should not have to call for technical help or ask someone about a price detail. This plan for organization design is useful, then, whenever the individual organization member must represent the organization without contact with other organization members. This plan for organization design does not give the individual member access to much information in transactive memory outside that available already in personal memory. For this reason, the individual member is not particularly dependent on the organization for informational support. The person could easily slip off and perform the appropriate functions alone or with another organization. In this structure, moreover, individual members who are already installed in the organization seldom benefit by getting together to compare notes. Because their knowledge bases are already duplicated, their conversations seldom bring together different items of information under the same label and so only infrequently will produce new and creative integrations of disparate items of information.

The operation of a differentiated transactive memory in an organization is useful in producing new integrations. When many people in the organization perform different functions, each has access to knowledge that others may label and locate, but do not know. Discussions among people in this sort of organization can be confusing, for they bring together items from different locations that may be only vaguely related to the label that is currently being considered. However, these discussions produce creative group products. (Eventually, it might be noted, such integrative discussions can transform the differentiated organization into an integrated one.) The potential for knowledge storage and production in a differentiated organization is naturally much greater than that in an integrated organization. Because individual minds are not duplicating their efforts, there is a much more efficient use of storage. Each individual brings to the organization a wide array of new knowledge, and contact with the appropriate knowledge location experts in such an organization can yield much more information than any individual could produce. Unless all the members of the organization are connected with high-speed computer communications devices, however, the organization's encoding and retrieval processes will be sluggish indeed, resembling those of a brilliant slow person.

Many difficulties in organization management can be traced to the improper matching of transactive memory structures to organizational tasks. The wise manager would consider the properties of each of these structures in planning the layout of an organization. In putting together a retail store, for instance, one might assume that salesclerks are inter-changeable; certain benefits in the uniformity of training, the replaceability of workers, and the like would result from the strategy of organizing these people into an integrated memory structure. A customer asking a question about a product in the stereo department might be met with a blank stare by every employee in the store, however, and so leave one wondering whether an assembly of experts in the various retail areas would not be better. A more differentiated transactive memory would allow the organization to provide the information services that people often want to accompany their products. Depending on the kind of retail outlet one wanted to develop, then, very different transactive memory strategies would be appropriate. Of course, the integrated and differentiated structures need not characterize the entire organization uniformly. These could be mixed and matched in different departments of the organization, with the appropriateness of each to the task of each organizational unit taken into account.

Conclusions

The idea of transactive memory provides a useful way of understanding how people think together. The traditional theories of the group mind, aside from their aforementioned problems, have always suffered from an overly simplistic view of group mental operations. The notion of the group mind has always served as a shorthand for the uniformity of individuals' mental processes and behaviors. In the mass movements of a crowd, the majority decisions of an electorate, or the sweetly homogeneous mindlessness of people in love, theorists have only seen the *similarity* of individual minds as a hallmark of the group mind. Transactive memory describes a social network of individual minds that transcends such uniform agreement.

A transactive memory system is interesting precisely because it connects disparate minds. The fully integrated transactive structure is, in a sense, a deterioration of the richness and complex connectedness of individual minds that can be found in a group. When everyone thinks the same thing at the same time, there really is no reason to speak of a group mental entity—for there is nothing new added by the social context of the individual's thought processes. This, then, is the real departure that transactive memory theorizing makes from the tradition of group mind theory that characterized early social psychology. Transactive memory incorporates the system of interconnections that exists in individuals' communications of information and, hence, places direct emphasis on the social organization of diversity rather than on the social destruction of diversity.

Acknowledgments. I wish to thank Toni Giuliano for helpful comments on this chapter, and Kelly Johnson and Sharon Thoms for assistance in the conduct of research reported here. Address correspondence to the Department of Psychology, Trinity University, San Antonio, TX 78284.

References

Anderson, J., & Reder, L. (1979). Elaborative processing explanation of depth of processing. In L. S. Cermak & F. I. M Craik (Eds.), *Levels of processing in human memory* (pp. 385–403). Hillsdale, NJ: Erlbaum.

Archer, R. L. (1980). Self-disclosure. In D. M. Wegner & R. R. Vallacher (Eds.), *The self in social psychology* (pp. 183–205). New York: Oxford University Press.

Atkinson, J., & Huston, T. (1984). Sex role orientation and division of labor early in marriage. *Journal of Personality and Social Psychology, 46,* 330–345.

Bartlett, F. C. (1932). *Remembering*. Cambridge: Cambridge University Press.

Bishop, G. D., Sikes, L., Schroeder, D., McGregor, U. K., & Holub, D. (1985, August). *Behavior in response to physical symptoms*. Paper presented at the meeting of the American Psychological Association, Los Angeles.

Colligan, M. J., Pennebaker, J. W., & Murphy, L. (Eds). (1982). *Mass psychogenic illness*. Hillsdale, NJ: Erlbaum.

Davis, H. L. (1976). Decision making within the household. *Journal of Consumer Research, 2,* 241–260.

Flavell, J. H., & Wellman, H. M. (1977). Metamemory. In R. V. Kail & J. W. Hagen (Eds.), *Perspectives on the development of memory and cognition* (pp. 3–33). Hillsdale, NJ: Erlbaum.

Giuliano, T., & Wegner, D. M. (1985). [The operation of transactive memory in intimate couples]. Unpublished research data.

Graf, P., & Schacter, D. L. (1985). Implicit and explicit memory for new associations in normal and amnesic subjects. *Journal of Experimental Psychology: Learning, Memory, and Cognition, 11,* 501–518.

Harris, J. E. (1978). External memory aids. In M. M. Gruneberg, P. E. Morris, & R. N. Sykes (Eds.), *Practical aspects of memory* (pp. 172–180). London: Academic Press.

Hart, J. T. (1967). Memory and the memory monitoring process. *Journal of Verbal Learning and Verbal Behavior, 6,* 685–691.

Hayes-Roth, B., & Thorndyke, P. W. (1979). Integration of knowledge from text. *Journal of Verbal Learning and Verbal Behavior, 18,* 91–108.

Hegel, P. T. (1807/1910). *The phenomenology of mind* (Transl.). London: Allen and Unwin.

Hopper, R., Knapp, M. L., & Scott, L. (1981). Couple's personal idioms: Exploring intimate talk. *Journal of Communication, 31,* 23–33.

Janis, I. (1983). *Victims of groupthink*. Boston, MA: Houghton Mifflin.

Johnson, M. K., & Raye, C. L. (1981). Reality monitoring. *Psychological Review, 88,* 67–85.

Jung, C. G. (1922). *Collected papers on analytical psychology* (2nd ed.). London: Bailliere, Tindall, and Cox.

Leavitt, H. J. (1951). Some effects of certain communication patterns on group performance. *Journal of Abnormal and Social Psychology, 46,* 38–50.

Loftus, E. F., Miller, D. G., & Burns, H. J. (1978). Semantic integration of verbal information into a visual memory. *Journal of Experimental Psychology: Human Learning and Memory, 4,* 19–31.

Meacham, J. A., & Leiman, B. (1982). Remembering to perform future actions. In U. Neisser (Ed.), *Memory observed* (pp. 327–336). San Francisco: Freeman.

Pareto, V. (1935). *The mind and society*. New York: Harcourt-Brace.

Pennebaker, J. W. (1982). *The psychology of physical symptoms*. New York: Springer-Verlag.

Reiss, D. (1981). *The family's construction of reality*. Cambridge, MA: Harvard University Press.

Rousseau, J. J. (1767). *A treatise on the social contract*. London: Beckett and DeHondt.

Sackett, D. L., & Snow, J. C. (1979). The magnitude of compliance and non-compliance. In R. B. Haynes, D. W. Taylor, & D. L. Sackett (Eds.), *Compliance in health care* (pp. 11–22). Baltimore, MD: Johns Hopkins University Press.

Slamecka, N. J., & Graf, P. (1978). The generation effect: Delineation of a phenomenon. *Journal of Experimental Psychology: Human Learning and Memory, 4*, 592–604.

Wegner, D. M., Giuliano, T., & Hertel, P. (1985). Cognitive interdependence in close relationships. In W. J. Ickes (Ed.), *Compatible and incompatible relationships* (pp. 253–276). New York: Springer-Verlag.

Wood, D. J. (1980). Teaching the young child: Some relationships between social interaction, language, and thought. In D. R. Olson (Ed.), *The social foundations of language and thought* (pp. 280–296). New York: Norton.

Chapter 10

Theories of Group Behavior: Commentary

George R. Goethals

The nine preceding chapters consider a variety of group phenomena and theories about why they occur. The approach to understanding group behavior adopted in these chapters seems to be a rich and productive one in two respects. First, for the most part, the theories represented here consider the relevance to group behavior of concepts that have been applied to individuals. Second, they have been developed to explain a broad range of behaviors, not just particular, isolated individual or group phenomena (see Mullen, Chapter 1, this volume). Because of their applicability to both individuals and groups and their applicability to a broad range of behaviors, each of these theories, individually, has the potential to provide an integrative analysis of not only behavior in groups, but also of social behavior more broadly. If some integrative analysis and understanding is provided by each of the theories individually, what can we say about the degree of understanding to be derived from the theories collectively, that is, from the volume as a whole? We shall approach this question by addressing two issues in this commentary. First, how do the various theories relate to one another? How do they differ, how do they compete, and how do they cooperatively add to our knowledge? Second, once the theories are placed in comparative perspective, what do we know about group behavior, and what do we still need to know?

A useful starting point is two of the earliest theoretical papers on group behavior, Festinger's (1950) theory of informal social communication and his 1954 theory of social comparison processes (Festinger, 1954). The theory of informal social communication identifies two key group phenomena, "group locomotion," that is, successful completion of tasks and achieving of goals, and "social reality," a definition of right and wrong, good and bad, and true and false, with respect to which group members may achieve self-validation. Both group locomotion and social reality require opinion uniformity and create "pressures toward uniformity" in groups (see Goethals and Darley, Chapter 2). Pressures toward uniformity lead to social influence attempts and rejection of deviant members. Thus Festinger implies that a great deal of interpersonal behavior in groups entails social influence. Consistent with this implication is the fact social influence figures prominantly in most of the chapters in the present volume (Chapter 9 by Wegner being the exception). Of course group locomotion and social reality will have important consequences other than pressures toward uniformity. The need to complete tasks successfully so as to bring gratifications from their achievement into the group (group locomotion), and the need to define reality (social reality) should create strong pressures toward understanding and knowledge as well. Consistent with this implication is the fact that several chapters in the current volume consider social knowledge and memory. Another aspect of group locomotion and, especially, social reality is made more explicit in Festinger's (1954) theory of social comparison. Individuals have a need to evaluate their opinions and abilities and this is often done with respect to social reality. Actually Festinger (1950) implies that social reality creates pressures toward self-validation as well as a basis for self-evaluation. Consistent with Festinger's emphasis on the importance of self-evaluation and self-validation in these two theories is the fact that self-evaluation and self-validation also figure prominantly in several chapters of this book. We think we can usefully compare and contrast the various theories in this book by considering how they address these three issues suggested in Festinger's early theorizing: social influence, social knowledge, and self-validation.

Our approach is to group the eight theories presented in this volume into those which emphasize social influence, those which emphasize self-validation, and those which emphasize social knowledge. In addition, we think it is useful to discuss the theories in the order of emphasis they place on viewing individuals in groups as active vs. passive. The three theories that emphasize social influence processes—social impact theory, drive theory, and self-attention theory—emphasize passive responding to social influence rather than active initiating of social influence. In addition, they are passive in that they place little emphasis on active self-validation or the acquiring and organizing of social knowledge. The three theories that emphasize self-validation—self-presentation, social comparison, and cognitive dissonance theories—not only emphasize an active approach to self-validation, they also envision actively initiating as well as responding to social influence, and they give some attention to the active organization of social knowledge. The two threories that emphasize social knowledge—social cognition and transactive memory—stress an active approach to understanding the social world. They deal relatively little with social influence, from either the recipient's or the initiator's point of view, and they deal relatively little with self-validation. However, because of their very active approach to social knowledge we shall view them as the most active theories and treat them last.

In short, our comparative appraisal of the theories presented here uses an overall active vs. passive dimension to array the theories and provide an order for considering them. Within the overall active vs. passive continuum we consider the extent to which theories portray individuals in groups as active vs. passive participants in the social influence process, as active vs. passive in the pursuit of self-validation, and as active vs. passive organizers of social knowledge.

The Individual's Response to Social Forces

As noted above, three theories in this book emphasize the individual's response to social forces, although none of them deals directly or primarily with social influence or persuasion. These are the chapters on social impact (Jackson, Chapter 6), drive (Geen & Bushman, Chpater 5), and self-attention (Mullen, Chapter 7). The theory that portrays individuals in groups in the most passive manner is social impact theory (Jackson, Chapter 6). Following Stevens' (1957) analysis of the impact of physical stimuli, social impact theory proposes that the impact of social stimuli increases in relation to the strength, immediacy, and number of social sources. The more people there are, the closer, and the stronger, then the greater is their stimulus value or social impact. Social impact theory is impressive in its mathematical elegance and in the broad range of group phenomena to which it can be applied. It is also, it seems to me, impressive in the range of data that can be cited to support it, although there are debates in the current literature about the utility of the theory compared to other theories, notably self-attention theory (Mullen, Chapter 7).

Social impact theory assumes that people respond to social stimuli, but it never provides any rationale for that assumption. That is, why should they? It would seem that people would respond to the wide array of forces considered by social impact theory for very different reasons in different situations. Some of the other theories in this book suggest some of these reasons, for example, pleasing an audience, self-validation, evaluation apprehension, a desire to match to standards, etc. Social impact theory simply assumes, reasonably enough, that people respond to each other. How much they respond is specified in impressive detail.

If we regard social impact theory as a theory about the degree to which people respond to social pressure from others we can see that it implies more than passivity on the part of human beings. After all someone out there is exerting pressure or influence, or at least generating stimulation. However, the theory deals only with how the response is generated, not the stimulus. It tells us that the degree of response generated by social stimuli can be moderated if the object or target of influence can become a member of a group or subgroup through which the social impact can become diffused.

That is, one can diminish the impact of social pressure by hiding among others. Social impact imagines active generators of social influence but only details the behavior of passive receivers.

Social impact theory is high in specification and applicability but low in discussion of process. As Jackson indicates it seems almost a metatheory. It is compatible with other theories, which specify the processes through which people respond to social stimuli. It simply specifies how strongly those processes operate. The theory is useful as far as it goes. It does not tell us why individuals exert influence or why they respond. It does tell us a great deal about how much they respond to whatever stimulation is generated.

Drive theory (Geen & Bushman, Chapter 5) is similar to social impact theory in that it portrays individuals in a rather passive way and focuses on the way people respond to social stimulation. Both social impact theory and drive theory are distinctively marked by their derivation from the experimental psychology of the 1940s and 1950s. Drive theory offers us considerably more than social impact theory in terms of specification of process, but it offers less in range of applicability. Drive theory has been applied exclusively to understand the speed and effectiveness of performances given in social settings. The fundamental assumption is that other people produce increases in generalized drive or arousal levels and that these increases can positively or negatively affect performance. In this respect the theory is much like social impact theory. Other people provide stimulation, which in Miller and Dollard's (1941) formulation equals drive, and this stimulation or drive affects performance. How large the effects of stimulation or drive are on performance has not been considered within drive theory in any detail but it would seem that drive theory would be hospitable to the application of social impact principles. The degree of social facilitation produced by other people should follow social impact specifications. For example, more powerful other persons should produce increased stimulation or drive and more impact on performance. In short, although there has not been an integration of the social impact and social facilitation literatures, the two approaches seem entirely compatible. A recent study by Jackson and Williams (1985) which considers a drive approach to social loafing, a phenomenon considered by social impact theorists, may provide the foundation for such an integration.

The passivity and essentially automatic responses to other people that are portrayed in drive theory are not the whole story, however. Zajonc's (1965) original discussion of why other people produce drive seemed to portray people passively responding to others. The mere presence of others was apparently sufficient to produce drive. However, Zajonc's (1980) more recent discussion of uncertainty and Guerin and Innes' (1982) social monitoring idea indicate that people experience drive in the presence of others because they are preparing to respond readily with whatever behaviors may be required by the actions of the others. That is, the individual is seen as observing and actively processing information about the others in order to respond adaptively and effectively.

The evaluation apprehension explanation of socially produced drive increases introduces the idea that people are concerned with the ways that others evaluate them. This idea is highlighted in several other theories in the book as we noted above. Being concerned with the others' evaluation may be quite passive, but in discussing this concern drive theory suggests more than a black box responding to stimulation. A social information-processing, adapting individual is suggested. A sense of self is nearly, but not quite, suggested. People may be concerned with other people's evaluation and treatment quite apart from a sense of self. Overall, however the various explanations of the ways that other people can produce drive give us a richer sense of what individuals bring to social situations than we received from social impact theory. In terms of social impact theory, however, it is worth noting that several studies of the evaluation apprehension explanation of performance effects manipulated the strength (expertise) of the other persons presence and found significant effects (e.g., Henchy & Glass, 1968). This finding fits nicely with social impact theory and reminds us again of the good fit between the social impact and social facilitation literatures.

The third theory in this volume that discusses people's responses to social forces and social influence is self-attention theory (Mullen, Chapter 7). It portrays individuals passively in that it only considers their responses to self-attention produced by the presence of other people. However, it gives a detailed explanation of the within-individual processes and variables that affect those responses and thereby, like some accounts of drive theory, suggests an actively cognizing and adapting person. For the most part, however, as with social impact theory, self-attention theory views that person's behavior as largely under the control of external variables, specifically, the number of people and subgroups outside the individual or his subgroup. Self-attention theory argues that members of other groups cause the individual to become self-attentive and that self-attention leads people to attempt to match the salient standards of behavior in the group, providing that they expect they have the ability to do so. Self-attention theory is quite specific, using the Other–Total Ratio, in predicting the degree of matching to standards that individuals will manifest.

Self-attention theory has clear points of intersection with both social impact theory and drive theory. Like social impact theory, self-attention theory considers the ways people's responses are affected by the number of other people in the situation. Social impact theory uses a power function, specified only as being less than 1, to detail the effect of number. Self-attention theory offers the more precise Other–Total Ratio. Social impact theory considers both the number of sources and the number of targets as affecting the degree of social impact, directly and inversely, respectively. Self-attention theory's Other–Total Ratio also builds in a consideration of both the number of sources and the number of targets. Those in the Other subgroup can be considered sources, those in the Self subgroup targets. In addition, self-attention theory considers the additive effects of different Other subgroups in a group situation and therefore is able to make more precise predictions regarding the role of group composition than is social impact theory's consideration of undifferentiated sources and targets. While self-attention makes more precise predictions, with impressive success, regarding the nature and number of others, social impact theory considers the strength and immediacy of sources as well as their number. Mullen (1985, 1986) and Jackson (1986) have debated the power of social impact theory's predictions regarding the strength and immediacy variables. For our purposes it is sufficient to note that self-attention theory offers a more detailed account of the impact of numbers of different kinds of individuals in a group, that Mullen questions whether social impact theory's unique contribution, its discussion of strength and immediacy, is a significant one, and that the debate goes on.

Self-attention theory intersects with the evaluation apprehension explanation of why the presence of others increases drive. Evaluation apprehension theory suggests that others increase drive because we are apprehensive about how they will evaluate us, especially if they have the strength to have an impact on us. This explanation seems quite parallel to self-attention theory's concern about matching to salient behavioral standards when the number of others increases proportionally. The matching to standards occurs, according to self-attention theory, due simply to perceptually induced self-attention, although it is not clear just why self-attention should have this effect. Evaluation apprehension can be thought of as self-attention combined with awareness that one is falling short of standards and resulting negative affect. It seems plausible that this negative affect could further energize the matching to standards process. Thus we can see social facilitation phenomena as produced by attempts to match to standards produced by self-attention or self-attention plus negative affect, that is, evaluation apprehension. A study by Hormuth (1982) shows that self-attention produced by a mirror is sufficient to produce social facilitation effects. However, whether evaluation apprehension works in part through self-attention, or by energizing matching to standards, is not clear.

We can also consider the other side of the coin, self-attention adding to the independent effects of drive. Self-attention theory does not discuss drive or arousal. It is a perceptual approach. The more self-attentive one becomes, as a result of being figural, the more one matches to standards. However, one could also become self-attentive as a result of drive. A study by Wegner and Giuliano (1980) indicated that arousal from exercise increased self-attention. Thus it is plausible to imagine that drive itself can produce social facilitation but that drive combined with drive-produced self-attention, and resulting attempts to match to standards, can produce even greater effects.

These points of intersection of drive and self-attention theory suggest rich possibilities for future research.

There is another point of intersection. Self-attention theory is not specific about what standards are salient in a particular situatioin. In some cases they are the person's own internal standards or the standards of his or her subgroup. In other cases they are the standards of the Other subgroup. When the salient standards are those of the Other subgroup, we have a case where individuals become more concerned and apprehensive about matching the Other subgroup's standards or expectations as their proportional size increases. The parallel between the evaluation apprehension idea and self-attention theory is striking here indeed.

Self-Validation in Groups

Social impact, drive, and self-attention theories have considered the way individuals respond to the presence of other people in group settings. Together they usefully detail some of the ways that performance of a variety of behaviors is affected by others. Both behaviors that influence such agents as teachers and psychotherapists are trying to affect, and behaviors that other people in a group may have no concern with, for example, an individual's anagram performances, are considered in these analyses. That is, behaviors that others may intend to affect and behaviors about which they have no knowledge or interest are both considered. Both the evaluation apprehension approach to explaining drive and self-attention theory alert us to the pervasiveness of self-consciousness and self-evaluation in groups. People are concerned with the ways that others evaluate them, and they are concerned with the ways they match up to salient behavior standards, which in many cases are set by others. The next three theories we consider all discuss different aspects of these self-related concerns. Specifically, they consider aspects of self-validation in group settings. They are self-presentation (Baumeister & Hutton, Chapter 4), social comparison (Goethals & Darley, Chapter 2), and cognitive dissonance theories (Sande & Zanna, Chapter 3).

Self-presentation theory serves as a useful transition point from the three chapters that consider the impact of social pressure to the three chapters that deal with self-validation. It considers two motives, audience pleasing and self-construction. The first is the kind of self-presentation motivation we would expect if self-presentation theory were similar to social impact, drive, and self-attention theories in considering only the individual's response to social forces. Audience pleasing reminds us of evaluation apprehension and matching to standards. Not surprisingly, Bond (1982) has attempted to account for social facilitation effects in terms of self-presentation of the audience pleasing variety.

It is easy to imagine audience pleasing increasing with the strength, number, and immediacy of the audience members. Baumeister and Hutton in fact suggest it varies with the audience's power and importance. On the other hand, self-construction reminds us, more so than the other theories considered so far, that individuals in groups have something private, something reserved for themselves. Goffman (1961) was eloquent on this point, arguing that our status is backed by the solid buildings of the world, but that our self resides in the cracks, in what is private. Self-construction is not a private process, but it originates from the individual rather than from the audience. The motive in self-construction is to use the group rather than to please it. Still, we are reminded of the interdependence between self-conception and others' reactions. We try to persuade an audience to accept the fact that we possess a certain trait, but our uncertainty about it is what leads us to engage in the self-constructive influence attempt. There has to be some degree of agreement from others that we possess the trait before it can become part of our self-concept (Erikson, 1968). As Baumeister and Hutton argue, the relations between the public self and the private self are "complex, dynamic, and reciprocal."

It should be noted that self-construction involves matching one's self-presentation to one's own ideal self. This is, of course, essentially equivalent to self-attention theory's matching to standards. Self-attention theory considers matching to both public and private standards (Froming & Carver, 1981). The self-construction idea in self-presentation theory seems to emphasize standards set by oneself. However, William James (1890) noted long ago that one's own standards or aspirations are difficult to set independently of the standards of those with whom we interact. Perhaps then we can regard self-construction as matching to one's own ideal self as influenced by social standards.

The notion that we engage in self-construction in presenting ourselves to others, and that the self-construction process is successful if the audience acknowledges that we indeed possess desired identities (Schlenker, 1980), underlines the fact that one of the key processes in self-concept formation and self-validation is *reflected appraisal* (Gergen, 1971). That is, what we think of ourselves is influenced by what others think of us. Another key self-conception process, role internalization, is also considered in Baumeister and Hutton's chapter. When people behave according to the expectations of social roles, perhaps because of the audience-pleasing motive, they frequently internalize these roles. This internalization can be explained in terms of cognitive dissonance (Festinger, 1957; Sande & Zanna, Chapter 3), self-attribution (Bem, 1972), or the self-presentation process itself (see Baumeister & Hutton), though the details by which self-presentation has this effect are not well specified. Goffman (1959), for example, indicated that self-presenters could be taken in by their own act without specifying how. The key point is that while self-construction can result in rather deliberate changes in the self-concept, audience pleasing, through role internalization, can result in changes in the self-concept that are often unintended.

While self-presentation theory considers self-evaluation and self-validation largely in terms of the processes of reflected appraisal and role internalization, social comparison theory (Goethals & Darley, Chapter 2) emphasizes the way they are achieved through a third process, comparative appraisal (Jones & Gerard, 1967). We appraise ourselves according to the ways our behaviors and characteristics compare to others' in addition to the ways we are appraised by others and the ways we internalize roles. Can we gain further insight into the social comparison process by considering the implications of social impact, drive, and self-attention theories? Goethals and Darley argue that social comparison can be automatic or forced by the situation (Mettee & Smith, 1977; Allen & Wilder, 1977) whenever other salient people are present. That is, one kind of social impact that other people can have is to produce social comparison. There is no evidence to our knowledge that the amount of social comparison follows social impact principles, but whether it may is an issue worth considering and studying.

Social comparison theory holds that there is a drive to evaluate the self and drive theory principles can be applied to it. If self-evaluation is a dominant response then it ought to occur more often, and in an energized form, when other people are present. If it were to, social comparison would be a natural form for such self-evaluation to take. The others provide not only the impetus but the means for self-evaluation. The Gastorf, Suls, and Sanders (1980) study of the Type A behavior pattern and social facilitation, discussed by Geen and Bushman, Chapter 5, is consistent with idea that, at least for some people, there is a drive to self-evaluate. Self-evaluation may be a dominant response for Type As but not Type Bs. Thus the presence of others should increase self-evaluation, evaluation apprehension, and resulting competitive tendencies for Type As with exactly the performance effects that were found.

The evaluation apprehension approach to social facilitation assumes that evaluative concerns generate drive. Festinger's original social comparison theory would argue that drive generates evaluative concerns—not only how will I be evaluated by the other people, but how do I evaluate myself in comparison to them—but that engaging in self-evaluation reduces drive. That is, the evaluation apprehension idea holds that self-evaluation increases drive; social comparison theory would argue that self-evaluation reduces drive. It is interesting to note that the Festinger's idea that drive generates evaluative concerns is consistent with self-attention research showing that arousal increases self-attention. It is also consistent with Schachter's (1959) research on anxiety and affiliation, which grew out of Festinger's original formulation of social comparison theory.

The modified account of social comparison processes presented in this book views social comparison, and self-evaluation more generally, as ocurring automatically, in the absence of drive or in spite of a desire not to compare and self-evaluate (Brickman & Bulman, 1977). This revised account finds compatible the idea that in many situations, especially when negative consequences of comparison are expected, self-evaluation is likely to produce apprehension and increased drive rather than decreased drive. Moreover, revised social comparison theory, with its consideration of the pain of social comparison, as well as its potential to satisfy the self-evaluation drive, is consistent with the idea that evaluation apprehension occurs when others are present and that it may have energizing properties.

Social comparison theory seems compatible with the matching to standards concept of self-attention theory. Both theories suggest that people in the presence of others are concerned with how their own opinions or performance levels compare to those of others. For social comparison theory this concern stems from needs for self-evaluation or self-validation. For self-attention theory it stems from a process of matching to standards. Though people often match to private standards, in many cases the salient standards are others' beliefs about appropriate conduct, or manifestations of those beliefs in behavior, or ability-related performance standards. That is, self-focused attention can lead to social comparison with the standards set by other members of the group one is in. This idea is nicely illustrated by a study by Scheier and Carver (1983).

Self-attention theory's discussion of outcome expectancies is of interest to social comparison theory. People are predicted to attempt to match to standards, to self-regulate, if they feel they have a good probability of success. Where other people's performance levels constitute salient standards self-regulation can be seen as the kind of competetion or upward striving predicted to follow from social comparison information indicating one's performance levels are below those of other people in the group. If individuals do not feel they have a good probability of success, if they feel they are unlikely to meet the salient standards in the situation, they will withdraw. Withdrawal in this case can be seen as a form of cessation of comparison with the others in the group. It includes consequent tendencies to cease competing and to leave the field.

It is perhaps surprising that social comparison theory intersects as much as it does with the theories concerned with responses to social pressure, whereas the intersection with self-presentation theory, another theory concerned with self-validation, seems less. However, it can be recalled that two major consequences of self-evaluational and self-validational tendencies in groups are, according to social comparison theory, social influence and competetion. These two behaviors are very much part of what social impact theory, drive theory, and self-attention theory deal with. Competetion, for example, is easily explained in terms of drive theory, self-attention theory, and social comparison theory.

In discussing self-presentation theory we contrasted the rather passive audience-pleasing behaviors with the more assertive self-construction behaviors. Audience-pleasing behaviors presumably involve public match-ing to other people's standards, that is, conforming to their expectations. On the other hand, self-construction involves influencing others rather than being influenced. One attempts to get others to agree to a projected self-definition. The distinction between these two kinds of self-presentational behaviors parallels social comparison theory's distinction between chang-ing oneself and changing others as ways of achieving opinion or ability uniformity in groups. The first is passive; the second is active. Finally, note that we have used the language of self-attention theory, matching to standards, in discussing audience pleasing or changing self. All three theories, self-presentation, self-attention, and social comparison, deal with individuals changing in order to conform to group standards. Conforming to others is one way of achieving uniformity in groups, and, as self-attention theory predicts, quite reasonably it seems, it is more likely when those others are proportionally numerous. However, self-attention theory does not discuss a second, more active way of achieving uniformity, which does figure in social comparison and self-presentation theories, and that is changing others.

Self-presentation theory deals with self-validation through the concept of self-construction, matching to ideal standards, whereas social comparison theory considers self-validation as a motive underlying and a consequence of social comparison. Cognitive dissonance theory considers self-validation through the process of self-justification. The basic premise of dissonance theory, that people supply cognitions to justify their feelings or their behavior, grew out of the study of rumor. Festinger (1957) reports that studies of rumors near disaster-struck areas in India showed that rumors of further disaster were more numerous just outside devastated areas than inside those areas. After first wondering why people should spread fear-provoking rumors, Festinger concluded that the rumors were actually fear justifying rather than fear provoking. This insight led to the general notion that people would change or generate cognitions to justify feelings or behavior. While dissonance theory can easily be seen as a theory of self-justification (Aronson, 1969), and in fact has evolved from such a notion, it is generally seen as a cognitive consistency theory. In this form its basic premise is that people are uncomfortable when they hold two inconsistent cognitions.

Dissonance reduction is an active and in many cases creative process. When considered in the context of group decisions, as it is by Sande and Zanna (Chapter 3), we can see that it places special emphasis on the action and initiative of the individual rather than the group. People can reduce dissonance produced by group decisions by diffusing responsibility. Diffusion of responsibility is a somewhat antisocial and distancing psychological maneuver and Sande and Zanna argue that in highly cohesive or important groups individuals may be unlikely to use it as a means of reducing dissonance. However, people will reduce dissonance through responsibility diffusion if their purposes are best served by doing so.

Since dissonance theory was first presented by Festinger only 2 years after the publication of his social comparison theory, in Festinger, Riecken, and Schachter's (1956) *When Prophecy Fails*, it is interesting to speculate about points of intersection between comparison theory and dissonance theory. There are at least two. First, both concern self-validation in the domain of opinions, in the case of comparison through showing that our opinions are supported by others, in the case of dissonance through generating opinions that justify our actions. It is interesting that the *When Prophecy Fails* study has been used to support both theories. Proselytizing and seeking social support after the failure of a prophecy can be seen either as trying to reduce dissonance (Festinger *et al.*, 1956) or as attempting to engage in social comparison (Schachter, 1959). Second, both theories consider discrepancies between cognitions. Social comparison theory considers opinion discrepancies between group members and assumes such discrepancies frustrate the need for self-evaluation and self-validation; dissonance theory considers discrepancies among one individual's cognitions. That is, Festinger moved the focus from considering within-group cognitive discrepancies to within-person cognitive discrepancies. In discussing dissonance, Festinger (1957) subsumed social comparison theory. He emphasized that discovering other people's disagreeing opinions aroused dissonance more than that it frustrated the drive for opinion evaluation.

In addition to interesting connections with social comparison theory, not surprising in light of their common author, dissonance theory also intersects with several of the other theories we have discussed. First, there is a connection to drive theory. Dissonance is a drive and several studies have indicated that it has drive-like effects on performance similar to those produced by the presence of other people (Wicklund & Brehm, 1976). Research also shows that dissonance can be reduced if the arousal it produces can be attributed to sources other than counterattitudinal behavior (Zanna & Cooper, 1976). Second, dissonance is important in offering an explanation for the internalization of roles and self-presentational behavior discussed by self-presentation theory. Actually, some self-presentation theorists (Tedeschi, Schlenker, & Bonoma, 1971) have disputed dissonance effects and argued that they represent the desire to appear consistent rather than real opinion change. Baumeister and Hutton consider genuine attitude change following self-presentaton in the present volume. It seems that genuine attitude change produced by self-presentation must be explained in terms of a process other than self-presentation itself, a process such as dissonance reduction or perhaps self-perception (Bem, 1972). However, Baumeister and Hutton argue for a role for self-presentation itself in producing such attitude change. Further research awaits this issue.

In sum, self-presentation, social comparison, and cognitive dissonance theories emphasize an active process of self-validation rather than a passive set of responses to the presence of others. They emphasize the active individual in the group using the group to obtain self-validation. In the case of dissonance theory, there is even some emphasis on the individual psychologically distancing himself from others through the process of diffusion of responsibility, that is, seeing himself as less responsible and fellow group members as more responsible for group action. More than other theories we have discussed, dissonance theory emphasizes cognition, particularly how we think about ourselves and others in the group. This emphasis on cognition is continued in the chapters on social cognition and transactive memory.

Social Knowledge in Groups

The theories discussed so far have relatively little to say about the ways we think about other people. Social impact theory indicates we note how many people are present and how close they are, and also that we notice their strength. Various versions of drive theory assume we take note of what other people are doing or whether they are going to evaluate us. Self-attention theory suggests we consider how people in a larger group divide into various subgroups and that we consider their standards. Self-presentation theory suggests we are tuned to other people's opinions of us. Social comparison theory proposes that we consider other people's beliefs and abilities. Dissonance theory considers how we assess other people's responsibility for group decisions. However, these theories generally say very little about the ways we think about individuals or groups of individuals. The two remaining chapters, social cognition theory (Pryor & Ostrom, Chapter 8) and transactive memory (Wegner, Chapter 9), give much more attention to how we think about other people and how such thinking affects our behavior. At the same time these approaches make interesting connections with other chapters.

Social cognition theory emphasizes the fact that we organize information about people in groups in the same ways we organize information in general. We encode, represent, categorize, form schemas, make associations, and retrieve. A key aspect of perceiving people in groups is whether we individuate them, that is, impose a person organization, or see them simply as a member of a group, an instance of a group category. When our unit of analysis is the individual we see people as more responsible, we evaluate them more accurately, and we are more influenced by them.

Social cognition theory relates in an interesting way to dissonance theory's discussion of attributing responsibility to others. Social cognition theory argues that the leader is individuated and thereby held more responsible. Dissonance does not discuss individuation but seems to imply that other group members are distanced and deindividuated when responsibility for dissonant decisions is attributed to them. This apparent contradiction regarding the effects of individuation on attributed responsibility suggests the need to look at both motivational and cognitive factors that can affect our perceptions of our own and other people's responsibility.

Social cognition theory reminds us of the importance of cognitive processing in social comparison. One of the key aspects of social comparison is the categorization of individuals into in-groups and out-groups that is emphasized by Tajfel and Turner's (1986) social identity theory. A second key aspect is the perception of members of those groups as diverse and variable as opposed to similar or homogeneous. There are both social comparison and social cognition explanations for our tendency to perceive the in-group as more diverse (Goethals, Allison, & Frost, 1979; Quattrone, 1986). The key point is that our understanding of social comparison processes, especially across group comparison, is enhanced by social cognition's contribution to our understanding of the ways we perceive in-groups and out-groups.

The chapter on social cognition also reminds us of the centrality of social influence in groups. However, the emphasis is on the way we actively represent information about the world that others present to us and how we integrate it with what we already know. This emphasis stands in contrast to the less deliberate or rational responding to others that is suggested by social impact, drive, and self-attention theories. Social cognition theory relates to both social impact theory and self-attention theory as it discusses how much we are affected by groups of individuals. While social impact theory does not consider how we may organize information about the individuals who make up the sources of social force, social cognition research reported by Pryor and Ostrom makes it clear that the way we organize information about those individuals has an important effect on their degree of social impact. Self-attention theory, in its discussion of subgrouping, also gives attention to the importance of how we organize information about individuals in groups. Social cognition theory extends this emphasis on thinking about how we think about others. Along with self-attention theory it recognizes we sometimes process more information about others than how many there are.

The chapter on transactive memory (Wegner, Chapter 9) offers a new approach to thinking about interdependence in groups. Jones and Gerard (1967) distinguished information from effect dependence and considered effect interdependence in groups in some detail. Cognitive or information interdependence has not been considered heretofore. In proposing the concepts of transactive memory Wegner emphasizes the very active organizing of knowledge that people engage in individually and in groups. He also emphasizes the diversity and complexity of groups rather than their uniformity. Individuals in groups can play quite different roles according to their expertise and knowledge. Furthermore, in order for the transactive memory system to work, individuals participating in it must have some representation of the way knowledge is held by other members. Other members of the group must be individuated. Information about them must be characterized by person organization as discussed by social cognition theory. While group members may be aware of the knowledge structure of their own group, and the fact that different individuals play quite different roles, they may not appreciate that there is equal diversity in other groups as well. That is, there may not be person organization of the information about those others. This lack of person organization may contribute to the perception of other groups as less variable than one's own (Quattrone, 1986).

The overall emphasis on active processing of social information that highlights social cognition theory is repeated in the work on transactive memory. Transactive memory assumes that individuals actively and automatically process information about other people. It places special emphasis on knowing what others know. It also emphasizes the assumption of responsibility rather than the diffusion of responsibility that dissonance theory stresses. This differential emphasis on assuming vs. diffusing responsibility makes sense when one considers the two kinds of situations emphasized in the cognitive dissonance and transactive memory chapters.

Transactive memory theory emphasizes the organization of knowledge in cohesive, well-ordered groups. Transactive memory requires organization and appreciation of others and, not surprisingly, grows out of the consideration of aspects of intimate relationships. Transactive memory flourishes in groups where people know, trust, like, help, and rely on each other, and where they appreciate each other's unique abilities and contributions. Dissonance theory considers groups where individuals have collectively done something threatening to their self-concepts or interests and it typically explores the consequences of these actions in groups of strangers. Thus it is not surprising that it emphasizes diffusion of responsibility and the related social distancing that seems to go along with it. Again, dissonance theory argues that diffusion is not expected to occur in groups that are important to people and where they like the other people. They must deal with dissonance in other ways in these situations. The *When Prophecy Fails* study suggests they support each other and then seek more support as well.

Transactive memory intersects with social comparison theory in interesting ways. Both theories emphasize the impact of what we know, or think we know, about other people. In his discussion of individuals overestimating the capabilities of their transactive memory systems, Wegner suggests that making erroneous judgments about other people's knowledge "paves the way for the group to make poor decisions." Social comparison discusses the way pluralistic ignorance can lead to erroneous assumptions about other people's beliefs in the groupthink context. A key difference is that the person in the transactive memory situation makes an erroneous assumption about others knowing differently from themselves. In the pluralistic ignorance situation people assume that others believe the same. Either incorrect assumption can lead to poor decisions.

For the most part transactive memory emphasizes diversity in groups, whereas social comparison emphasizes uniformity. However, social comparison theory does emphasize diversity in one important respect. People can be most confident of their opinions when their group is uniform with respect to the belief being evaluated but diverse with respect to the perspectives they have on that issue (Goethals & Darley, 1977; Goethals *et al.*, 1979). The idea that dissimilar agreers triangulate an opinion and provide the greatest validation runs parallel to the transactive memory idea that groups have the greatest knowledge when they have a differentiated transactive structure.

In sum, the chapters on social cognition and transactive memory emphasize the active processes involved in knowing each other and the world around us. While they have a different tone than the other chapters, they seem complementary rather than antagonistic. Indeed, a consideration of all the theories together gives a rather full understanding of various aspects of group life. Perhaps we can best see how the different theories work together in increasing our understanding by considering how they may attempt to understand a single process that is central to group functioning, that is, the process of group decision making.

Group Decision Making: An Integrative Account

All of the theories represented in this volume have something to say about group decision making. Let us consider what they have to say, and whether they imply that groups are likely to behave in ways which foster sound decisions. The three theories considering the impact of social forces, as we have seen previously, tell us little about how an individual or subgroup within the larger group will initiate a proposal or suggestion in the group. They have little to say about leadership, role structure, interpersonal relations, or trying to make a sound decision. They tell us a good deal about how individuals are affected by the ideas and actions of others.

Social impact theory specifies how much any targets of group influence are affected by the sources of that influence. Regardless of the kind of stimulus the sources provide, individuals are affected according to the strength, immediacy, and number of those sources and according to the strength, immediacy, and number of fellow targets. An individual in a small, weak, and dispersed group will be highly influenced by strong, close, and numerous others.

Drive theory suggests that individuals are more likely to perform dominant responses in the presence of other group members. This suggests that decisions in groups are likely to be quite conventional and to reflect dominant norms, except in those groups where creative ideas are individuals' dominant response. It also suggests that as drive increases individuals' cue utilization may be deflected from relevant information. The narrowing of attention produced by drive is likely to be particularly troublesome in the case of complex decisions where a great deal of information needs to be considered.

Self-attention theory suggests that individuals are more likely to match to standards, perhaps standards endorsing conventional decisions and dominant norms, as they feel proportionally outnumbered by others who define appropriate standards of behavior. Unless those standards dictate careful weighing of information and drawing of conclusions, and perhaps creative thinking, the decision is unlikely to be aided by self-attention. Furthermore, self-attention may draw attention away from relevant information just as drive does. On the other hand, self-attention theory suggests that the individuals who make up the predominant Other subgroup will match to salient standards, their own or others, less as their proportional predominance increases. They may lose sight of dominant norms and conventional standards and push the group in the direction of behavior that may be creative, reckless, or antisocial. Thus the smaller subgroup may attempt to match whatever standards are salient, provided they think they can. The larger subgroup will not. There may be an ironic situation where the smaller subgroup matches to standards typically endorsed by the larger group, the larger group's standards being the salient ones in the group decision-making situation, while the larger subgroup becomes quite casual about these standards. It is difficult to predict whether the stronger impact on the group decision will be the smaller group's matching to group standards or the larger group ignoring them. Research on minority influence suggests that the minority can be successful by appearing autonomous, consistent, and rigid (Moscovici, 1985). The smaller subgroup may not appear to be autonomous, however, if it is matching to group standards.

The three theories concerned with self-validation each suggest quite different issues in group decision making. Self-presentation theory suggests that individuals in groups may conform to other people's opinions in order to please them. It is also possible for individuals to be assertive in the service of their self-construction motive and to try to lead the group toward a novel position. They may also conform in the interests of self-construction, presenting themselves as "good soldiers," willing to go along in order to get along. In short, opinions will be adopted by individuals in order to serve motives that have little to do with making a sound decision—unless contributing to a sound decision serves their principal concerns, pleasing others or validating a desired identity.

Social comparison theory suggests that people may be caught between motives to make a sound decision and motives to obtain self-validation through agreement from others. If they are truly concerned with evaluating their opinions they may behave in ways that push toward sound decisions. If they are simply interested in self-validation, their concern may simply be group consensus. Either motive could lead to the exclusion of deviant opinions, which may mean the elimination of creative thinking and fresh analyses. However, there are other possible effects of concerns with self-validation. One is group polarization, as each members tries to be as true or truer to group values as other members. Social comparison theory also suggests that some individuals may strive for leadership positions in order to satisfy their "unidirectional drive upward" for abilities. Competition for leadership may foster sound decisions or it may simply lead to nonproductive oneupsmanship. To the extent that the decision affects another group, comparison with that out-group may produce aggressive decisions. Whether those are sound depends on the group's interests.

Cognitive dissonance theory incorporates social comparison theory and suggests that disagreeing opinions produce dissonance and pressures toward their elimination. Its major focus is on the ways individuals behave after they have made an irrevocable decision. One possibility is considerable self-justificatory attitude change. Another is diffusion of responsiblity, blaming others if things go wrong, and dissension within the group. Dissonance has little to say about sound decision making except that later decisions are less likely to be sound if earlier decisions are bolstered by self-justification rather than appraised through objective reality testing (Janis & Mann, 1977).

The two theories emphasizing social knowledge suggest less to get in the way of sound decision making than do the other theories in the book. Social cognition theory suggests that individuals will make every attempt to master their environment and behave effectively in it. They will attempt to make sound decisions free from fear of force from others, cognition limited by drive or self-attention, or a concern with self-validation. The only limits on sound decision making are biases arising from the ways people in a group or perceiving a group process information. Decisions will be sound or flawed depending on whether individuals' information-processing capacities and habits are suited to the problem at hand.

Transactive memory theory suggests that individuals may be able to organize a structure of information exchange that is well suited to making sound decisions. Like social cognition there are no irrelevant motives or drives to get in the way. What limits the soundness of a decision is each individual's own cognitive limits and errors built into the transactive memory system, such as overestimating its capabilities. The good news is that people can use transactive memory to increase their individual cognitive reach and genuinely improve the chances of a sound decision.

In sum, each of the theories illuminates a different aspect of group decision making. Our knowledge from these theories seems cumulative. What we know from one adds to what we know from another. Whereas the theories compete in many instances (for example, social impact vs. self-attention), for the most part they collaborate. Let us consider now what we know, and what we still need to know, about group behavior from the theories presented in this volume.

Conclusion and Future Considerations

We began by considering the emphasis on social influence, social knowledge, and self-validation that was implicit in Festinger's (1950, 1954) early theories of behavior in groups. In this context it was no surprise to see that our chapters deal extensively with, and could be organized around, these three topics. We have learned a tremendous amount about these issues. At the same time it seems clear to me that there is much that future theories of group behavior must consider more than the present theories have. The largest gap concerns our knowledge of socioemotional behaviors in groups. Transactive memory theory grows out of considering close relationships but does not tell us very much about them. We know about self-validation, which is one aspect of the socioemotional side of group behavior, but we learn virtually nothing about liking or social support from these theories. Social comparison and cognitive dissonance theories tell us something but not very much. Second, we know very little about social organization in groups. Transactive memory, social comparison, and self-attention theories have some implications, but again we know little in this area. Third, we know little about the forming and adjourning aspects of group evolution (see Mullen, Chapter 1). Most of our theories concern storming, norming, and performing. Fourth, in spite of the fact that social influence is very important in most chapters, we know little of face to face influence in groups. These are just a few of the areas about which we need to know a great deal more. However, the enterprise of psychology is to find out more, and it is clear we have exciting psychology still lying ahead of us. We hope this volume will stimulate some of that psychology.

References

Allen, V.L., & Wilder, D.A. (1977). Social comparison, self-evaluation, and conformity to the group. In J.M. Suls & R.L. Miller (Eds.), *Social comparison processes: theoretical and empirical perspectives* (pp. 187–208). Washington, DC: Halsted Press.

Aronson, E. (1969). The theory of cognitive dissonance: a current perspective. In L. Berkowitz (Ed.), *Advances in experimental social psychology* (Vol. 4 pp. 2–34). New York: Academic Press.

Bem, D. (1972). Self-perception theory. In L. Berkowitz (Ed.), *Advances in experimental social psychology* (Vol. 6 pp. 1–62). New York: Academic Press.

Bond, C.F. (1982). Social facilitation: A self-presentational view. *Journal of Personality and Social Psychology, 42,* 1042–1050.

Brickman, P., & Bulman, R.J. (1977). Pleasure and pain in social comparison. In J.M.

Suls & R.L. Miller (Eds.), *Social comparison processes: Theoretical and empirical perspectives* (pp. 149–186). Washington, DC: Halsted Press.

Erikson, E. (1968). *Identity: Youth and crisis.* New York: Norton.

●Festinger, L. (1950). Informal social communication. *Psychological Review, 57,* 271–282. M4104

Festinger, L. (1954). A theory of social comparison processes. *Human Relations, 7,* 117–140.

Festinger, L. (1957). *A theory of cognitive dissonance.* Stanford, CA: Stanford University Press.

Festinger, L., Riecken, H.W., & Schachter, S. (1956). *When prophecy fails.* Minneapolis: University of Minnesota Press.

Froming, W.J., & Carver, C.S. (1981). Divergent influences of private and public self-consciousness in a compliance paradigm. *Journal of Research in Personality, 15,* 159–171.

Gastorf, J.W., Suls, J.M., & Sanders, G.S. (1980). Type A coronary-prone behavior pattern and social facilitation. *Journal of Experimental Social Psychology, 38,* 773–780.

Gergen, K.J. (1971). *The self-concept.* New York: Holt, Rinehart, and Winston.

Goethals, G.R., Allison, S.J., & Frost, M. (1979). Perceptions of the magnitude and diversity of social support. *Journal of Experimental Social Psychology, 15,* 570–581.

Goethals, G.R., & Darley, J.M. (1977). Social comparison theory: an attributional approach. In J.M. Suls & R.L. Miller (Eds.), *Social comparison theory: theoretical and empirical perspectives* (pp. 259–278). Washington, DC: Halsted Press.

Goffman, E. (1959). *The presentation of self in everyday life.* New York: Doubleday.

Goffman, E. (1961). *Asylums.* Garden City, NJ: Doubleday.

Guerin, B., & Innes, J.M. (1982). Social facilitation and social monitoring: a new look at Zajonc's mere exposure hypothesis. *British Journal of Social Psychology, 21,* 7–18.

Henchy, T., & Glass, D.C. (1968). Evaluation apprehension and social facilitation of dominant and subordinate responses. *Journal of Personality and Social Psychology, 10,* 446–454.

Hormuth, S.E. (1982). Self-awareness and drive theory: comparing internal standards and dominant responses. *European Journal of Social Psychology, 12,* 31–45.

Jackson, J.M. (1986). In defense of social impact theory: A comment on Mullen. *Journal of Personality and Social Psychology, 50,* 511–513.

Jackson, J. M., & Williams, K. D. (1985). Social loafing on difficult tasks: Working collectively can improve performance. *Journal of Personality and Social Psychology, 49,* 937–942.

Janis, I.L., & Mann, L. (1977). *Decision making.* New York: Free Press.

Jones, E.E., & Gerard, H.B. (1967). *Foundations of social psychology.* New York: Wiley.

Mettee, D.R., & Smith, G. (1977). Social comparison and interpersonal attraction: the case for dissimilarity. In J.M. Suls & R.L. Miller (Eds.), *Social comparison processes: theoretical and empirical perspectives* (pp. 69–102). Washington, DC: Halsted Press.

Miller, N.E., & Dollard, J. (1941). *Social learning and imitation.* New Haven: Yale University Press.

Moscovici, S. (1985). Social influence and conformity. In G.L. Lindzey & E. Aronson (Eds.), *The handbook of social psychology* (Vol. 2). New York: Random House.

Mullen, B. (1985). Strength and immediacy of sources: A meta-analytic evaluation of the forgotten elements of social impact theory. *Journal of Personality and Social Psychology, 48,* 1458–1466.

Mullen, B. (1986). The effects of strength and immediacy in group contexts: A reply to Jackson. *Journal of Personality and Social Psychology, 50,* 514–516.

Quattrone, G. (1986). On the perception of a group's variability. In S. Worchel & W.G. Austin (Eds.), *Psychology of intergroup relations*. Chicago: Nelson-Hall.

Schachter, S. (1959). *The psychology of affiliation*. Stanford, CA: Stanford University Press.

Scheier, M.F., & Carver, C.S. (1983). Self-directed attention and the comparison of self with standards. *Journal of Experimental Social Psychology, 19*, 205–222.

Schlenker, B.R. (1980). *Impression management: The self-concept, social identity, and interpersonal relations*. Monterey, CA: Brooks/Cole.

Stevens, S.S. (1957). On the psychophysical law. *Psychological Review, 64*, 153–181.

Tajfel, H., & Turner, J.C. (1986). The social identity theory of intergroup behavior. In S. Worchel & W.G. Austin (Eds.), *Psychology of intergroup relations* (pp. 33–48). Chicago: Nelson-Hall.

Tedeschi, J.T., Schlenker, B.R., & Bonoma, T.V. (1971). Cognitive dissonance: private ratiocination or public spectacle? *American psychologist, 26*, 685–695.

Wegner, D.W., & Giuliano, T. (1980) Arousal-induced attention to self. *Journal of Personality and Social Psychology, 38*, 719–726.

Wicklund, R.W., & Brehm, J.W. (1976) *Perspectives on cognitive dissonance*. Hillsdale, NJ: Erlbaum.

Zajonc, R.B. (1965). Social facilitation. *Science, 149*, 269–274.

Zajonc, R.B. (1980). Compresence. In P. Paulus (Ed.), *Psychology of group influence* (pp. 35–60). Hillsdale, NJ: Erlbaum.

Zanna, M.P., & Cooper, J. (1976). Dissonance and the attribution process. In J.H. Harvey, W.J. Ickes, & R.F. Kidd (Eds.), *New directions in attribution research* (Vol. 1 pp. 199–217). Hillsdale, NJ: Erlbaum.

Author Index

Subject Index

Springer Series in Social Psychology

Springer Series in Social Psychology

The Social Construction of the Person
Kenneth J. Gergen/Keith E. Davis (Editors)

Entrapment in Escalating Conflicts: A Social Psychological Analysis
Joel Brockner/Jeffrey Z. Rubin

The Attribution of Blame: Causality, Responsibility, and Blameworthiness
Kelly G. Shaver

Language and Social Situations
Joseph P. Forgas (Editor)

Power, Dominance, and Nonverbal Behavior
Steve L. Ellyson/John F. Dovidio (Editors)

Changing Conceptions of Crowd Mind and Behavior
Carl F. Graumann/Serge Moscovici (Editors)

Changing Conceptions of Leadership
Carl F. Graumann/Serge Moscovici (Editors)

Friendship and Social Interaction
Valerian J. Derlega/Barbara A. Winstead (Editors)

An Attributional Theory of Motivation and Emotion
Bernard Weiner

Public Self and Private Self
Roy F. Baumeister (Editor)

Social Psychology and Dysfunctional Behavior: Origins, Diagnosis, and Treatment
Mark R. Leary/Rowland S. Miller

Communication and Persuasion: Central and Peripheral Routes to Attitude Change
Richard E. Petty/John T. Cacioppo

Theories of Group Behavior
Brian Mullen/George R. Goethals (Editors)